Little Will and Clink Carrot

The basic facts in this late nineteenth century story are believed to be essentially correct. Some names have been altered to avoid unlikely, but possible, embarrassment to descendants or collateral relatives of some of the characters portrayed. Minor characters are, inevitably, fictional as are certain events for which no complete records exist but, although the origins of this account lay in 'Grandad's' tales, as the author explains in his Foreword, what at first seemed to be no more than 'yarns' have on closer investigation turned out to be at least based on documented fact. How close the author's reconstruction of events has been to reality must be left to the reader, and possibly later research, to assess.

This is the first of a planned trilogy which will follow the family fortunes in Lincoln and eventually to Sheffield, Manchester and Malaysia.

Below: *The photograph shows 'Little Will', at the age of fifty nine or sixty, on the right. He is standing next to his younger daughter who was the author's mother. On the far left is his elder daughter. The child on the donkey is the author and next to him his grandma – 'Polly'.*

Above: *The only known photograph of 'Herbert Everton' taken from his obituary notice in 1925.*

LITTLE WILL
AND CLINK CARROT

TWO BOYS IN LINCOLN

by PETER GASTON

Illustrated by Roger Kidd

19 90

RICHARD KAY

80 • Sleaford Road • BOSTON • Lincolnshire • PE21 8EU

© 1990 Peter Gaston – text
© Roger M Kidd – drawings

British Library Cataloguing in Publication Data
Gaston, Peter *1931* –
Little Will and Clink Carrot.
I. Title
823.914 [F]

ISBN 0–902662–88–0

Set in 10 point Bookman type on an AppleMac Macintosh Plus using Microsoft
Word and PageMaker as a package supplied by Gestetner Ltd. Great Britain.

Printed and bound in Great Britain
by
Woolnough Bookbinding, Irthlingborough, Northants. NN9 5SE
Tel. (0933) 652444

CONTENTS

ILLUSTRATIONS

A photograph of Little Will with some of his family, including the author, will be found as a frontispiece facing the title page together with the only known photograph of 'Herbert Everton' reproduced from his obituary notice.

Other illustrations will be found on
pages: 33 • 83 • 117 • 150 • 197 • 229 • 241 • 308

To my Grandparents:
William Herbert and Mary Frances,
now long gone,
but without whom my life might have been very different

FOREWORD

My grandfather was born in the city of Lincoln in 1875 and married my grandmother, a headmaster's daughter from Staffordshire, in Lincoln in 1898.

Looking back to my childhood, it is difficult to remember any time when my grandparents were not present. My own parents were not happily married and were eventually divorced and my grandparents home, although much humbler than my own, became a refuge from the constant arguments and recriminations. Like most children in an unhappy marriage, I did not really care what the arguments were about; I just wanted a happy home with both parents present.

My grandfather was a great storyteller. I clearly recall the small kitchen with its scrubbed, wooden table and its 'Zebo' polished black side oven heated by a roaring, open fire. Here, after school, I would sit down to tea and hear my grandfather's slow and deliberate tread crunching up the back garden path as he returned from work. This would be followed by a heavy stamping as he knocked off the dirt from his boots, and his first job on entering the house was always to remove the old-fashioned, leather leggings which secured the bottoms of his trousers.

Tea over, we would sit around the fire and discuss the happenings of the day. My own stories would be of school, my grandmother might tell of some event concerning the neighbours, but my grandfather's stories were inevitably of his boyhood in Lincoln. He would slowly ram the Erinmore Flake into his pipe, tamp it down with the edge of his matchbox, and light it several times. Then, leaning back in his chair, he would exhale a cloud of pungent smoke all over the tiny kitchen, his deepset eyes would sparkle and he would say: 'I remember when I was a lad . . .'

Sometimes he would be cut short as my grandmother would turn from washing the pots at the sink and say: 'Just remember, father, we don't want any of those mucky tales'.

I do not recall that he ever told any really 'mucky tales', but as his story progressed, the clattering of the pots would cease and even my spinster aunt, a dear soul of unusual eccentricity, would cease her continuous chatter and listen. Occasionally she would nod her head and say, 'I remember that', even though the event being recounted had taken place before she was born!

In placing these stories on record I have taken some liberties with both events and characters to make the narrative flow smoothly, but in essence the substance of each chapter remains as I heard it so many times all those years ago. Indeed, in pursuing the necessary research it has been little less than amazing how many events frequently discounted by the family as 'one of Dad's tales' have been found to have a solid basis in fact.

I will give you just one instance of this.

My grandfather always said that at one time his great friend, Clink, lived 'in a little house on Burton Road, just by the drive to the workhouse'. He also said that Clink's mother never acknowledged the existence of her husband, much as she adored him. In an old Lincoln directory I found an entry for a Mrs Carrot, living at 8, Burton Road. This address, now a laundrette, is by the side of a drive leading through to a housing estate. The housing estate is on the site of the old Union workhouse. The drive was indeed the entrance to the workhouse, the very name of which would cause my grandfather to shudder.

Quite which Carrot was 'Clink' I do not know. Having found the entry for my grandfather's admission to the North District School, Lincoln, on 23rd January, 1884, (having formerly attended a 'private school') I found quite a number of 'Carrots' of the same age group. As I never knew Clink's true Christian name, I was unable to establish which entry related to him.

The school is now an hotel, but on my many visits to Lincoln in the research for this book I have never been able to stay there. Perhaps I fear the ghosts of childish voices echoing along the cold corridors, but just as many times as I have picked up my telephone to make reservations there, so I have put it down again. . . 'There are more things in Heaven and Earth, Horatio . . .'

I must apologise to the reader that I have taken the Spring

viii.

Heeled Jack incident out of chronological order. This event would seem clearly to be tied down to the year 1877. At this time my grandfather would have been no more than two years of age and I now realise that his recall of this story must have been second-hand! However, that such a character did exist cannot be doubted, and my explanation of his demise is no more far fetched than any of the others which have been put forward over the years.

This, then, is the story of my grandfather's upbringing by strict parents and of his early life in the city of Lincoln at the end of the last century. I do not doubt that it is typical of the life led by many children of that time and, indeed, my grandfather was probably considerably better off than most children of his day in terms of the basic necessities of life such as food, shelter, and clothing. However, like most of us, his character was formed by the events of his childhood and, as an old man, he appeared to outsiders to be cantankerous and bitter, the cutting edge of his tongue tempered only by the unswerving loyalty of my grandmother, a sweet and loveable person. To the day of his death he carried an abiding fear of ending his days in the workhouse.

'Little Will' was a product of the age in which he lived; a gifted man denied expression of much of his natural talent by his upbringing. If this volume goes some way to illustrating his abilities as a storyteller, then I shall be more than satisfied.

I must acknowledge with deep thanks the assistance of Mr Maurice B Hodson who has carefully checked my drafts for accuracy. He and his family actually jogged around Spring Heeled Jack's route to make sure that it was possible and he has always been free in imparting his boundless knowledge of Lincoln and its people. Without his assistance I am sure that I could not have given the stories the essential authentic background which I desired. I am also indebted to another local historian, Mr Tony Gadd, for his valued comments and constructive criticism.

My thanks go to the staff at the Central Reference Library, Lincoln, for the patient and courteous manner in which they have answered my many queries. I am also indebted to the staff in the

Search Room of the Lincolnshire Archives Department, The Castle, Lincoln. They have shown incredible patience in assisting me and, as a sideline to this novel, I have now firmly established 'Little Will's' line of descent to the village of Withcall in the sixteenth century. The staff at the Reference Library, Boston, Lincolnshire, have also been most helpful.

Above all, I am indebted to Little Will and his family. They gave me the greatest gift anyone can give to a child; a secure home, a shoulder to cry on, and a great deal of love.

Peter Gaston.

July 1989.

x.

CHAPTER ONE

THE BEGINNING . . . .
. . AND LUCY MATCHBOX

IT WAS AN APRIL DAY in the year 1876 and Sarah Jane was dying.

She had been ill since the birth of her second child, a son named William, in the June of the previous year and had seemed gradually to wither away as if she had no will to live.

A pale shaft of early Spring sunlight came through the window and showed her drawn, grey face against the snowy white sheets. Her eyes, dark-rimmed and deeply sunk, suddenly seemed to glow with a new light and she stretched out one thin hand towards her husband, sitting at the side of the bed.

Herbert Everton was twenty-five years of age and already on the way to establishing himself as a successful business man. He was short and stocky with deep set, piercing eyes below heavy eyebrows. A neat pointed beard seemed to emphasise the heavy, aquiline nose and more than once he had been likened to a bird of prey ready to pounce.

He grasped the extended hand but, with a new found strength, Sarah Jane pulled it away and stretched it out beyond him to where her two children were together in a corner of the room.

Annie was just three and her tear-stained face was drawn and thin. William could not hold himself upright, but Annie held his hand until their father beckoned and brought them forward to be by the bedside.

Sarah Jane made a great effort and, helped by the doctor, raised herself on her pillows to see her children, then turned towards Herbert and murmured something. He put his ear close to her lips and strained to hear the words she was so desperately trying to utter. Finally he understood.

'My little boy', she whispered. 'My little boy! Look after my little boy.'

Big Tom, high in the tower of Lincoln Cathedral, struck three o'clock and with a deep sigh Sarah Jane Everton died.

One of the few tears he ever shed in his life ran down Herbert's face and he put his head in his hands. Already a hard man, Sarah Jane's death was to make him even harder, and the fact that her last few words had been for her son was always to affect the relationship he had with William.

William grew up to resemble his father very greatly, inheriting the deep, flashing eyes and prominent nose and always being short in stature. Early in his school days he acquired the nickname 'Little Will' and this stayed with him all his life, although it caused many a bloody nose in the school yard and not a few in public houses in later years.

His father seldom had much to say to him, devoting his time to making a great success of his business, that of cabinet maker and funeral director, and just as soon as he could get William exempted from attendance at school so that he could work in the yard in Motherby Lane, he did so.

Whilst other boys played, William worked, and he was often to be seen riding through the streets of Lincoln on the back of the pony trap, picking up timber from the merchants or taking a coffin down to some bereaved household.

He remained short of stature, always well below average, and as he struggled to unload planks twice his own length from the cart, the children at the neighbouring school would lean over the railings and shout at him. 'Look, there's Little Will, getting ready to nail someone else in a box.' If no teacher was in the schoolyard, the epithet was more likely to be 'Shortarse', but to those he knew the rather pathetic little lad was always known as 'Little Will' and thus he was to be called all his long life.

It was nothing for him still to be working late in the evening and to be seen dragging his weary feet up Asylum Road and Drury Lane towards the family home in Burton Road.

On one occasion he was passing the White Hart when he

2.

heard a familiar voice booming forth from the dining room. Scrambling up onto the buttress below the window, he could just see into the room and there, sure enough, with a glass of port in the one hand and a large cigar in the other, was his father. The remains of a sumptuous meal littered the table and a uniformed waiter glided between Herbert and his cronies, refilling glasses as necessary.

Will struggled to keep his balance, the toes of his hefty boots scrabbling against the wall, whilst he thought of the sort of meal he would have to prepare for himself when he got home and compared it with whatever his father had been eating.

A hand tapped him on the back, and he looked down to see Lucy Matchbox, tray of matches balanced on her shoulders, giving him a disapproving glance.

Lucy was a well-known figure in Lincoln and could normally be found selling her matches outside either the White Hart or the Saracen's Head. She was tall and thin with finely cut features and her long auburn hair, which hung down over her shoulders in rather untidy ringlets, was streaked with grey. Sometime in the past she had acquired a red tunic and this hung, almost overwhelming her, from her thin shoulders. She wore a stout pair of leather boots and long grey socks which reached to her knees. Ragged mittens completed the picture except for a woollen cap with a bright red bobble on the top.

No one seemed to know anything about Lucy. She had appeared in the city some twenty years earlier, complete with red tunic and tray of matches, as if from nowhere. There were occasions when she disappeared from the city for several days at a time and local gossip said that she went home to visit her rich parents and fill up the box of sovereigns which rumour said she kept beneath her bed. Certainly there were times when her accent became very refined and precise, but as these were mainly when she had taken a few swigs from the bottle she often carried beneath her tunic in the cold weather, no one took much notice.

Will scrambled down the wall, boots scrabbling on the rough brick, and stood in front of Lucy Matchbox, rubbing the sleeve of his jumper across the end of his nose.

'Now then, Will,' said Lucy, 'that's no way for a gentleman to wipe his nose. Your handkerchief should be tucked up your right sleeve and brought down with a flourish . . . so!' And with a swoop of her long fingers she dangled her own handkerchief in front of his face. The careful observer would have noted that for one so neglected in appearance it was a very fine silken handkerchief indeed, held in a very clean and well manicured hand.

Will gave his nose another defiant upward sweep and finished it off by wiping his sleeve across the seat of his pants.

'I haven't got a handkerchief, Lucy', he said. 'No more than I've got a silk shirt or a tweed jacket or boots with no holes in.'

'I bet your father's got a silk handkerchief . . . and a tweed jacket . . . and fine leather boots, hasn't he?' said Lucy. Before Will could answer she added: 'Him with all those fine clothes, travels in a carriage and pair and hobnobs with all the gentry in the White Hart and drinks a bottle of port a night, but you can't have a decent handkerchief to blow your nose on! A crying shame, I calls it!'

Will shuffled his feet uncomfortably and looked at the ground.

'My father says that I can't have those sort of things until I can pay for them myself out of my wages.'

Lucy put her head close to his ear and whispered.

'Wages?' she said. 'Wages? And how much wages does he give you then? What's the rate for a twelve year old boy today? Two shillings a week?'

Will squared his shoulders.

'My father gives me five shillings a week,' he said proudly.

Lucy's jaw dropped open and a quick 'Saints alive!' escaped before she recovered from her surprise.

'Of course', said Will, 'I have to pay him for my board and lodging.'

'Pay your own father to live in your own house?' said Lucy in disbelief. 'Your poor mother must be turning in her grave. And how much does old skinflint Herbert charge for that? Three bob,

4.

I'll be bound.'

Will shuffled his feet and looked at the ground again and mumbled something under his breath.

'What? What did you say, then?' badgered Lucy. 'Don't be mumbling like a great girl, Will Everton. Speak up and let's hear what you have to say.'

'Four shillings and threepence', said Will in a low voice.

'Four shillings and threepence?' cried Lucy, That leaves you ninepence for a hard week's work, then?'

'I suppose so', said Will, 'but I'll get a raise when I'm twenty-one, my father says.'

'I bet he does', said Lucy. 'Now then, Little Will, there's no business about this night, so you're coming home with me. We'll have a bite of supper and chat about how to increase your wealth.'

Will didn't need much persuading. He was very tired and the prospect of the bread and cheese which probably awaited him at Burton Road was hardly calculated to turn down an invitation. Lucy's little room at the corner of Michaelgate and Steep Hill always had a warm glow to it. On the window sill stood an oil lamp with a red cranberry coloured bowl which seemed to cheer every passer-by on a cold night.

Will took the tray from Lucy and carried it off down the hill. As he passed the end of Wordsworth Street a portly gentleman in evening dress bought a box of matches from him, touched his tall hat to Lucy, and gave Will a penny for himself.

'There you are,' said Lucy, 'it would take you . . . er . . . six hours hard work for your father to earn a penny for yourself. Two minutes with old Lucy and you're on your way to becoming rich!'

Lucy's room was over a public house, the Harlequin, but she had her own little door at the side of the pub and her own key. As they stood outside the door she delved her hand down the front of her old red tunic and triumphantly flourished a latch key on a piece of string. She opened the door and Will stood aside to let her pass.

'Thank you, kind sir', she said, dropping a mock curtsey, and together they commenced to climb the steep staircase. They had barely reached halfway before there was a knocking at the door and, with a muttered exclamation, Lucy had to climb down again to answer it. It was quite gloomy on the unlit stairs and as Lucy opened the door all Will could see over her shoulder was a mop of bright, red hair. In fact he reflected that it was the brightest red hair that he had ever seen in his life.

As the owner of the hair appeared on the staircase, Will recognised a boy of about his own age whom he had occasionally seen around the city, normally hanging around the market. Will remembered that one time when he had been with his father, Herbert had remarked that the red haired boy was up to no good.

'Mark my words, Will,' his father had said, 'there's nothing more ungodly than a boy with nothing to do. Ask yourself, Will, what good is that boy doing? Is he working? No, of course he's not, he's too idle for that. Is he propping the wall up? Will it fall down if he moves away? No. Of course it won't! Therefore he isn't even doing a service for his fellow citizens. He's idle, Will, idle! Whilst you and I toil and stream with honest sweat to earn our daily bread, he does nothing but hang around seeking to rob us all. Work, Will, work! The salvation of all of us, that's what it is'. And with these words of godly advice he had sent Will to collect his monthly accounts and entered the Blue Boar for a four course lunch.

The room at the top of the stairs was warm and cosy.

Lucy stirred the dull embers in the fireplace and dancing flames lit up the room, flickering off the walls and reflecting from the large mirror at the end of the room. She turned up the oil lamp and put the kettle on the fire. There was a small sofa in front of the fire and Lucy sat the two boys there whilst she busied herself with a small cooking pot which she placed in the side oven.

Warily they eyed each other up.

The new boy was taller than Will, although much thinner. His flaming red mop crowned a freckled face which seemed to have a permanent grin on it. He had a large hole in the elbow of his woollen jersey, his short trousers were covered with mud and his socks draped around his ankles as if they were trying to cover his battered boots.

Neither of them spoke until Lucy stood between them, hands on hips, and said 'Will, this is Edgar. . .'

The red haired boy grimaced and made a mock retching sound.

Lucy clouted him half-heartedly around the ear and continued.

'Although he doesn't like it, Edgar he was christened and Edgar he remains. In fact, to give him his full title, this is Master Edgar Carrot of Gordon Road in the city of Lincoln.'

Will burst into laughter, his shoulders heaving as he pointed at Edgar and spluttered. 'Carrot? Carrot? He looks like a carrot with that red hair! Edgar Carrot! What a name!'

The freckles became suffused with a dull red glow as Will continued to laugh as if he would never stop. Suddenly Clink leapt across the settee and dragged Will down onto the floor where they rapidly became a whirling mass of arms and legs, 'ouches' and 'oos'!

Having twice told them to stop and been ignored, Lucy waded in with a heavy wooden spoon to restore order and soon pushed them, breathless and red-faced, to opposite ends of the settee.

'Gentlemen!' she said, 'What disgraceful conduct in a lady's chambers for two young men to get up to! If there's any more of this, outside you go where you can fight to your heart's content! Now, to continue. This other gentleman, Master Carrot, is William Everton of Burton Road in this city. Perhaps you know him better as Little Will.'

'I know him better as Shortarse,' laughed Edgar. 'He spends all his time putting folks in coffins for his father! They lay 'em out in that workshop in Motherby Lane, 'im and his father, and before they nails the lid down they pulls out all the gold teeth and cuts off their fingers to get the gold rings!'

'Liar!' shouted Will and the two boys once again became a whirling mass on the floor of the little room.

It took quite a time to sort them out again into separate bodies and, when she had done so, frail Lucy was panting heavily and the wooden spoon drooped from her limp wrist as if it weighed a ton.

Taking a deep breath she threw out her chest and pointed dramatically to each in turn with the wooden spoon, bosom heaving and eyes sparkling angrily.

'You will now shake hands,' she gasped. 'Shake hands like gentlemen. Each of you will say loudly and clearly to the other "I apologise for my ungentlemanly behaviour" and you will never again behave like this in my presence.'

Noticing a distinct reticence on the part of either of them to do anything, she continued: 'If you do not, then you will both leave at once and you, Edgar Carrot, will no longer be my friend. You, Will Everton, will never become my friend, and I shall not speak to either of you again.'

By this time, the fire had taken hold merrily and the room looked much more cosy than the world outside. In addition, the first faint aroma of a tasty stew was emerging from the saucepan on the hob.

'Well?' said Lucy, taking hold of the door handle.

Will shuffled his boots, held out his hand and mumbled something indistinct.

'On your feet sir!' ordered Lucy. 'And speak clearly and distinctly so that I can hear every word.'

Will shuffled slowly to his feet and started to hold out his hand.

Edgar positively shot out his and before Will could say a word, he grasped him firmly by the hand and apologised in a loud, clear voice. Then he turned to Lucy and apologised to her.

Lucy nodded her head in approval and remarked that he might even yet make a gentleman, then turned to Will with an expectant look on her thin face.

'I apologise', he said, and held out his hand.

Lucy put an arm around each of their shoulders and smiled, hugging them both to her.

8.

'As you go through life, you will find that true friends are very rare. Let's make a vow that we shall always be friends, all three of us.'

And she dived into a cupboard and brought out a bottle and three glasses. The two boys watched as she poured an inch of golden liquid into each glass.

'Now then', she said, 'a toast to our friendship. Raise your glasses, gentlemen, and down it in one gulp.'

It took about five seconds for the raw spirits to hit Will like a sledgehammer and he staggered and spluttered as if he was in imminent danger of choking to death. Clink seemed to have weathered the brandy with no ill-effects and, indeed, was already holding out his glass for a refill which was quickly refused.

'Drink, young Edgar, is a very evil thing,' she said. 'Why, look at little Will here, eyes streaming, gasping for breath and as red as a turkey-cock! Give him his pony and trap now and he'd be riding up and down Bailgate like a champion, knocking down all in front of him, wouldn't you, Will?'

'I don't think I could do anything 'til I've got my breath back,' he spluttered. 'If drink is so evil, why did you give it to me Lucy?' he asked.

'Purely for medicinal reasons,' she replied. 'Purely for medicinal reasons. And as I'm a lot older than you are I need a lot more medicine than you do, so I'll have another tot.'

Thus saying, she measured a generous helping into her glass and downed it in one gulp, smacking her lips in obvious relish at her own brand of medication.

The meal was a huge success and when the last vestiges of stew were scraped from the plates with chunks of home-made bread, both boys sat back on the settee with a contented sigh.

'Now then, master Edgar, did you bring me anything tonight?' she asked.

'Do they really call you Edgar?' Will interrupted.

Edgar shuffled his feet and seemed to be searching for an answer; he started to say something, changed his mind and then suddenly burst forth in a torrent of words.

'I suppose you'll have to know,' he said with an embarrassed grin, the freckled face lighting up with a curiously shy smile. 'My mother calls me Edgar because that's what I was Christened, leastways I think I was Christened. Anyway, no one else, except Lucy, calls me Edgar any more. They all call me Clink!'

'Now, Edgar,' said Lucy . . .

'No, I want to tell Will,' he said. 'If we are to be friends, real friends, then we mustn't have secrets. Everyone calls me Clink because my father is always in clink . . . in prison, you see. He's there now and he won't be out until Christmas.'

Will was wide-eyed and asked 'What did he do, then? Is he a burglar or a robber? He's not a murderer, is he?'

'Not exactly', said Clink. 'He threw a bailiff through our window and out onto the pavement. My mother shouted to him to open the window first, but he didn't. Anyway, there was lots of blood everywhere and the bailiff ran off down the street and fetched back two policemen. By this time my dad was really angry. He was cursing and swearing and my mother was crying and shouting. Constable Peasgood told my dad to be quiet and to go along quietly with him to the police station, but my dad just hit him square on the nose and sent him flying . . .'

Constable Peasgood was one of the best-known policemen in Lincoln. He was more than six feet tall with shoulders like an ox. He was the heavyweight boxing champion for the local force and when the fair came to Lincoln he would take on all comers in the wrestling contests. His very appearance in the four ale bar was enough to send rowdies back to their seats with sheepish grins on their faces.

'He flattened Constable Peasgood?' said Will in awe.

'That he did,' said Clink. 'Put him out for the count and threw the other one straight out into the street like a sack of feathers!'

'Cor,' said Will, his eyes popping like organ stops. 'What happened next then?'

'They brought up the wagon from the police station and when my dad heard the horses' hooves pounding up the street, he went straight out into the middle of the road and stood there, waving his arms and shouting, "Come on, then, I'll floor the lot of you! I'll pound you into splinters, every last one of you!"'

'Cor,' said Will again.

'Anyway, they stood in our street, circling round each other like cockerels at a cock fight. Every time my dad moved forward, the peelers moved backwards. Every now and then, one tried to get around behind him, but when my dad turned round, he'd back off. I reckon they'd have gone on like that for hours if my dad hadn't backed into the horse. It shied up and kicked him on the head and all the coppers fell on him in a heap while he was still on the ground, dragged him up and threw him into the wagon. I reckon that he won, though, 'cos it wasn't the coppers that knocked him down, it was the 'orse!'

'I reckon he won at that!' said Will. 'Cor, he flattened Constable Peasgood!'

Clink continued: 'When he came to proper, they sent him in front of the beaks and my dad said that just because he was out of work and couldn't pay his rent he wasn't going to let anyone break his home up and take away his furniture, and particularly his piano. It was only an old piano and half the strings were missing, but my dad loved that piano. He used to get out his Sankey's Sacred Songs and Solos and sing *Fight the Good Fight* every Sunday dinner time when he got back from the pub. Fair blasted it out, he did, you could hear him down at the White Hart sometimes.'

'The beaks said that if he didn't pay his rent, he must expect that the bailiffs would come. Honest businessfolk couldn't be driven into bankruptcy because scoundrels wouldn't pay their rent, they said . . . and they sent him to clink for eighteen months.'

'I can't believe that anyone could be so wicked, said Will. 'Who would do such a thing? Why, only last week when my father read the lesson in church, it was all about helping the poor and needy.'

A quick glance passed between Lucy and Clink and the subject was quickly changed.

'Back to business, Edgar,' said Lucy. 'What have you brought me tonight?'

Clink dipped deep into his pockets and brought out a paper bag containing about a dozen empty matchboxes. He carefully laid them out in a row and Lucy examined each one, paying particular attention to the sandpaper strip on the side. She threw out one box which had a grubby corner and then put the remainder into a cupboard and gave Clink a ha'penny which she took from a tin box.

'There, Master Will,' she said, 'a ha'penny earned is a ha'penny gained and Master Edgar here has earned himself an extra ha'penny and at the same time has helped me to earn a few extra pennies.'

'A ha'penny for a few dirty, old matchboxes? They're not worth that,' he said. 'I can find fifty in the High Street any day.'

'Can you now?' said Lucy, going to the cupboard and taking the boxes out again. 'Look carefully, Will Everton. How many of these boxes are "dirty, old matchboxes" like you said then? Look at them, Will, and count the dirty ones.'

William turned them over and over, looking at each one.

'Well' he said, 'they're not really dirty, I suppose, but I still don't see what use they are.'

'They're worth a ha'penny!' chimed in Clink, 'So they got to be some use, ain't they?'

'Use the eyes God gave you,' said Lucy. 'Every one of those boxes is brand new, not even a strike mark on the side. Now look at these full boxes and see what it says on the side about how many matches are in each box . . . see, there, it says: "Average contents fifty matches". Now, average means that it doesn't have to be exactly fifty, it might be fifty-two or, then again, it might be forty-eight.'

So saying, she took out two matches and put them on the table. Then she took a further carton of new boxes from her store cupboard and took two matches from each of them. Then she counted out forty-eight matches very carefully and put them in one of Clink's boxes, tapped it on the table, and then put it with her stock.

'There you are', she said, 'do that a few times and I have increased my stock to make a couple of pennies extra and Edgar here has earned an honest ha'penny!'

Will looked rather dumbfounded.

'But that's cheating!' he said.

'Cheating?' said Lucy. 'Who's being cheated? The factory that makes the matches doesn't lose anything. The chap that buys the box of matches doesn't lose anything – he still gets "Average contents, fifty matches" even if there's only forty-eight. Certainly, I've never seen anyone count the matches in a box. have you? And me and Edgar here, down at the bottom end of the ladder as you might say, we can afford a pot of jam now and then. What's dishonest about that?'

Will was lost for words and he listened eagerly as Clink told him the best places to find the clean, unused boxes. Everywhere the toffs go, was Clink's way of describing it. The gents with fancy match holders on their watch chains would buy a box of matches, fill their vesta cases, and then throw the empty box away, often with a few matches still remaining in it. Clink told Will that he could sometimes make sixpence in a week and that on one occasion he had made a shilling in a single day at the races. However, as Clink put it, there ain't no justice in the world because the last box he found there got him arrested as there appeared to be some doubt as to whether the box had been thrown away or whether it was still in the owner's pocket when Clink 'found' it. Fortunately for him, as he was being removed from the racecourse by an enthusiastic young policeman, Constable Peasgood had appeared on the scene and taken Clink into his own custody.

The constable had taken him back home to Gordon Road and mother Carrot with her large brood, where he had received a firm talking to from all parties plus a clout round the ear from his mother for good measure, and a silver threepence had mysteriously appeared in his hand from heaven knows where. All in all, a very confusing day.

The two boys would have talked all night, but Lucy looked at the clock on the mantelshelf and sent them packing.

Although it was not on his way, Clink agreed to walk home with Will and as they wended their way through the gaslit streets they chattered excitedly as boys will. Perhaps it was the effect of the unaccustomed brandy mixed with fresh evening air, but Will felt strangely happy and elated.

He had never had friends, even at school, for when school was finished there was always work to be done. Long hours in the workshop had made him seem old beyond his years and always there was his father talking about the value of hard work and how it would one day earn Will a place in Heaven. On the credit side of his life-style was the fact that, even at twelve years of age he had an uncanny ability to work with wood and could handle a plane or a saw as well as many twice his age.

Will really felt that he had made a friend that night.

'I know,' said Clink. 'Let's sing a song!'

'I know a good song,' said Will. 'It's called: "Hold the Fort for I am Coming!" and it's a real rousing one. We can walk past the barracks in Burton Road and march like soldiers as we sing it.'

Clink also knew the song and volunteered to sing the first chorus on his own. He had a loud voice for one so young and the words seemed to echo and re-echo around the streets.

  'Hold the fort for I am coming
  In a donkey cart,
  The wheels are rotten
  And the shafts are broken
  And the donkey wants to fart!'

Will looked horrified and glanced around to see who might be listening, but the streets appeared to be empty. By now they were outside the barracks where a lone sentry stood outside the great wooden doors. Efforts to quieten Clink proved fruitless and he burst forth into a second verse.

  'Hold the fort for I am coming
  In my sister's pram,
  She's nought but a tot

14.

And she's peed on the lot
And it looks like yellow jam!'

By this time Clink was really enjoying himself and he stood straight in front of the sentry and sung the whole lot all over again. The soldier looked straight ahead, standing in the 'at ease' position, and, it seemed without moving his lips, hissed loudly at Clink like an angry snake.

'Piss off, or I'll shove this bayonet straight up your arse!'

What might have become a very painful experience for Clink was forestalled by the silent appearance of the sergeant of the guard. He suddenly loomed out of the shadows, grabbed hold of Clink by the shirt front and pushed his face within an inch of Clink's nose. His spiked moustache positively bristled, his rapidly reddening face clearly visible in the flickering gaslight. The row of medals glistened as they clanked about as the sergeant restrained the struggling Clink with great ease, using only one hand. With the other he grabbed Will by the scruff of the neck.

'What 'ave we 'ere, then,' he said in a marked Cockney accent. 'A pair of music 'all performers, no doubt. Or is it a pair of choir boys from the Cathedral? Do you think they're choir boys, sentry?'

The sentry crashed his feet to attention.

'No, sergeant!' he shouted in a loud voice. 'These is a pair of ragamuffins what is makin' fun of 'er Majesty's soldiers!'

By this time the sergeant's face had become as red as the scarlet sash which he wore around his shoulders and even Clink had been silenced whilst Will was positively trembling. A small crowd of sightseers had now gathered as if from nowhere and were giving the sergeant a variety of advice varying from: 'Let 'em go, you bully.' to: 'Give the cheeky young buggers a damned good hiding!'

The sergeant appeared to think for a moment and then, with an exaggerated wink at the crowd said, 'Seein' as 'ow these lads is so interested in the army, I shall invite them in (he pronounced it "hin") to our guard room and lock 'em up in the cells!'

This appeared to meet with general approval and before they

could say a word the two lads found themselves in the guard room surrounded by half a dozen grinning soldiers.

'Corporal,' said the sergeant, 'open me a nice, big cell for our guests.'

Will and Clink stared at each other as the heavy steel door clanged open.

'Cor, you've done it now Clink,' said Will 'I don't want to be locked in there, even if you do!'

'As I sees it,' said the sergeant, 'there's just three courses open to you lads. Firstly you can accept my judgement, 'cos I'm the orderly sergeant and the sergeant of the guard, and I reckon that would mean I'd 'ave to 'aul you up in front of Captain Walmsley-Browne in the mornin' and he'd give you at least three years in the glass'ouse, don't you reckon, lads?'

All the soldiers in the guardroom nodded wisely and one said they would get four years rather than three. 'Very serious offence, insultin' the Queen's soldiers,' said one of them.

'Or,' continued the sergeant, 'you could elect to go the 'ouses of Parliament and be tried by them. Now if you was found guilty – and bein' as we was all witnesses to your 'orrible crimes I don't doubt as you would be – then they'd lock you up in the Tower of London and after that . . .' He made a rattling noise and drew his hand across his throat.

'Or, there's a way not to get punished at all . . . you know, lads,' he said, winking at the assembled men. 'The THIRD choice!'

'The THIRD choice? Ain't that a bit 'ard on the lads, sergeant?' said one of them.

'No, it's too easy on 'em,' said yet another. 'Send 'em off to London and the Tower!'

Will took a deep breath and stepped forward, drawing himself up to his full (and rather insignificant) height. Although there was a tear in his eye and a catch in his voice he faced the sergeant square on.

'Sergeant,' he said, 'my friend is very sorry that he annoyed the sentry and I would bet my life he won't do it again, will you,

Clink?'

Clink shook his head eagerly.

'All you have to do is let us go,' said Will.

Sergeant Cuthbert wrinkled his brow and mumbled under his breath to himself, until he finally said: 'Well, I don't reckon as 'ow I can do that. You see, Sergeants is a bit special and 'as to uphold the law, particularly when one of 'er Majesty's subjects is insultin' her soldiery. Why, Corporal Fletcher 'ere would tell you, when we was on guard at Buckingham Palace last year, 'e was standing at the gates and I was inspectin' 'im, when there's a shout from up on the balcony. . .

"Come up 'ere" says this voice, (Sergeant Cuthbert performed this phrase in a loud falsetto tone) and me and Fred goes up this great gold staircase and there standin' at the top as large as life is "er Majesty . . . ain't that right, Corporal?'

Corporal Fletcher appeared to be about to choke, but he tried to look serious and nodded.

The sergeant continued, the two boys with jaws agape listening to every word.

'Now then,' says 'Er Majesty, 'I've called you up 'ere, Clarence ('cos that's my name, Clarence, and I don't mind the Queen calling me that) . . . I've called you up 'ere, Clarence, to tell you that there's far too much of this insultin' of my brave soldiers by ragamuffins what ain't got no respect for law and order. You got to stop it, Clarence, afore it gets out of 'and. So in future, when you catches one of these ragamuffins, you gives 'im the THIRD choice, 'stead of clappin' 'im in the Tower. Besides, that there 'eadsman's gettin' tired, swingin' that great axe all day long, poor chap, 'e needs a rest, like.'

The sergeant went to a small cupboard and drew out two forms, giving one to each boy.

'Now, my brave lads,' he said. 'The third way out is to join this Regiment, the finest in the British Army, and become a soldier. Out in Burma there's a mad King called Thebaw an' 'e's choppin' up our lads as fast as we can send 'em out there. Now we need two good drummer boys . . . ' He looked at Will and added: 'It don't matter that there ain't much of you, 'cos when old Thebaw's finished choppin' you about there won't be much left of you, any'ow!'

This fascinating lecture on the sanguinary habits of King Thebaw was brought to a close by a loud voice from the guardroom door.

'What's this, Clarence?' asked Constable Peasgood. 'Still press ganging 'em into the Lincolnshires, are we?'

Both boys instinctively went and stood at his side as he put his arms out towards them.

'Now, then, John' said the sergeant. 'Just a bit of 'armless fun to stop the lads being cheeky to the sentries. I couldn't really 'ave enlisted 'em, now could I?'

'Misbehaviour by the civilians is my job,' responded the policeman. 'Both these young gentlemen is my responsibility and you 'ad no right to bring them into the barracks.'

He took out his notebook, licked the end of his pencil and continued, 'I reckon I shall have to enter this in my notebook and make a report to Captain Walmsley-Browne in the morning. Can't have innocent civilians being terrified by the soldiers 'ere in Lincoln. The magistrates is dead against that, I do know Clarence, and after your last appearance in front of their worships I have a feeling that you'd soon be Private Clarence Cuthbert. Add to that, it's forbidden to bring young lads into the barracks as we both well know. . . oh, yes, I would think you'd get about three months as well, don't you, Clarence?'

Sergeant Cuthbert turned a bright shade of scarlet again and rubbed his hands together. The soldiers of the guard were grinning at him quite openly, for he was not the most popular of NCOs, and he felt a great rage building up inside him. With great difficulty he controlled his emotions and held out his hand towards the constable.

'Now, John,' he said, 'there's no harm done. No one hurt you, did they lads? And look, 'ere's a sixpence each to show you that Sergeant Cuthbert is your friend.'

The boys took the proffered sixpence and looked at each other.

18.

What had appeared to be turning into a disaster was now being transformed into a turn of good fortune.

Constable Peasgood put away his pencil and notebook and put an arm around each of the boys.

'Very well, then, Clarence,' he said. 'like you say, there's been no harm done and perhaps these two did deserve what they got. I was brought here by a report of disgustin' songs being sung in the street and there can't be too many small boys with flamin' red 'air singing lewd songs at night. However, I won't have the law being taken into your own hands, soldiers or no soldiers. In this part of Lincoln I'm the law and anyone who thinks otherwise can answer to me at any time.'

He clenched a ham-like fist and waved it around the room, but no-one appeared to wish to dispute the point and with this final gesture he ushered the boys through the barrack gates and out into the street.

The air was shatterd as Sergeant Cuthbert gave vent to his wrath on the unfortunate guard.

'What the 'effin' 'ell are you starin' at, Lumsden? Get that rifle cleaned, it's bloody filthy! Larfin at me, are you Brown? Get your pack on and double around the perimeter ten times . . go on lad, don't stand there waitin' for your bleedin' mother to 'elp you . . . go on . . . 'eft 'ight, 'eft 'ight, 'eft 'ight . . . go on lad, faster, faster . . . '

Constable Peasgood laughed quietly to himself and shepherded Will and Clink up the road until they were near the big house, where Will lived.

Having given them a stern lecture on their behaviour and expressing surprise that young Will was 'getting into strange company' he took Clink back down the hill and left Will to walk home alone.

Unbeknown to Will, his escorted journey home had been witnessed through the parlour window by his father who had returned home early from the White Hart. Having been in the hotel since late afternoon and having consumed more than his fair share of alcohol, he was not in a mood to stand any form of behaviour which might reflect badly. Working a small boy until he dropped he deemed to be good for the boy's soul and eventual salvation. Being escorted home by a policeman, he saw as a blot upon his efforts to secure himself a higher place in Lincoln society.

Will had barely got through the front door when a stinging blow around the head sent him staggering against the heavy oak sideboard. His father took him by the shoulders and shook him violently.

'What have you been up to?' he shouted. 'Why have the police brought you home? Why were you with that dreadful Carrot boy?'

Will fought back the tears, put a hand to his burning ears and asked: 'How do you know who he is Father?'

He was answered by another blow.

'Don't talk back to me, boy,' screamed his father. 'All the neighbours will have seen Peasgood bringing you home. Don't you realise that I'm looked up to in this town? It's bad enough that I lost your mother through you, without you turning into a criminal and bringing shame on us all. I'll ask you for the last time. Where have you been and what have you been doing?'

Will stumbled through a brief resume of the evening's events, missing out Lucy Matchbox altogether, and pretending to have met Clink in the street on his way home from work. He made out that the soldiers at the barracks had been bullying them and that Constable Peasgood had saved them from being pushed into the army at gunpoint.

Herbert ranted and raved for several minutes and threatened Will that if he ever saw him with Clink again he would be forbidden to go outside the house on his own, even on his way home from work.

'I'll have old Walter bring you home from the workshop every evening if you can't be trusted,' he said. 'I've worked hard since your mother died to make a name for myself in this city and I'll not have you ruin everything by associating with a jailbird's son. If I have to, I'll turn the whole family into the street rather than have you make friends with that boy!'

'How could you do that, father?' asked Will. 'He lives in Gordon Road and doesn't harm us.'

'Because I own that row of houses in Gordon Road,' said his father. 'The Carrot family have never been up to date with their rent yet and I might as well turn them out and get someone in who will pay properly. I'm not a bloody charity, giving home and shelter to all the idlers in Lincoln.'

Any deep loyalty that Will felt for his father began to evaporate from that moment. There is always a strong bond between father and son and in his heart of hearts, each boy emulates his father, but Will had much of the gentleness of his mother in his make-up and in this instance his sympathies were with his new found friend. He knew now who had sent the bailiffs into Clink's home and who, in his mind, was responsible for Mr Carrot senior going to prison. From this fateful night in the Spring of 1887 Will started to grow up and to see the world as it really was.

Despite his father's warning, the friendship between the two boys ripened rapidly during those early months. Fearful of his father's anger, Will would meet Clink at Lucy's rooms where they would laugh and joke and make a few coppers from finding the empty, clean matchboxes. There was always a cosy fire, a warm meal and a genuine welcome from Lucy who understood only too well the bond that was springing up between them.

It was during this time that Will learned to fish, play football and take part in all the other things that other boys of his age were doing, and in his short life he could never remember having been happier.

Old Walter, the foreman in the Everton workshop, turned a blind eye to Will's absences on sunny afternoons and on the rare occasions that Herbert came into the workshop and asked after his son, Walter would make the excuse that he had sent him out on errands or to the timber yard for wood. Walter had worked for the Evertons before Will had been born and remembered Will's mother.

Once, when he had been working late in the evening and had

consumed several bottles of brown ale, he had confided in Will of his great affection for Sarah Jane.

'Do you know, Master Will,' he said, 'I used to see her walking down to the shops some mornings when I was out delivering in town. She was tall and slender like a willow rod and her long, black hair used to gleam like ebony in the sunlight. She always wore bright, pretty dresses and she turned every head as she passed by. I was bold enough to bid her good-day once and she gave me such a smile that I felt as if my legs had turned to jelly and my heart thumped like it was going to jump out of my chest and run away up the street shouting for sheer joy . . . '

Will laughed. Of course, he remembered nothing of his mother but he loved to hear others talk of her.

Walter continued, 'I had never had a mind to marry, though when I was young I knew a sweet, young thing I went to school with. When she was only seventeen she was carried off by the consumption and I never had a mind to marry anyone else. But Sarah Jane were different . . . I never saw a lovelier woman in my life. Of course, I was much older than she was, but every time I saw her I felt like I was seventeen again . . . then she met your father with his fine ways and fancy clothes and I knew that there would never be any chance for me. Anyway, I could still see her from time to time and that was something, I suppose.'

Walter cleared his throat and drew out his silver hunter from his waistcoat pocket. He looked at the time and told Will that it was time he went home.

'Mind you, no stopping at Lucy's on the way home,' he said. 'It's late already.'

Will looked startled.

'Don't worry lad,' said Walter, 'I won't tell your father about your friends, but take care. He has a dreadful temper and if your sister finds out, Annie will tell him for sure.'

Will never understood about his sister who seemed to be the apple of his father's eye. She was three years older than he was and was beginning to blossom into a young woman. She could never have been called pretty, in fact she was quite plain and not at all like her mother. She rarely smiled and was forever telling him how fortunate he was to have such a loving father. Her evenings were spent at church functions such as bible classes and she was already a junior Sunday School teacher. Finding that her bosom was beginning to expand and believing that it was quite shameful for this to show, she had once bound it as flat to her chest as she could before taking her Sunday school class. By the time she had walked a few hundred yards down Bailgate to the church she was turning a bright shade of red when she walked into her classroom filled with small children.

She opened her bible and read half a dozen sentences then suddenly fainted and fell to the floor. It was quite embarassing when Mrs Clute, the vicar's wife, unravelled the several yards of broad bandage so that she could breathe again and she was even more embarassed when Mrs Clute explained that the Lord had intended the female of the species to have bosoms which, as she put it, she might well find useful in later life. This story was repeated several times throughout the congregation and lost nothing in the telling. In fact, Clink's version of the incident was positively obscene, but he was very careful not to tell it to Will.

Conscious of the smirks and giggles, Annie became sterner and more forbidding in appearance and seemed convinced that Will had something to do with the stories which were circulating. In fact, if sheer embarassment had not stopped her, there is little doubt that she would have reported the incident to her father and Will would have received a sound thrashing, for Annie's word was never questioned.

On one occasion, walking around the outskirts of the Cathedral on a Sunday afternoon, a young man who was a near neighbour had raised his hat and endeavoured to get into conversation with her. Although the approach was perfectly innocent, she had run back through the Exchequer Gate, panted up Bailgate and puffed up Westgate to the house in Burton Road as if pursued by the devil, collapsed on the sofa and told Herbert a story of near abduction and rape.

Without any attempt to question the girl, Herbert had battered his neighbour's door almost into a pulp, threatened to call the police and would have beaten the young man senseless if it had not been for the interference of the youth's father who had witnessed the whole innocent event from a seat in the Cathedral grounds. Herbert fumed over the incident for days and bad blood existed between the two families from that day forth. But Annie's word was never doubted.

Walter's warning was a wise one and Will knew that he had to heed it.

There were three events happened during that year which wove themselves together into a story that Will was to remember all his life.

Firstly, his father was elected to the board of guardians of the Burton Road workhouse. As he did much of the joinery for the establishment and handled many of the paupers' funerals which took place from there, it was felt by a number of well-meaning individuals that he was a suitable candidate for the post. On more than one occasion he had read the morning lesson in the workhouse chapel and had impressed the elders with his booming voice proclaiming the inmates' good fortune and the fact that surely they were the chosen of God, for only by poverty and suffering would they find their way to Heaven.

Secondly, it was the year of Queen Victoria's Golden Jubilee, and amongst the many processions which would take place would be one in which Will's father would be walking in the dignity of his new position.

The third event was a sadder one, the death of Lucy Matchbox.

Lucy had not been seen in the city for some days. This in itself was not remarkable for she had disappeared for short periods before, but had always told the publican below that she was going away and asked him to keep an eye on her rooms.

When the publican finally sent for the police and together they entered her lodgings, they found Lucy sitting in her velvet-covered armchair, feet on a small stool and her head resting on her shoulder at an angle as if she had fallen asleep. Her scarlet tunic was draped loosely around her shoulders and that, together with the pale sunlight filtering through the cranberry glass lamp and falling softly upon her face, made her look as if she was just taking a nap instead of having passed on to a better life. She had been there for several days; rigor mortis had set in and there was the sickly smell of death in the room.

In front of her on the small oak table was an inkwell, a pen and a letter sealed with red sealing wax. The wax bore a seal of two intertwined snakes and a dragon's head.

It was a great shock to Will, for it was he and old Walter who were sent for to move her body. Although he was only twelve years old, he was no stranger to dead bodies, but the sight of Lucy made the tears roll down his cheeks.

'Now then, young Will,' said Walter, 'Don't take on so. See, she's got a smile on her face and wherever she is now she knows that her friends have arrived and are going to look after her. Take yourself outside, Will, and sit in the sunshine for a few minutes. Then ask Mr Ferris, the landlord, to help me carry the coffin upstairs and I'll do the rest.'

Walter was glad that Will did not have to put Lucy in the plain, wooden coffin for she was so rigid that it was not a pleasant task. Together with Mr Ferris he carried the coffin downstairs, loaded it on to the back of the cart and covered it with a couple of blankets.

'Send the hearse for Lucy?' Herbert had laughed in Walter's face. 'Paupers' burials are worth practically nothing to me; next thing, you'll want the four black horses, plumes and all. Take the cart and she's lucky to get that.'

Lucy's coffin was put on two trestles in the workhouse chapel and probably there the matter would have ended with but two mourners and an unmarked grave.

However that evening there was a knock on the Evertons' door and when Will opened it there stood Josiah Otter of Otter, Oxberry and Oxby, solicitors. He was wearing his usual frock coat, winged collar and cravat and mournful expression; indeed, it was said in Lincoln that none of the three partners ever smiled except when presenting their account and again when receiving payment of it.

Mr Otter asked to see Mr Everton 'on official business' and Will showed him into the drawing room. Herbert and Josiah were often to be found together at the White Hart and much of the affairs of the dead and dying were resolved in the bars and dining rooms of that establishment.

Will was told to leave the room, Herbert brought out the decanter and Josiah took a formal-looking document from his pocket.

'What I am about to say, 'Bert, is rather irregular and, strictly speaking, I suppose that I should not mention it. However, you and I have often had . . . er . . . mutually satisfactory business arrangements . . . and therefore in the interests of my client . . . . strictly in the interests of my client, I might say . . . I feel justified in drawing this . . . er . . . highly confidential matter to your attention.'

Herbert noticed that Josiah's glass was not quite filled to the top and hastened to remedy the omission.

'I am given to understand that you have removed the mortal remains of my client, Lucinda Letitia Hathergoode-Smythe, to the workhouse chapel where she lies in a cheap coffin without even a candle to light her departure from this world. My client was always a God-fearing woman who placed great importance upon the religious and sacred formalities being observed; she has left me precise instructions as to the manner of her funeral and interment and it was certainly NOT her wish to lie in a workhouse chapel like a pauper!'

'Lucinda Letitia who?' said Herbert.

'Lucinda Letitia Hathergoode-Smythe, my client,' said Josiah. 'Perhaps better known to you and to the citizens of this fair city as Lucy Matchbox. Miss Hathergoode-Smythe has been a client of our firm since she first came to the city and, indeed, your employee, Walter Smeed, brought to me her last will and testament from her lodgings this morning and which she had only just finished when she shuffled off this mortal coil and passed on to better things.'

Mr Otter delicately dapped at the end of his long nose with a silken handkerchief.

'Lucy Matchbox with a solicitor?' queried Herbert. 'That's one of the daftest things I ever heard of in my life. She didn't have two brass farthings to scratch her arse with!'

'On the contrary,' said Mr Otter, 'my client was not, and indeed never has been, impoverished. Her family, were I to mention the name, would immediately spring to your mind as having many thousands, nay millions of . . . er, brass farthings to scratch their . . . er . . . anatomies with.'

Herbert was still quite staggered by all this.

Josiah Otter took a healthy swig of his port and cast his eyes towards the decanter. Herbert caught the glance and made haste to refill the glass.

Josiah regarded his full glass with great satisfaction, holding it up to the light and perusing the rich, ruby liquid with a contented smile on his face. He didn't often have the advantage of his crony and was quietly savouring the moment and in no mood to expedite matters. Eventually, having downed half the glass and been given one of Herbert's best cigars from a silver box, he puffed a pungent cloud of cigar smoke towards the ceiling and volunteered the reason for his visit.

'As is customary in my profession,' he said, 'the will has been opened by me and has been found to be quite in order . . . this is all in confidence, of course . . . '

Herbert nodded eagerly, leaning forward on the edge of his chair and anxious not to miss a word.

Mr Otter continued: 'There will, of course, be an official reading and at this stage I feel it my duty as your friend to advise you that your son, William, will be required to be present as surprisingly, he is named as one of the beneficiaries together with another boy, one Edgar Ponsonby Carrot . . . '

Herbert nearly spluttered port all over his fine Indian carpet.

'Ponsonby Carrot?' he said. 'Whatever next. You mean the Carrots from Gordon Road? Father in jail and mother with a houseful of small children?'

'The very same,' said Josiah. 'But the best is yet to come. Miss Hathergoode-Smythe has left adequate funds to pay for a fine funeral, plus a fine brass plaque in memory of a gentleman friend to be placed in the Cathedral and . . . '

He drew a long inhalation of cigar smoke into his lungs, savouring the moment for all he was worth.

'And,' said Herbert. 'And?'

'And the balance of her estate is to be left to one Herbert Everton, cabinet maker, joiner and funeral director, subject to my being happy that her every wish in respect of her funeral arrangements has been carried out. So you see, Herbert, it all depends upon me . . . '

Where money was concerned, Herbert was not one to beat about the bush.

'How much?' he snapped.

'Money would be totally inappropriate,' said Mr Otter. 'However, Mrs Otter was greatly admiring the china cabinet that you made for Mr Oxby and also the dining table which you made for Mr Oxberry . . . ?'

Thus was the bargain concluded and Josiah Otter left.

Lucy Matchbox was removed from the workhouse chapel that very evening and arrangements were made for her to lie at rest in St Michael's Church where she had worshipped every Sunday. The vicar was not pleased at being called out so late but when it was explained to him that a fine funeral was in prospect, he brightened visibly. By the time that it was explained to him that full services of choir and organ were required and that the church was to be decked with the finest flowers, he was positively beaming.

The plain wooden coffin caused him to raise an eyebrow, but when he was told that this was only a temporary receptacle and that the following afternoon the deceased would be placed in the finest oak coffin that money could buy, complete with genuine brass fittings, and that it was not unlikely that a bequest to the church would be made, he invited Herbert round to the vicarage for a glass of spiritual comfort.

Will was sent round to Walter's house to tell him to be at the workshop at crack of dawn and that no expense was to be spared in the making of Lucy's coffin nor in the matter of fittings. It was to be the finest coffin that could be made. The engraver was to cut a fine, brass plate with Lucy's name on it and this was to be affixed to the lid.

In all the bustle and excitement, Herbert had almost forgotten the procession which was to take place the following day and which was to mark the commencement of the Golden Jubilee celebrations and it was not until he returned to Burton Road that night and saw his new suit hanging ready on his wardrobe that he realised that the great day was almost upon him.

Early the following morning he was at the workshop with Walter and Will and gave precise instructions as to the making of the coffin and its transport to the church. Walter had estimated that it would be ready by about two o'clock which, by coincidence, was also to see the start of the procession to the Cathedral to give thanks for the fifty glorious years of Her Majesty's reign.

Headed by the band of the Lincolnshire Regiment, the procession was to assemble in Silver Street, which was to be closed to all forms of traffic from one o'clock. The processional route was to be a simple one. Moving off from Silver Street the procession would walk up the New Road, then via Pottergate to the Minister Yard. However, on that very morning a part of the New Road collapsed into a Roman cellar beneath and the route was hastily altered to take in a number of side streets to avoid the resultant crater in the road. Walter was given strict instructions that the plain coffin was to be returned to the workshop in Motherby Lane - 'No doubt we'll find someone to fit it soon enough!' said Herbert.

'On no account are you to come anywhere near the procession,' said Herbert. 'This is a joyous occasion and I wouldn't want anyone to think that we were so grasping as to be carrying on our rather painful business on this particular day. All the shops and houses will have flags and bunting out and the whole city will be celebrating. In fact, take the cart, not the hearse. Black horses and plumes would be quite out of place. Mind you cover up the coffin, both coming and going, just put a few old sacks over it so's no one will pay it any particular attention.'

By one o'clock the new coffin was ready, and Walter decided to take it along before the procession started. Already, excited crowds waving Union Jacks were on the streets in large numbers, the Cathedral bells were chiming and the flags and banners were waving in a light breeze. It was fine and warm and an air of gaiety hung over the whole city. Children were in their best clothes and the adults were displaying the finery normally reserved for Sundays. At the top windows of Boots, the new chemists, and also at Murfin's, the grocers, there were large crowns with the royal cypher 'VR' on each side, whilst the Saracen's Head was positively ablaze with red, white and blue bunting. Some shops had hung banners from one side of the High Street to the other and these loudly proclaimed Lincoln's loyal greetings to their Queen. 'Long to reign over us' and 'God Save the Queen' seemed to be the two most popular ones. Above all, there was a hum of excitement which grew as the hour of the procession drew nearer.

Taking a roundabout route, Walter and Will delivered the new coffin to the church. The vicar was waiting and had already provided two helpers to assist with the unpleasant task of transferring Lucy from from one coffin to the next. During this procedure the vicar ran around the church with a handkerchief held to his nose, whilst the verger sprayed perfume all over.

At last the grisly task was done and Walter called Will in from outside and handed him the screwdriver.

'She was your friend, Will, perhaps you'd like to make sure that she's fastened in safe and sound?' said Walter.

Will wasn't sure that he wanted the job, but it was one that he had done many times before.

The job done, they went out into the churchyard and sat on a tombstone whilst they ate their sandwiches. Walter fetched across two tankards of ale from the local pub, 'to drink the 'ealth of the departed!' as he put it. Perhaps it was the combination of excitement, ale and the sun, but Will felt decidedly merry and, hearing the noises from the High Street, tried to persuade Walter that they should return leaving the plain coffin until later and go and watch the procession.

'And what if your father should spot us in the crowd?' asked Walter. 'What do you think he would say? Blame us for wasting his precious time, I wouldn't wonder.'

At last they compromised by agreeing that they would drive the cart down Steep Hill – no mean feat – and turn along Danes Terrace and Danegate to bring themselves to the junction with the New Road. From this vantage point they could sit on the cart and watch the procession go by and, if Will's father did spot them, they could say that they had been held up by the crowds and couldn't get through.

When they reached the end of Danegate they found it blocked solid with people. Walter shrugged his shoulders, lit his pipe, and sat back to enjoy the parade, whilst Will dismounted and put the nosebag on the horse, who was becoming a little restless at the noise all around him.

The empty coffin soon acquired a troupe of flag-waving small boys who, seeking a vantage point to see over the heads of the crowd, had not hesitated to jump aboard.

'Mind you behave' warned Walter 'or off you go, the lot of you! And don't move them sacks, what's under there is nothing to do with you.'

From further down the street a crash of cymbals and martial music announced the beginning of the parade and there was a loud cheer from the crowd. Those at the back of the crowd strained forward to see and there were cries of 'They're coming! They're coming!'

It took some time for the head of the procession to reach them, but soon the scarlet tunics of the soldiers were passing by. Two officers were at the head, riding horses and carrying swords. They made a fine sight and the crowd gave them a cheer. Bayonets gleaming, the soldiers stared straight ahead and marched in strict time to the beat of a drum, for the band had stopped for a few moments to draw second wind for the climb up New Road.

At that point, two things happened simultaneously.

Firstly, the bandmaster gave a shouted command and the band struck up with a rousing rendition of 'The Lincolnshire Poacher' and secondly, a small boy who had been denied a place on the cart by his friends gave the horse a whack over the rump with his flag in a fit of temper.

Old Nellie was an aged horse of great patience, but all the noise and excitement had made her nervous and these two events proved the final straw.

She reared up, whinnying in fear and anger, and small boys scattered from the cart like leaves in a storm. The crowd in front of her screamed and parted like the Red Sea before Moses as Old Nellie reared high, her hooves clattering on the cobblestones as she strained to get away from Walter's tight grip on the reins.

Fearful of the horse's antics, Walter tried to guide her gently to one side but, feeling the grip on the reins loosen, Nellie did a sharp right turn and set off down Silver Street, scattering the oncoming dignitaries like chaff before the wind. Will hung on like grim death, shouting to the horse to 'Whoa!' but Nellie knew the way back to Motherby Lane blindfolded and had made up her mind that that was where she was going.

At the far end of the procession, resplendent in frock coat and beaverskin hat, his diamond stickpin glittering in the sun, Herbert viewed the oncoming apparition with mounting horror.

'It's thy horse, Herbert,' shouted one of his fellow dignitaries. 'Stop the damned thing!'

No one could ever have called Herbert a coward and as Walter fought with the reins, Herbert stood out in the middle of the street and waved his arms from side to side, calling on the horse to stop.

Nellie recognised a familiar voice and saw a familiar figure. Not being quite a youngster any more, she decided that enough was enough, veered sharply to one side and stopped, causing the cart to career across the road at an angle where it smashed into the front of Nelson's the pork butchers. Mr Nelson, being aware that after the procession there would be a demand for something

33.

special for tea on this festive day, had raised the shutters and made a beautiful display of pork sausages on his marble slabs.

The cart stopped abruptly, but the coffin, Will astride it, carried on going. It shot out from beneath the sacks, tipped Will into the street, and completely demolished the sausage display, scattering pork sausages far and wide. The good people of Lincoln were not slow to respond and whilst Walter calmed the horse and Will rubbed his bruises, they collected the sausages from the street and some were returned to Mr Nelson. Others were trampled into the cobbles and some people were seen running off down the side alleys with links of sausages hanging over their shoulders. All in all, it was quite an exciting event and, as no one had suffered more than a fright and a few bruises, the clamour soon turned to a titter of laughter and then a positive roar of heartfelt mirth.

Mr Nelson stood outside his shop, fists clenched and arms waving, danced up and down and threatened Herbert with all the might of the law to repair his shop and to compensate him for the loss of his stock. Herbert stood motionless in the middle of the street, arms spread wide still, whilst his eyes looked for someone to blame and his face slowly assumed a shade of violent purple.

Spying Will getting up from the cobbles rubbing his rump, he was stimulated into motion and made for him, arms outstretched and mouthing inarticulate threats. What would have happened to Will would have been anyone's guess, but Herbert appeared to slip on the squashed sausage meat. He was caught by none other than the redoubtable Constable Peasgood, who continued to hold him up when it seemed that he might logically have let him go.

'Very heroic, Mr Everton,' he said. Then, turning to the crowd raised his voice and repeated the praise.

'A right hero, I reckon you are, Mr Everton,' he shouted. 'If you hadn't stopped that runaway horse, who knows how many of us might have been run down and killed! What do you say, then?'

Someone in the crowd started cheering, then someone else and soon it spread up and down the street and people were clammouring around Herbert and patting him on the back. A chorus of 'For he's a Jolly Good Fellow' ran around the crowd and Herbert positively glowed with pleasure.

When Mr Cornthwaite, the chairman of the workhouse guardians, shook his hand and said 'I knew you were the right man for us, Everton!' Herbert's cup was full to overflowing and he even expressed concern for Will and Walter that they had not sustained any injuries.

As for Mr Nelson, he was promised that his shop would be restored better than new the following morning and that he, Herbert, would gladly pay for all his lost and damaged stock. This further endeared Herbert to the crowd, and another cheer went up whilst Mr Nelson shook him by the hand and said he was a proper gentleman.

In the White Hart that evening, Herbert waxed eloquent as to his valiant behaviour and his way with horses. Cigar in one hand and a glass of brandy in the other, he told an enthralled gathering how he had seen Old Nellie thundering down the street a quarter of a mile away and made up his mind then and there to stop her.

'You see, gentlemen,' he said, 'I'd seen Old Nellie and, what's even more important, she'd seen me and realised that I'd stand no nonsense even though she was a quarter of a mile away!'

'Why, Herbert,' said a wag from the back of the room, 'that's progress for you! You must have fitted your horses with spectacles!'

Herbert joined in the laughter. Nothing could dampen his spirits on this day and the thought of the terms of Lucy's will made him look around his companions almost with scorn. If only they knew! But they didn't know and Josiah Otter, sitting quietly in a corner with his port, was not about to tell them. Mrs Otter had been most gratified to hear that her husband had bought her both the china cabinet and the dining table and that they should be hand made to her own measurements and requirements.

The following day, the *Lincoln Gazette and Times* sang Herbert's praises: 'Local hero averts disaster . . . brave Mr Everton of Burton Road stops mad horse!'

Lucy's funeral had the whole of Lincoln talking for many a day, for it was done in such style and pomp as left people who had known her gasping in amazement. The church was decked out in great masses of lillies, each pew being draped with a black silk covering. Her fine oak coffin, brass handles and fittings gleaming, laid on a tressle in front of the altar, tall brass candlesticks on either side and a single wreath of deep, red roses on the lid. The order of service was printed on fine vellum in gold typeface and concluded with the words: 'It is more blessed to give than to receive. Amen!'

The vicar preached a fine sermon, speaking of the wonderful and mysterious ways of the Lord. Who had not seen Lucy in the streets of Lincoln, he asked, and wondered at her strange apparel? Hearing her refined voice who had not wondered as to why she was little more than a beggar (Herbert visibly winced) when she had obviously known better times? Why, the vicar was convinced that she had heard the voice of the Lord, calling her to go forth and speak his word to the heathen, casting out sin and spreading light all around. Will, resplendent in his best suit and sporting a new pair of bright, black boots, wondered what the vicar was talking about, for he had never heard Lucy preaching anything anywhere except: 'Buy my matches, fine sir! Have a thought for one of life's less fortunates!'

Herbert himself acted as pall bearer, immaculately dressed, and holding his beaverskin hat in the crook of his arm, two black ribands trailing behind. Walter had also been equipped with a new suit ('purely a loan, you understand,' said Herbert) and a top hat with two ribands and the other two pall bearers had been warned to be smart and tidy upon threat of not being paid if they didn't.

The hearse was a picture to behold, newly varnished it shone and glistened at every slight movement. Cone-shaped vases of white lillies were at each corner and Herbert himself mounted the box for the short journey to the churchyard. The two black mares which pulled the hearse had been groomed for hours and their coats shone like ebony. Black ostrich plumes tossed up and down on their heads and their harness was gleaming with silver fittings. People gathered in large numbers to see the sight and lined the roadside, the men doffing their hats and caps and the ladies bowing their heads as the cortege passed by.

A plain, white marble cross was already lying by the side of the grave. It simply said 'Lucinda Letitia Hathergoode-Smythe. Born 2nd January 1857. Died 6th August 1887. Called to the Lord.'

The reading of the will took place in the offices of Otter, Oxberry and Oxby the following morning. The gathering included Herbert, Will, Clink, accompanied by his mother, and Mr Otter's clerk who ceremoniously placed a folder in front of Josiah Otter.

Mr Otter placed his rimless spectacles upon the end of his nose, opened the folder, and addressed his eager audience.

'Before I commence reading the will proper, it was my client's wish that I should give to you all some detail of her background. She felt that there were many who did not understand why she had taken to her way of life, and she did not wish to leave this earth without her friends knowing her reasons,' he said.

'Miss Hathergoode-Smythe, as she chose to be known, came from a noble and distinguished family. When she was but a girl in her teens, she met a soldier and fell in love with him. As the soldier was a common private, her family obviously could not approve of him and the thought of marriage to such a person was out of the question. Failing to convert her family to her way of thinking, she entered into a . . . er . . . er . . . a relationship with the gentleman.'

Knowing looks passed around the room.

'Not to put too fine a point on it,' continued Mr Otter, 'her family disowned her and that is how she came to Lincoln, following her . . . er . . . er . . . friend when he was sent to the barracks here. At the same time, I received instructions from Lord . . . ' Mr Otter quickly corrected himself ' . . . from her family, that she was to be provided for within certain limits.'

'Within reason, all might have been right, for the secret was well kept by everyone, but the soldier was transferred to another regiment, the twenty-fourth regiment of foot, I believe, and he was sent to fight the Zulus in Africa. Sadly, he was killed at a place called Isandhwlana and this seemed to have an effect on my client's mind.'

'Miss Hathergoode-Smythe had been quite well-informed on the stock market and had made some advantageous purchases over the years. Many of these she realised and I was instructed, under vow of strict confidence, to give the profits to charity and to reinvest the capital sum in other ventures.'

Herbert looked considerably cheered by this news.

Mr Otter now secured his spectacles more firmly on his nose, took the will from the folder and commenced to read.

'I, Lucinda Letitia Hathergoode-Smythe, of the Harlequin Tavern (Mr Otter wrinkled his nose slightly as he read this) in the city of Lincoln in the county of Lincolnshire, being of sound mind . . .'

Mr Otter glanced over the top of his spectacles at his audience and said: 'If no-one has any objections, I propose to dispense with the formal preambles . . .?'

No-one had any objection to getting down to the main part of the matter and Mr Otter continued.

'Er . . . let me see . . . ah, yes . . . do give and bequeath as follows . . . etc., etc. Ah yes, let me see . . . .' By now the tension in the room had become almost a solid object and even the rustle of Mr Otter's frock coat as he slightly adjusted his position on his chair was clearly audible.

'To William Everton of Burton Road, my friend and confidant, I leave a token of our friendship that he may remember me in the years to come.'

Mr Otter nodded to the clerk who opened the steel box on a side table and handed a leather pouch to Will.

Will took the pouch and looked across to Mr Otter.

'Go on, Will,' he said. 'Open it!'

Will opened the pouch to reveal a silver hunter pocket watch and albert. Eyes shining, he pressed the crown of the watch and the back sprang open. He read the inscription out aloud.

'Corporal John William Hathergoode. Killed at Isandhwlana,

22nd January, 1879. He died for his country.'

Will was quite speechless. He had never owned anything like this in his life. Eventually he got his breath back and stammered out his thanks to Mr Otter.

Mr Otter smiled a rare smile.

'Don't thank me, Will,' he said. 'Thank Miss Hathergoode-Smythe. That watch was returned from the battlefield by an officer friend of my client's family. I think that perhaps she valued it more than anything else she possessed.'

'Cor,' said Clink, wondering what was going to be his lot.

'To continue,' said Mr Otter. 'To the said William Everton I further leave the sum of one hundred pounds, the same to be invested on his behalf by my solicitors, Otter, Oxberry and Oxby and the proceeds to be given to him solely and exclusively upon his twenty-first birthday.'

Mrs Carrot, who had sat uncomfortably on the edge of a chair up to now almost fell from it and uttered an amazed 'Cor, Luvaduck!'.

Even Herbert was impressed and silent for a moment, then he recovered his composure and put an arm around his son's shoulders. Will automatically ducked from the anticipated blow around the head, but Herbert patted him on his tousled hair and said 'Quite right! Quite right! I've always said friendship was its own reward.'

The solicitor carried on reading: 'To Edgar Ponsonby Carrot of Gordon Road, my friend and confidant, I bequeath the sum of five pounds that he may immediately go into the city and buy himself some token to remember me by. I further bequeath him the sum of one hundred pounds, the same sum as I left William Everton, and to be invested for his benefit in the same manner and the proceeds to be given to him upon his majority . . . that means when you are twenty-one years of age, Edgar,' explained Mr Otter.

Mr Otter's clerk took a small purse from the steel box and carefully counted out five gold sovereigns on the desk in front of Clink. Clink stared at the gold coins as if hypnotised and made no effort to take them. He had never seen such a sum of money in his life. The clerk pushed a piece of paper in front of him and indicated that he should sign it. Dipping a pen into the inkwell, he passed it to Clink who made his cross on the bottom and the clerk then signed it as a witness.

Herbert could scarcely restrain the feelings of joy and impatience he felt. If twelve year old boys received a hundred pounds, then what might his share of the estate be worth. It was with great difficulty that he stopped himself from rubbing his hands in anticipation.

'The next portion of the will refers to you, Mrs Carrot,' said Mr Otter, reseating the spectacles in their precarious position and smiling as Clink still sat mesmerised by the five gold sovereigns.

'Where are we now, ah yes . . . to continue . . . To Mrs Charlotte Carrot, mother of the said Edgar Carrot etc., etc., I leave the sum of ten pounds to be paid immediately that she may pay off any arrears of rent which have befallen her due to the imprisonment of her husband, largely due to the wicked and heartless actions of her landlord . . . I think we can perhaps out of charity miss out the next few sentences.'

For the first time, Herbert felt a strange twinge of uneasiness.

'I furthermore leave to the said Charlotte Carrot the sum of one half-sovereign, to be paid each Friday between the time of my death and Christmas Day, 1887 . . . '

'My God,' said Mrs Carrot, 'she must have known that she was dying.'

Mr Otter coughed loudly and carried on as if he had not heard.

' . . . and thereafter the sum of one sovereign and one half sovereign each Friday until such time as her husband shall have found gainful employment, the wages of such employment to exceed thirty shillings per week. This second sum shall be paid for not more than twelve consecutive Fridays and on the thirteenth Friday the said Charlotte Carrot shall be paid the sum of twenty sovereigns in final discharge of this, my bequest to her. Mrs Carrot, do you understand the substance of my client's wishes?'

Charlotte Carrot nodded slowly, large tears running down her face, and rocked back and forth in her chair as she sobbed to herself 'I thought no-one cared. I thought no-one cared!

'We now come to the final bequest,' said Mr Otter, 'and this concerns the manner of Miss Hathergoode-Smythe's funeral and the remainder of her estate . . . ahum . . . er . . . yes, to continue to be sure . . . In the manner of my furnishings and various items in my lodgings at the Harlequin Tavern (Mr Otter sniffed again), it is my wish that the contents of my rooms be sold, being worth at least fifty pounds, to the first person willing to pay that sum and that the said fifty pounds shall be given to the workhouse in Burton Road for the benefit of its inmates . . . .'

He had hardly taken a breath before Herbert said in a loud voice, 'I'll give you the fifty pounds. I don't want the bits and pieces, but the good woman's wishes must be respected. Everyone here is a God fearing person, I'll be bound.'

The clerk pushed forward a piece of paper and Herbert, who by the most amazing coincidence had fifty sovereigns in a leather pouch in his pocket, paid over the cash and the clerk signed a receipt.

The voice droned on . . . 'It is most important to me that my funeral shall be carried out in a dignified manner and that I shall be laid to rest in a christian churchyard with a white cross to my grave, and in this respect I have left certain instructions with my solicitors in a separate document, desiring them to instruct Herbert Everton, a well-known funeral director of this city, to carry out my wishes. If my solicitors be satisfied that my wishes have been carried out to the letter, then I give and bequeath the rest of my estate to the said Herbert Everton, funeral director, such estate to include all monies, properties and possessions without let or hindrance.'

'At this stage, ladies and gentlemen, let me say that my partners and I are quite happy that Mr Everton has complied with Miss Hathergoode-Smythe's wishes to the very letter.'

Herbert did his best to look surprised and muttered: 'Why, I had no idea . . . what a kind and noble lady, indeed.'

The clerk then dragged in a leather portmanteau and Mr Otter handed a labelled key to Herbert.

'My late client's remaining possessions and titles etc., are, I gather, contained in this portmanteau and you Mr Everton, will please now open it in my presence that I may see the terms of the will carried out.'

Herbert opened the portmanteau with the key provided, standing it on end to get at the lock. His shaking hands failed to hold the lid secure and the contents of the case spilled out onto the carpet.

There was a washleather purse containing four shillings and eleven pence and two hundred and forty-seven boxes of matches!

CHAPTER TWO

. . . AND A HAPPY NEW YEAR

THE DAYS THAT FOLLOWED the reading of Lucy Matchbox's will were not easy ones for Will. His father was still positively seething a week after the event and everyone, friend and foe alike, got the sharp edge of his tongue. In Will's case he also not infrequently received the even harder edge of his hand, for he blamed Will and Clink for his misfortunes in the affair. At least a dozen times he told Will that he felt sure that the reason he had been treated so shabbily (as he thought) was because the two boys had been telling tales against him. 'Why else should the woman alter her will at the last moment?' he kept asking himself.

He sought to have the will made void, arguing with Josiah Otter that as she had obviously been making the will just before she died she could not possibly have had it properly witnessed. Josiah conceded that this was indeed a point and investigations were made of the witnesses. However, it was established that a few days prior to her death, Lucy had gone down into the bar of the pub below her rooms with a blank sheet of paper and asked two of the regulars to witness her signature.

Herbert was triumphant. How could the witnesses be legal when there was nothing written on the paper? Josiah pointed out that there did not need to be anything written there. The witnesses did not have to be party to the contents of the will; they were doing no more than certifying that the signature had been made in their presence by the person wielding the pen and the will itself had obviously been drawn up later by Lucy just before she died.

Although Herbert had been correctly recompensed for the funeral expenses, there was much for which he could not claim reimbursement. The special preparation of the hearse, the hire of the four black mares, the great masses of flowers in the church were all discounted by Josiah Otter as they had not been strictly in the brief given to Herbert. Josiah argued that Herbert could have used his own pair of horses, that the special varnishing of the hearse was a normal part of the business and that although Lucy had asked for flowers, it had not been necessary to provide so many.

As for Walter's new suit and Will's new boots, it was up to Herbert to provide his staff with 'uniforms' and his son with footwear, said Josiah, and any request for additional payment for these items just caused him to shake his head. In fact, if truth be known, Josiah was quite enjoying Herbert's discomfort and he was not alone in this respect for Herbert had pulled off more than one sharp deal in the city in his endeavours to rise in social status.

Herbert experienced severe embarassment on more than one occasion when he went into the White Hart.

'Now then, Bert,' shouted one of his friends, 'you'll be entering that nag of yours in the Lincolnshire Handicap, then . . . that's if you've got any money left to back it with!'

The room erupted with laughter and it was all Herbert could do to restrain himself from clouting the wit over the head with his walking stick. Instead, he smiled a sickly smile and dropped hints that everything was not quite as straightforward as it seemed and neither had everything been made public about the terms of the will.

'You might think that, Herbert,' said one crony, 'but the way old Ma Carrot was telling the yarn in the Butter Market yesterday, she's got a damned sight more out of the will than you have, and that's a fact. Why, even her lad got five pounds out of it!'

The humour was beginning to wear thin, largely due to the fact that Herbert had taken to imbibing his evening glass with a couple of close associates in the Saracen's Head, rather than the White Hart, in order to let the tumult die down. One evening, he was sitting quietly at a table working out a business deal with one of them when in came Mr Nelson, the gentleman whose pork butcher's shop had been half wrecked by the panic stricken horse.

Mr Nelson went straight to the bar and purchased a large glass of brandy which he took over to Herbert and placed on the table in front of him.

'Your very good health, Mr Everton,' he said and gave him a large sheet of paper.

'Now then, what's this?' asked Herbert.

Mr Nelson smiled, nay positively beamed, and advised him that it was the account for repairs to his shop.

Herbert's eyes ran slowly down the paper, his face becoming redder and redder as he got further down the sheet. By the time he had reached the last line his face was almost scarlet and he seemed to be having difficulty in breathing. He fumed and spluttered, his cheeks swelling and puffing, but no words seemed able to emerge.

Suddenly, in one furious explosion of sound, he screamed 'What the hell's this? I told you I'd pay for the repair of your bloody shop, not to rebuild the bloody thing! Thirty-three pounds? THIRTY-THREE POUNDS? The whole damned shooting match isn't worth that!'

And he screwed the bill into a ball and flung it down at Mr Nelson's feet.

Mr Nelson slowly bent down and picked it up. He carefully unravelled it, placed it flat on the table and smoothed it out, then took Herbert's right hand and gently placed the paper in it. The whole room strained to hear as he got hold of Herbert's shirt front, placed his face within an inch of Herbert's and positively hissed, 'You promised to pay for the damages to my shop. You promised to pay. I heard you, Constable Peasgood heard you, half of bloody Lincoln heard you. Now I expect to receive this money tomorrow morning. If I don't, I'll be here, or at the White Hart or I'll come to your home in Burton Road and I'll knock seven sorts of shit out of you!'

Nodding to the customers in the bar he turned on his heels and walked out, leaving a badly shaken Herbert trying to smooth out his shirt front and salvage what little dignity he could.

Walter duly delivered the required amount to Mr Nelson's establishment the next morning.

Herbert's next move was to try to get hold of Will's one hundred pounds by arguing that Will was a minor and therefore not responsible enough to handle such a large sum of money and that he, Herbert, as the boy's father, should take the cash into his care until Will reached twenty-one.

Josiah Otter smiled sweetly and pointed out that indeed Will was not mature enough to have charge of such a sum, but then again, of course, Will didn't have the money and would not until he reached majority. He, Josiah, would see to that.

Herbert eventually accepted defeat and appeared on the surface to have cast the whole matter from his mind, but underneath it gnawed at him and he was as much upset at the loss of face as at the financial tragedy.

Clink took his five pounds into the city, accompanied by Will and, after much debate, purchased a silver hunter pocket watch just like Will's for the sum of seven shillings and sixpence. A further sixpence was paid and the jeweller engraved the word 'Lucy' in the back of the case whilst he waited. It was a curious name for a boy, observed the jeweller, when he recounted the incident to his wife later in the day but then, what was the world coming to? Small boys with a sovereign to spend!

Thereafter, they bought two hot pies and two bottles of pop and sat with their feast on a bench by the Waterside and watched the barges go by. They discussed what they would do with their fortunes when they were twenty-one and planned, amongst other things, the opening of a bank – 'You can never be short of money if you own a bank!' reasoned Clink – sailing to a far away place and digging for gold, and owning a circus. Thus do small boys dream, and the Almighty is wise enough not to let them see the life that lies ahead of them and He lets them dream.

Of the four pounds, eleven shillings and fivepence left, Clink insisted that Will should have five shillings, kept five shillings for himself and turned the rest over to his mother.

Mrs Carrot had been walking on air ever since the day in

46.

Josiah's office. She had payed off the arrears of rent and each Friday went along to the office to collect her half-sovereign. Whilst her husband was in prison this was to be a godsend for she could pay her rent and, with care, could manage out the rest of the week. She took in laundry and did cleaning at the local pub three mornings a week whilst her smaller children were at school. Truth to tell, she had never been quite so well off in her life. She missed her husband terribly for, despite his rough ways and his affection for the products of Dawber's brewery, he was a kind man and a good father, but the relief from financial strain whilst he was away had given her a new lease of life.

With the change from the original ten pounds given to her to pay the rent, she had taken her four younger children on the horse-drawn tram into the city and had purchased new clothes for the two boys from Frederick Choice. Mr Choice was also a pawnbroker and, as he jovially remarked, it was nice for both of them that Mrs Carrot was giving him money rather than the reverse. Then they went on to Bainbridge's, where there was a sale taking place, and bought new clothes for the two girls. A gentleman in a smart suit, sporting a watch chain and with a silken handkerchief in his top pocket, brought Mrs Carrot a chair and addressed her as 'Madam'. This really made her day, and by the time she ushered them into a small tea shop for cakes and lemonade, they were all bedecked with parcels and quite excited. Such free spending of money had never been known before in the Carrot household.

Henry Carrot, languishing in prison, heard of all the good fortune with disbelief. He had always been a receiver of the slings and arrows of outrageous fortune and, once he had grown accustomed to the idea, the knowledge that his family was now provided for whilst he was away made his days seem a little shorter. Sitting in his cell it had taken him a little time to work out that once he was released he would have a weekly income of thirty shillings for at least twelve weeks, but he worried for he knew that he would never find a job paying that much money. However, he had a very sharp cell mate who soon enlightened him.

'Look 'ere, 'enery my lad,' he said, 'I reckon that old Lucy knew very well that you would never get a job at thirty bob a week. I bet you ain't never 'ad more than ten bob a week in your life. So what does old Lucy want you to do? She wants you to 'ave three months rest with your family, that's what she wants. Why, I reckon as 'ow she's a sittin' up there on a white, fluffy cloud, playing her 'arp and wishing that you'd understand that. After that you get another twenty quid? Gor blimey, 'enery, you're on easy street, mate!'

Henry slowly absorbed matters and realised that he was indeed on easy street, at least a damned sight easier street than he had ever been on before in his life, and when he was sent with a working party to clear some rubble from the back of the prison yard he waded in with such a will that the warders gazed upon him with awe. Beams that two other men could barely lift, he threw onto the cart with joyous abandon single handed, rendering a few lines of his favourite hymns into the bargain.

The weeks passed slowly by. Summer turned to autumn and the workshop in Motherby Lane was chill when Will entered early in the morning. He and Walter would build up the fire in a grate in the corner of the shop and make a brew of tea before commencing the work of the day. On one occasion, Herbert appeared unexpectedly and found them sitting by the fire with steaming tin mugs. He knocked the mug from Walter's hand with his walking stick, sending it clattering across the floor, screamed at the top of his voice that he didn't pay him to drink tea and on Friday knocked sixpence off his wages for time-wasting. Will received a clout across the ear that sent him staggering across the floor and also had sixpence docked from his wages. Any natural affection that Will felt for his father had been knocked out of his head before his thirteenth birthday.

Eventually Christmas Eve arrived. Herbert informed Will that he and Annie would be spending Christmas Day with an uncle in Market Rasen. Will was not to go, although he had been invited. Someone had to keep an eye on things, as Herbert put it; after all, people didn't stop dying just because it was Christmas and who would call Mrs Gambage to lay them out if Will wasn't there? If they all went away it would be tantamount to handing over the business to their competitors. He, Herbert, would be back on Boxing Day to attend to the business aspect of any funerals that might be required. Thus saying, he gave Will half a crown, wished him 'Merry Christmas', and departed with Annie in the pony and trap.

Will stared at the half crown and then put it into a purse with the florin he had been given by another uncle. He looked around the well furnished room, furniture all hand-made by his own father, heavy carpet on the floor and rich velvet drapes to the windows and would happily have swapped it all for a family gathering around the Christmas festive board such as he saw pictured in books and heard other children talk about. He had never really had a traditional Christmas as far as he could remember, and when he heard people say that Christmas was the happiest time of the year for children, he felt very sad indeed. He stood at the window and stared into Burton Road. A house opposite had a Christmas tree in the window and the road positively bustled with people hurrying into town to buy last minute gifts. A pony and trap passed by, the harness dressed with festive trimmings and the pony with a sprig of holly on its head-piece. A small boy sat in the carriage between his mother and father, chattering excitedly and revelling in that very special feeling that is Christmas.

Will pulled up his long woollen socks, rubbed his sleeve across his nose and cried. He sat in the chair by the window and sobbed in a low voice, 'Mother! Mother! Why did you leave me?' The tears flowed freely down his face and his shoulders shook with grief. He had never felt so desperately alone in his life and he longed for the warmth and comforting arms of the smiling woman that Walter had described to him that day in the workshop.

There was a tapping on the window and Clink's ginger hair suddenly rose above the window sill as he heaved himself up to look through the window. He beckoned Will to come to the door.

Will shouted 'Just a minute!' and dashed into the kitchen to rub a damp cloth over his face before he opened the door. Clink looked at the red-rimmed eyes and started to say something, but then he stopped and fidgetted his feet awkwardly.

Eventually he said: 'I saw your father and Annie going off in the trap, Will, so I knew you'd be alone. They've released my father a day early and he wants you to come round to our house to meet him.'

Clink gazed into the hall and added, 'Course it's nothing like your house, and if you don't want to come and see us my Dad says that doesn't matter and he'll meet you another time . . . but it is Christmas and he 'specially wants you to come.'

Will took his cap from the hallstand, jammed it on his head and locked the heavy wooden door behind them. He breathed a sigh of relief as the heavy lock rammed into position; the last place he wanted to be on that day was in that house.

As the boys walked down Burton Road and along Westgate, Will found himself brightening up. It was hard not to be caught up in the general excitement of that day before Christmas. The air was crisp and cool and a few flakes of snow occasionally drifted in front of them and this provoked a discussion as to why it always snowed at Christmas, at least in pictures they saw. Shop windows were full of pictures of snow scenes and robins.

Gordon Road, where the Carrot family lived, lay just off Bailgate and close to the Assize Courts. Strictly speaking, it lay in the 'Above Hill' section of the town where the better-off inhabitants of Lincoln society reputedly lived. In effect, some of the worst slums of the city were to be found in the area. When Will's father had purchased the property he had inherited the Carrot family as tenants, together with a number of other working class families who had somehow found their way into the area. Always behind with the rent, they formed a constant source of annoyance to Herbert, but there was method in his madness.

Families such as the Carrots could always be brought to heel by the bailiffs and the better-off would turn up their noses and say that it served them right. No stigma would attach to Herbert for pressuring them for his rent and, indeed, when the matter was queried in the lounge bar of the White Hart, he would chide his inquisitors by saying: 'They're all God's creatures, Mr So and So, not so fortunate in life as you and I, but nevertheless God's creatures. They have to live somewhere. Would you have them live down in Straw's Court, then? Far better for them to live near their betters where hopefully you and I may discharge our Christian duty by showing them a better way of life. Thus we give them a purpose, a goal towards which they may strive.'

Thus saying, he would stick his hands in the corners of his waistcoat, puff on his cigar, and order another bottle.

Will entered the little house by the front door and was immediately impressed by the cosyness of the room. A roaring fire was in the grate, the black side oven gleaming with a combination of Ma Carrot's elbow grease and 'Zebo' grate polish. A mouth-watering aroma of baking bread filled the place and the large, white wood table gleamed like ivory, scrubbed almost every day to pristine virginity. On the hearth was a set of brass fire tongs and poker, likewise polished to perfection.

But it was Henry Carrot who filled the room.

He was sitting in an armchair by the fire, a glass of ale at his right hand. Looking at him sitting in the armchair, Will was reminded of a cork squeezed into a bottle. His corduroy trousers seemed stretched so tight over his massive legs that they must burst. He wore a flannelette shirt, but no collar and one could but guess at the size of the neck around which the neckband strained to make an impression. His prison haircut had left him with a bare half inch of grey hair which covered his square-set head like stubble in a cornfield, whilst his ruddy complexion would have done credit to a scarlet poppy. His sleeves were rolled up above his elbows and on his right forearm was a tattoo of a heart pierced with an arrow and the word 'Mother' in a fancy scroll. His left forearm was totally covered by a writhing dragon which breathed fire down as far as his fingers, whilst on his hairy chest Will could make out a three-masted schooner in full sail before a strong wind.

On his left knee sat the two youngest of the Carrot brood, Emily who was two, and Sophia who was three. On his right knee sat his other two sons, Nathan who was five and John who was six: Will was reminded of sparrows sitting on the branches of a huge oak tree.

The mountain stirred from the chair, casting children onto the rug in front of the fire with great tenderness, and stood up to his full height of six feet four inches.

Will looked up at him with awe. Never in his life had he seen anyone so huge. He gazed at the proferred hand which resembled the prize ham he had seen in the butcher's window that very morning and hesitantly offered his own. The handshake took in his own hand and half his forearm in the massive palm and, as Will waited for them to be crushed to a bloody pulp, the gentle giant took his other hand into the grip and held them as tenderly as Will could remember anyone doing.

'You'll be master Everton, I'll be bound,' he said. 'Welcome to our 'umble 'ome, Master Everton. In this last few hours since I left 'er Majesty's establishment I've been 'earing a great deal about you and as how you've been a great friend to my son, Edgar. You'll understand, I'm finding all this quite 'ard to get used to, what with the will and everything, but Mrs Carrot 'as advised me of all your adventures and I'm fair out of breath with the wonder of it all. 'Ere I am, just out of prison, but not owing any man a penny, there's money in the missus' purse, half a sovereign in my pocket to go down to the Lord Nelson and treat all my mates and all of us looking forward to the most wonderful Christmas we have ever 'ad. What a miracle, what a miracle, indeed!'

Will wasn't quite sure how to respond. He was totally overwhelmed by Mr Carrot and soon found himself sitting by the fireside, playing with the younger children. Clink bombarded his father with questions about life in prison, but Henry just shook his head and said that he had no intention of going back there and that as soon as Christmas was over, he would be seeking a job and in future he would cause no trouble to anyone. In truth, Henry Carrot had never intended to cause any trouble, but he had a strong aversion to injustice in any form and this, combined with a formidable capacity for strong beer, had been his downfall on many an occasion. Being an uneducated man, he was not able to put his protests into words and thus tended to express himself by actions. Whereas an ordinary mortal in a bar brawl might raise a chair and threaten, Henry would raise a chair and suddenly find that he had broken off all four legs. Henry had a lot to contend with in life, and most of it he found hard to comprehend.

They chatted a while about Lucy Matchbox and that day at the solicitor's office and Henry's main contribution was an occasional muttered 'thirty bob a week, now fancy that!'. Then they all sat around the white wooden table and Mrs Carrot served a lamb stew, her small brood chattering like magpies all the time until she had to remind them of their manners. Henry said a very brief garbled grace and they all tucked in with a will.

By the time they got around to the home-made fruit pie and custard Will had lost the unhappy feelings with which he had started the day and was laughing and joking with the rest of them.

After the meal, Henry squeezed himself back into the armchair, lit his pipe and looked across to the other side of the fireplace where Mrs Carrot was sitting, cuddling Emily and Sophia to her ample bosom. Then he looked across to Will and nodded.

'Will,' said Mrs Carrot, 'Edgar has been telling us that your family has gone to Market Rasen and that you will be on your own tomorrow.'

Will nodded, the old familiar lump seeming to suddenly reappear in his throat. The warmth of the Carrot dwelling had fully enfolded him now, and the thoughts of spending Christmas Day on his own at Burton Road filled him with positive horror. He saw the happy family around him and was filled with longing. He fought back a tear and mumbled that he would be alright, rubbing his sleeve across his nose as he spoke.

'Damn it, woman,' said Henry, 'a twelve year old lad on his own on Christmas Day. It's neither human nor civilised and his father should be sent down to prison for allowing it.'

He raised his massive fists in protest and Mrs Carrot had to calm him down.

'The fact is, Will', said Mrs Carrot, 'we would like to ask you to spend Christmas Day with us. We know that our 'ome is not all what you're used to. We haven't got any fine china or silver dishes and there's no velvet curtains at the windows, but we're God-fearing people and we'd make you feel really welcome. There'll be a warm fire, a few Christmas carols and we honestly want you to come.'

It was all too much.

Will could control himself no longer and the tears flowed like water. His shoulders heaved as all the misery of his life seemed to descend upon him like a great torrent. Apart from Lucy Matchbox, he had had little to look forward to in his daily round and when Lucy had died after such a short friendship it had left a great gap in his young life. Clink was virtually the only friend he had. His own sister had no thought or love for him and it seemed to him that his father saw him only as a worker. The longing for a mother of his own was a great, solid mass in his chest and, try as he would, he could not hold back the tears.

Mrs Carrot put a tender arm around his shoulders and guided him into the kitchen where Clink tried to follow. Gently but firmly, she pushed him out and closed the door behind her. She hugged the small boy to her, shushing him and uttering words of comfort until the heaving shoulders subsided. Then she took a towel and wiped his face. Holding him by both shoulders she forced him to look her straight in the face.

'Will Everton', she said, 'life's never very fair to anyone, be 'e small or great, but it seems to me that you're getting more than your share of burdens for one so young. I'm sorry you 'ave no mother and I feel deeply for you, but your mother's gone and you'll not see her again in this world, God rest her soul. But mark my words, your mother loved you and, wherever she is, she still watches over you and loves you. Them's facts and no one can change them. But if you let me, I'll be a mother to you and I'll love you like one of my own.'

Will spent the rest of that day with Clink and his family, returning to Burton Road in the early evening in case there should have been any call for the firm's professional services. However, it appeared that no one in Lincoln had died that day, or if they had, they preferred their funeral arrangements to be handled by someone else.

At the last minute, just before the shops closed, he went out to buy Christmas presents for the Carrot family. For each of the four small children he bought a Christmas stocking. The stockings were made of net and sealed at the top with a large and bright picture of Father Christmas. Through the mesh you could see the contents, a bright orange rubber ball, a game with a paper board and counters, a squeaker with a feather at the end and lots of sweets and toffees together with a huge lollipop. For Clink he bought a mouth organ, for Clink's father a large cigar and an ounce of pipe tobacco but for Mrs Carrot he did not seem able to find anything suitable.

As he passed Fox's on the High Street his eye was caught by a bright red scarf draped across the corner of the window. In the busy commotion of Christmas Eve the window display had become rather jumbled and the price ticket had fallen off the scarf. Will carefully counted his remaining money. Taking into account that his father would expect a present for himself and Annie when he returned, Will reckoned that the most he could spend on the scarf would be two shillings and ninepence. He then realised that he had not yet bought any coloured paper in which to wrap the presents and quickly amended his available finances to two shillings and sevenpence.

Will looked at the red scarf again. It would, he told himself, be just the right colour for Mrs Carrot with her bright red hair and freckled face. In fact the more he looked at it, the more he determined that he must buy it and thus he marched into the shop and asked to see it.

The assistant, a pretty young girl with long hair falling on her shoulders, got it from the window and spread it out on the counter beneath the flickering gaslights. She moved an oil lamp on the counter a little nearer so that its light caught the square of silk and made its colours positively spring to life. Then she draped it around her shoulders and did a pirouette to demonstrate how pretty it was. Finally she spread it back on the counter and asked Will if it was to be a present for his mother.

'I don't have a mother,' said Will. 'Well, I don't but I do, if you follow me . . . that is, I just sort of got a new one today, but she's really someone else's mother not mine.' His face blushed with embarassment and to cover his confusion he blurted out a quick enquiry as to the price.

The disappointment showed on his face when the girl said it was three shillings. Despite the temptation, he dare not risk spending money which he had set aside for his father's and sister's gifts. He looked again at the coins in his hand, counted them three times but couldn't make them add up to any more, then said a choked 'Merry Christmas' to the girl and turned his back to depart.

As he reached the door, a male voice called him back into the shop.

'How much have you got, young sir?' enquired the dignified gentleman in the frock coat and very shiny shoes. Will told him two shillings and sevenpence.

'Miss Cooper,' said the gentleman, 'you may sell the scarf to the gentleman for that price. After all, it is Christmas Eve and almost closing time. I wish you a Merry Christmas sir, and many of them. I hope that your mother likes the scarf.'

Miss Cooper smiled a dazzling smile at Will, winked at him, and wrapped up the scarf in a pretty parcel tied with a bow of pink ribbon. Will paid his money and the gentleman opened the door for him as he left the shop.

Will was quite breathless with excitement and could barely stammer out his thanks.

'That's alright young man,' said the proprietor, 'I can remember many years ago when my mother's Christmas present was the most important thing in the year. It should be that for every young gentleman.'

And Mr Fox himself, for he it was, smiled a sad smile.

56.

Will went home with his packages and spent a busy hour making them up into gift parcels. When he got to Mrs Carrot's scarf, he found that his remaining piece of wrapping paper was far too small to make a neat parcel. Nothing daunted, he went outside into the outhouse where various bits and bobs were kept and took a piece of the white silk material used for lining coffins. When he had put the piece of ribbon around it and stuck a piece of holly on, he felt that it looked quite fine and was very pleased with his handywork.

Early next morning he made his way to Clink's house, humming merrily to himself. It was a cold, crisp day and the cathedral bells rang clear through the fine air. The Carrot household had been transformed since the previous afternoon. The windows were dressed around the edges with cotton wool to look like snow and behind the shining glass Will could see a Christmas tree. Inside, the little room was decorated with paper chains. The festive table was already set, spotless white cloth covered with a bright red lace one in stark contrast. Beside each place setting was a paper napkin decorated with holly. Mrs Carrot was busy in the kitchen but when she heard his voice she came out rubbing her hands on her apron and gave him a huge kiss.

The younger children made a great fuss of Will and showed him their gifts. Then he handed out his own gifts. There was much tearing of paper and great excitement. Will felt quite shy of handing his parcel to Mrs Carrot, but when she unwrapped it she flushed with joy, took Will in both arms and smacked a great wet kiss on his cheek. Then she fastened the scarf around her neck where it remained for the rest of the day.

Henry Carrot went to a cupboard and took out a parcel which he handed to Will. Egged on by everyone, Will opened it and found himself gazing at a thick and beautifully bound book, 'The Children's Book of Knowledge'. Will skimmed through the pages and wondered at the many coloured illustrations. Truly, it was a wondrous volume and his pleasure showed in his face.

'We all clubbed together to buy this for you,' said Clink. 'You see, neither my Dad nor I are very brainy, but we know you are.'

'Knowledge is a wonderful thing, Will,' said Henry. 'You're such a bright lad, I thought it was right for you.'

Will didn't know quite what to say, but was spared the embarassment of trying to think up something to say by a loud knock at the door. Clink answered it and a loud voice said, 'Package for Mr 'enry Carrot!'

Henry went to the door and his jaw dropped open in wonderment. There on a small horse cart was a piano . . . no, there on a small horse cart was THE piano!

'Bless my soul,' said Henry. 'It's my old piano, I'd know it anywhere. Look, mother, there's that chip out of the side where I 'it it with my 'ead when I was taken ill with the vertigo.'

'Taken ill with Dawber's disease, more like,' said Mrs Carrot.

Henry went out to the cart and lovingly stroked his hand across the battered wood, muttering to himself all the time, 'Well, I never!' 'Well, I never!'

Then he clambered up onto the cart, lifted the lid, and burst forth into an impromptu and rather toneless version of 'Good King Wenceslas' which reverberated around the quiet streets like a sudden thunderstorm. The old pony, who obviously had deep-rooted objections to working on Christmas Day anyway, reared in great alarm whilst the carter struggled with the reins and it took a great deal of effort to stop the piano sliding off the back of the cart. Finally, Will, Clink and Henry duly assisted the carter to carry the instrument into the living room where, with a little re-arranging of the furniture, it was finally restored to its former pride of place.

Mrs Carrot had seen the piano sitting in the window of a second-hand shop a few days previously and, using three pounds of her new found wealth, had bought it back for her husband's Christmas present. That Henry was deeply moved no one could doubt for a huge tear rolled down one ruddy cheek as he took Mrs Carrot into a bear-like hug and proclaimed his good fortune at having the best wife in the world. Then followed a jolly sing-song with all the favourite Christmas tunes being hammered out with great enthusiasm if not a lot of musical talent.

58.

Finally it was time for Christmas dinner.

Will looked at the groaning table and thought that it was the most beautiful thing he had ever seen. Two large red candles had been lit and cast a warm glow across the laden dishes. The goose sat in the middle on a blue and white dish, so hot you could see the heat rising from it. It was a rich brown, and the roast potatoes around its sides seemed to shine like golden nuggets. There were dishes of sprouts and peas, cauliflower and carrots. As Mrs Carrot called them to sit down, the children were chattering so excitedly that she had to shout to make herself heard.

Clink picked up his knife and fork as if he couldn't wait to start, but Mr Carrot gave him a firm crack across the knuckles with the carving steel and announced that he intended to say grace. If Mrs Carrot was surprised, she concealed it very well, and they all bowed their heads over the table.

'God bless this house and all who live in it,' commenced Henry. 'We thank thee, Lord, for this wonderful table placed before us today and for bringing a good friend to join us Little Will. 'E's welcome 'ere, and always will be and 'e's welcome to share whatever we 'ave. Especially we remember Miss Lucy who made all this possible and was thinkin' about us even when we never gave her a thought . . . in fact, if I'd known she was thinkin' about us I'd have bought a few boxes of matches of 'er sometimes. Thank you, God, for releasing me from prison and I promise you that I won't go there again. The bad times is be'ind this family now, so 'elp us all, Lord to be a bit better than we 'ave been, and particularly ask John Peasgood to forgive me for swipin' 'im so 'ard. He's a constable and was naught but doin' his job and didn't deserve to be belted like that . . . and, by the way, God, Merry Christmas to you, too!'

Thus Christmas dinner was enjoyed in a spirit of great optimism and when the final bones had been picked and the last scrap of Christmas pudding coaxed from the dishes, no one there could have eaten another mouthful. Mrs Carrot looked around the now silent table and spoke for everyone when she said softly 'Amen!'

They sat down around the fire, the four younger children ready to doze off, replete with Christmas dinner and lulled into drowsiness by the warmth of the glowing coals. Henry lit his pipe and after puffing for a while showed Clink how to play his mouth organ. His playing of this instrument was rather like his playing of the piano, full of gusto but rather lacking in finesse. Will browsed through his book, in which pastime he was soon joined by Clink who had needed only a few minutes to convince himself that he did not have the makings of a musician. As a background to this tranquil scene, the bells of Lincoln Cathedral chimed out a joyous celebration of this, the most holy day of the year.

In mid afternoon there was a gentle knock at the door and Mrs Carrot, wiping her hands on her apron, as she had been disturbed from washing the pots, opened the door to find Constable Peasgood standing on the steps. He saluted her, touching the peak of his helmet with gloved hand, and asked to see Henry, who lumbered to the door clenching his fists and much like an angry bear disturbed from its winter hibernation. The good wishes for the constable which he had uttered in his Christmas prayer were fading rapidly, for to Henry, police meant trouble.

'Now then, Henry,' said the constable, 'calm yourself down. I did but call to shake your hand and to satisfy myself that there's no hard feelings between us on this Christmas Day and to congratulate you on your good fortune.'

He held out his hand and, after a moment's hesitation, Henry seized it and shook it so violently that John Peasgood cried out in mock terror and asked to be released. At Henry's bidding he stepped into the room, removing his helmet as he did so.

'Mrs Carrot,' he said, 'my job isn't always a pleasant one, but I hope you'll forgive and forget. I only did what I had to and I'd have to say in all truthfulness that if the same thing happened again, I'd have to act just the same as I did before except I'd duck a lot quicker than last time!'

Everybody laughed and the atmosphere became very relaxed. The policeman produced some sweets for the younger children and let Clink try on his helmet. He declined Henry's offer of a mug of ale, but downed a glass of lemonade in one mouthful and ate two of Mrs Carrot's delicious mince pies. They all laughed as he related how he had saved Will and Clink from being enlisted in the army and sent to Burma to fight the savage King Thebaw, and then they all chattered at once as they told Henry about Lucy's funeral and the horse and cart going straight through the butcher's window.

Constable Peasgood's face took on a more serious note as he spoke to Will.

'I'd not turn a boy against his father, Will, but mark my words, your father will never forget that day. Oh yes, he liked the heroics of stopping the horse and all the praise that got him, but that day cost him a pretty penny when you add it all up and you finished up with a hundred pounds, so I hear. Your father won't forget that in a hurry!'

The constable looked at his watch and put his hand on Will's shoulder as he rose to depart.

'I knew your mother, Will, a very fine lady she was and respected by us all. If ever you need a friend, then John Peasgood's your man. Mind you, if ever you break the law then I'll lock you up as quick as the next man and never you forget it.'

With this advice he turned to Henry Carrot and held out his hand saying 'I'll take that pint of ale with you some evening when I'm off duty, Henry Carrot. It's been a great wonder to me to see you all here together at Christmas time, all your cares gone and something to look forward to at last.'

He shook his head in wonderment and said: 'And all thanks to a little lady that most of us never gave a passing glance to. All except you, young Edgar, that is, for she regarded you as a true friend and took you at face value. And it was through her that you and Will became friends and so she remembered Will as well and despite the humble life she led, she saw more than most of us did and rendered fair judgement on us all, God bless 'er.'

He held out his hand to Mrs Carrot and said: 'Truly, Mrs Carrot, the Lord works in mysterious ways and He's smiled on you at last, I'm pleased to say.'

. Ma Carrot ignored the proferred hand and seized the constable to her ample bosom and planted a great, wet kiss on his rapidly reddening face.

'Down at heart, you're naught but an old softie, John Peasgood!' she said with a laugh as he hurried through the door with his face bright scarlet and mumbling that he had to report to the police station that very minute or he'd be in trouble with the Sergeant.

The rest of the day passed off in great spirit and when Will departed for the cold, empty house, he felt very happy indeed. It was the most wonderful Christmas that he could remember in his short life and the spirit of optimism which pervaded the Carrot family had rubbed off on him. After all, with such wonderful friends, how could anything possibly go wrong? Thus comforted he fell into a deep sleep and dreamed the wonderful dreams which are the privilege of the very young.

His father returned in the afternoon of Boxing Day.

Annie had barely got her coat off before she pirouetted in front of Will in a lovely wine-coloured velvet dress trimmed with white lace. She had a pair of maroon ankle boots and carried a matching purse on a string.

'See, Will!' she smirked. 'Look what father bought me for Christmas. And we had such a wonderful time.'

Slyly she rubbed in the intended hurt.

'What did you buy with your half-crown, Will?' she asked. 'And what did you do with yourself here alone all day? Did you cook yourself a good Christmas dinner?'

Will was about to retort that he had had the most wonderful Christmas of his life, but then remembered his father's opinion of the Carrot family in general and Clink in particular and thought silence to be the wisest course. In the past he had made the error of trusting Annie by taking her into his confidence and every time she had told his father within a matter of minutes.

'Oh, I bought myself a few things, went to the Cathedral to hear the carols and then had a most wonderful roast goose for Christmas dinner, followed by plum pudding and all the trimmings', he said nonchalantly.

'Will Everton,' screamed Annie, 'Father's right about you. You're an idle boy and you tell lies into the bargain!'

As she flounced out of the room Will managed accidentally to clump his heavy boot onto one of the dainty new shoes, scratching its polished surface to smithereens. The ear-piercing wailing of his sister seemed to make the inevitable clout across the head well worth while.

Later in the day he came into the house and surprised Annie sitting in the parlour with a young man whom he had seen going in and out of a large house further up Burton Road. Herbert was out and Will lost no time in threatening Annie that he would tell father when he came home that she had been entertaining a gentleman friend whilst he had been out, something she had many times been forbidden to do.

The young man had heard of Herbert's fiery temper and with a few stammered excuses he grabbed his cap and made off rapidly down the road, whilst Annie went into a tantrum, positively dancing up and down in rage as she threatened to get her own back.

'You do,' said Will, 'and I'll tell him who it was and then father will go round to his house and shout and scream at his father and before you know it, they'll be fighting in the road – just like them common Carrot family!'

His smile as he gazed at Annie's tear-stained face was positively angelic. He had often heard the vicar use the phrase 'Truly, my cup runneth over!' but he had never experienced its true meaning before. Perhaps life was really taking a turn for the better.

As New Year's Eve approached, Will could sense something in the atmosphere. His father was strangely pre-occupied with the house, something in which he had not previously had a great deal of interest. The old carpet in the hallway was taken up and replaced by a magnificent rug and there was a general cleaning by two busy charladies from down the hill. Everything was cleaned and polished and scrubbed and tidied. One evening Herbert gave

Will twopence and told him to go into the town and spend it just to get him out of the house. Will was quite shocked but grabbed it and went to meet Clink to help him spend it on sticky toffee. Something, he mused, something was definitely in the air.

It was the day before New Year's Eve when Herbert called Annie and Will into the parlour.

He stood with his back to the fireplace, deep-set eyes gleaming in the gathering gloom, beard trimmed to perfection and his diamond tiepin flashing against the dark silk of a neatly tied cravat. Placing his thumbs in the pockets of his waistcoat, he rocked back and forth on his heels, then spoke to them.

'Tomorrow is New Year's Eve,' he said, 'and we shall be having a party in this house!'

He paused for effect, but it was hardly necessary. Will and Annie looked at each other. Neither of them could ever remember having a party in their own house and each was equally dumbfounded. For once they shared something, even if it was only astonishment.

Annie recovered first.

'Why, father,' she said 'how wonderful! Who will be coming? Can we invite our own friends?'

'To answer your first question, Annie,' he said, 'I have invited quite a number of my colleagues on the workhouse guardians, a number of my business friends and . . . a very special lady!'

He paused for a moment to let the information sink in and was not slow to note that both children appeared to be rather taken aback at the mention of his 'special' lady. There was an uncomfortable shuffling of feet and both children were looking at the floor.

'Your dear mother has been dead these twelve years', he said, 'and I feel very lonely. You, Annie, are now fifteen years old and growing into a very pretty young lady . . . '

Will shuddered. He thought his sister was anything but pretty. In fact, more than once he had compared her to the Judy he had seen in Punch and Judy at the annual fair. With her tall, angular frame, protruberent teeth and metal rimmed spectacles, her hair tied back in a bun, he thought she was positively ugly.

Herbert continued: 'and I do not doubt that many a young gentleman has his eye on you at this very moment . . . '

Will's chuckle was quickly stifled by a ferocious glare from his father.

'There are certain matters which are best discussed between ladies and which I, as a father, feel totally unable to communicate to you due to their delicate nature. You need the guidance of a more mature lady in these things and I have been mindful of this for some time. Will, you are of a rather wilful nature Despite my advice, it is obvious that you are more set upon childish things than considering your position as my son. You make friends of people of whom I strongly disapprove and fill your spare time with idleness. You have been a burden to me ever since your mother died and she must be looking down on you from Heaven and wondering what has happened that you are going so sadly astray.'

Will felt a tear spring to his eye. He was not particularly aware that he had ever done anything very wicked and as for spare time, he hardly ever had any. He could not help but wonder what made him so different from other boys of his age, boys whose spare time was filled with cricket, football, kite flying and other wonderful things. Their fathers seemed always to have time to play with them, but Will could never recall enjoying even a game of battledore and shuttlecock with his own father.

Herbert continued: 'With these thoughts in mind I have decided that it is time I took another wife. I have approached a suitable lady and she has indicated that she will marry me. You will meet her tomorrow evening at the party.'

There was no time for argument or comment as Herbert went on to tell Annie that she was expected that very day to purchase a new dress and shoes for the occasion and Will was told to polish his shoes and try on the new suit which even now was lying on his bed.

Annie departed hastily to the town, the money her father had given her burning a hole in her purse. Will went upstairs and tried on the suit which he found to be slightly too large. A hole in one of the pockets and some slight fraying of the trouser hems led Will to believe that it most certainly was not new and, having donned it, he went down into the sitting room to show his father.

'Very smart, Will' said his father, 'Very smart indeed. A bit of blacking on your boots, a smack of brilliantine on your hair and your best shirt and tie and you'll look very presentable indeed!'

'Please, father' said Will, 'This isn't really new. There's a hole in the pocket and it's frayed on the trousers. Look, there's a mark on the jacket. Can't I have new clothes like Annie?'

Herbert put down his pipe, rose from the chair and went a shade of red tinged with purple. He seized Will by the shoulders and thrust his burning eyes within an inch of Will's face.

'Ingratitude,' he spluttered, 'damned ingratitude for you! Jealous of your own sister. You're full of pride, Will, full of sinful pride. You want to strut around your friends looking like a peacock whilst I work my fingers to the bone to keep you!'

No one in Lincoln could ever have compared poor Little Will with a peacock and the blow around the head that knocked him to the floor was yet another nail in the inevitable rift that was to occur between father and son.

'Read your bible, Will. Read your bible,' raved Herbert. 'Pride goeth before a fall! You see, isn't that just what's happened to you? You were only thinking about your appearance, pride it was, sinful pride. And where are you now? On the floor, Will, on the floor! Pride goeth before a fall! That suit's a good suit and my friends must see that my family are always well-clothed, Will. Here I am, doing my best for you, trying to rise in this world . . . not for myself, mind you, I have no vain ambitions. I'm doing this for you Will, for you and your sister, just like your mother would have wanted me to do.'

It would have been pointless to argue and even Will realised this. He murmured an apology and went up to his room to change back into his old clothes. He was very disturbed at the thought of a new mother, yet strangely excited. Would she be like Mrs Carrot, all fat and jolly and would it mean that they could have a wonderful family life like so many of the boys he knew? Would there be holidays at Skegness and Mablethorpe? Will had never seen the sea in his life, but he knew that it was something wonderful and he had seen the posters on the railway station . . . 'Come to Sunny Skegness' they exhorted and there was a bright picture of mother, father and two children relaxing on the beach.

By the time bedtime came around he had almost grown used to the idea and had talked himself into believing that this was the point at which his life would change for the better. A new mother would surely be the answer. His father could not possibly be so unfeeling if there were a woman in the house, a woman like his own mother whom everyone had described as being beautiful, smiling and gentle. He settled into a deep sleep, disturbed only by dreams of warm sunshine and the lapping of the sea on golden sands.

The following day was full of movement and excitement such as Will had never seen in the house before. The two ladies who had cleaned the house returned, dressed in white aprons. They covered the dining room table with spotless white cloths and, as the various tradespeople arrived with their baskets, laid out in splendid array the hams, cheese, cold chicken and other meats.

There was a splendid centrepiece made out of various kinds of fruit which rose from the table like a mountain of pure colour. Apples, oranges, and grapes cascaded in splendour around the base of the silver bowl and the whole display was set off by bright red candles in silver holders..

When Will returned from the workshop in the afternoon he wondered whether he had come to the right house, everything appeared so splendid. There was even a trio rehearsing in the living room. A rather stout lady played the piano and two gentlemen played the violin and 'cello. Will thought that the music sounded very dull and wished that they would play something a little more exciting.

His father was in the kitchen arguing with Mr Pratt from the wine and spirit merchants on the High Street. There were several crates of bottles on the floor and on the kitchen table and Mr

Pratt had his hands on one of them as if he intended to take it back out to the cart. He was obviously getting very agitated and was becoming quite red in the face.

'Look here, Mr Everton,' he said. 'Sale or return means just what it says. If you return it, we haven't sold it, so you don't pay for it. But everything you don't return you pay for! We won't take back any bottles that's been opened and if you smash any, then you don't get allowed the penny on 'em that I normally give you. As for discount, I've already told you I'll give you a discount of six-pence in the pound, seeing as we're both in trade in the city, but sixpence it is and not a penny more ... and before you say another word, no, I don't find myself overjoyed by the discount on my funeral that you've offered me because I reckon it might be a damned long time afore I take advantage of it!'

Herbert was nothing if not a tryer.

'Now then, Percy' he wheedled, 'There's no need to get upset about it. After all, we all have to make a bit of profit to live, but as this is the biggest order I've ever given you I think it's worth a bit more than a tanner in the pound. Now then, I'll tell you what I'll do. Make it a shilling in the pound and I'll send the lad to mend that broken flap on your shop counter at no charge. Now, how's that, eh?'

Mr Pratt still had both hands on the crate.

'Ninepence, Herbert,' he said. 'Ninepence, and that's it! One more argument and it all goes back on the cart!'

Herbert held out his hand.

'Done!' he said. 'You're a hard man to do business with and that's a fact, Percy.'

By the time that Will had got washed and changed into his new suit, Annie was already down and preening herself in her new dress. It was of a bright blue velvet with a white lace collar and cuffs. She had a matching blue bow in her hair which was tied back behind her head to make a long pony tail and she wore new ankle high boots which buttoned down the side.

Will thought that she looked like a story book illustration of Little Miss Muffet except in his story books Miss Muffet looked a lot prettier than Annie. She was practising her curtsey in the hall mirror and saying in a simpering voice: 'Pleased to meet you, Mr Otter, a pleasure I'm sure.' Then she turned to the other side and performed another little bob of the knee: 'Pleased to meet you, Ma'am, how kind of you to come!'

Will bit into an apple he had taken from the hall table.

'You look a right nitwit, Annie,' he said. 'Who do you think's coming? The Queen?'

Annie put both hands on her hips and looked Will up and down.

'At least if the Queen was coming, Will Everton, she'd notice me and I'd know what to do. Look at you, tie all to one side, boot-laces undone and a tidemark around your neck I'll be bound. You wait until our new mother sees you, she'll be sorry she came here.'

Will looked himself up and down in the mirror with all the ac-quired dignity of his twelve years. He straightened his tie, took out his handkerchief, spat on it and used it to remove a grubby mark on the end of his nose and rubbed the toes of his boots on the back of his stockings in an endeavour to make them shine. This was somewhat disastrous as he had been rather liberal in the application of boot blacking, much of which he had now transferred to his stockings so that each had a huge black patch on the back.

Annie laughed and promised: 'I'll tell father. Look what you've done, you've ruined those stockings. He'll be ever so an-gry.'

Herbert appeared at the top of the stairs, the very picture of a dignified gentleman. His suit was of a pearl grey, the jacket edged with a velvet cord. His waistcoat had pearl buttons and across his paunch was a fine fetter link watch chain of gleaming gold. His spotless white shirt had a ruffled front supporting a deeper grey cravat in which flashed the inevitable diamond stickpin. His thick black hair was swept back from his forehead on either side of a centre parting, his moustache was trimmed to the last hair and his pointed beard looked as if it had been trimmed with a slide rule, each side perfectly balanced.

Even Will was impressed.

'Will, get yourself changed and put on those new clothes' he said. 'Our guests will be arriving shortly.'

Will started to say something but his father cut him short. 'Go on boy,' he said. 'I know you've been at work but it's time to get ready now. Look sharp about it and change those damned awful socks and put some blacking on your boots.'

Will went up the stairs and didn't know what he ought to do. However, he was saved from disaster by the intervention of Mrs Brundage. Mrs Brundage was from down the hill and had been hired by Herbert for the night to attend to the ladies' coats and wraps. The one and sixpence he was paying her might have seemed generous, but as Mrs Brundage owed him rent she had a feeling that she would never see it anyway.

She helped him clean his shoes, changed his socks and put a stiff brush over his suit. With a re-knotted tie and a clean handkerchief in his breast pocket he looked quite presentable, particularly when Mrs Brundage mysteriously produced a pot of brilliantine and smoothed down his tousled hair. She looked him up and down, holding him by both shoulders at arms length, then she gave him a quick hug and a peck on the cheek.

'Get off with you now, Little Will' she said. 'You know your father doesn't like to be kept waiting. You look a real little swell, you do. Your mother would have been very proud of you.'

'Thank you, Mrs Brundage,' said Will, as he left the room. He stopped at the door and turned in time to see Mrs Brundage brushing a runaway tear from her cheek.

'Don't cry,' he said, 'I'm getting a new mother tonight, you know.'

And he ran off down the stairs, leaving the good lady with her jaw agape and not believing what she had heard.

There was a clattering of horses' hooves as the first of the guests arrived and soon a small crowd had gathered outside the gate, the ladies uttering 'Oohs!' and 'Ahs!' as they surveyed some of the splendid gowns and their owners alighting from their carriages. Herbert stood inside the sheltered porchway and greeted every guest, ushering them into the hallway where a maid took the coats and wraps. Will's job was to take the guests into the drawing room and offer them drinks from the huge sideboard. 'Mind you, Will' his father had warned him, 'Don't open one bottle until the previous one is quite empty. Small measures for everyone. We aren't going to encourage drunkenness in this house! Oh yes, the empty bottles. Make sure they're taken into the scullery right away. We don't want anyone cutting themselves on broken bottles.'

Will knew quite a number of the guests and they knew him. The way in which Herbert treated his son was often a talking point amongst the business community of Lincoln and it seemed that Herbert himself was the only one who did not know it. Although Herbert saw his son on this evening as being a smart, well-dressed young man, everyone else saw a small, rather shabbily dressed little boy looking very dull and insignificant amongst all the finery. This may have accounted for quite a number of threepenny and sixpenny pieces he found pressed into his palm as he very efficiently played at being a barman. In fact, he found it becoming so profitable that he was truly sorry when his father called him and his sister into his study.

Closing the door behind him, Will found himself facing two ladies. The younger of the two was short like himself, but much older. Will calculated that she must have been at least twenty, but despite that he took an instant liking to her. She had auburn hair which fell over her shoulders in ringlets. Tiny pearls adorned her ears and matched the string she wore around her neck, whilst the hand which she extended towards Will bore two pearl rings. Her plump face was covered with freckles and Will thought her smile was the loveliest he had ever seen. He fell in love with her at once.

There could not have been a harsher contrast with the older woman. She was tall and thin, with a prominent nose and rather staring eyes which seemed to flit restlessly about from one person to the next. Her front teeth were quite enormous and her black hair was swept straight back and tied into a bun at the back. In contrast to every other guest at the party she wore very plain, dark clothes, high at the neck and sweeping down to the floor. Pince nez were on a long cord around her neck and her long, scraggy fingers played with them as if she were ill at ease. For no reason at all she went into a fit of coughing in the middle of the introductions and then blew her nose with the ferocity of a train whistle. Immediately, her daughter, for mother and daughter they were, went to her aid, put her hand around the elder lady's shoulder and ushered her to a chair whilst Herbert made suitable concerned noises. Will decided he didn't like her at all.

It was then that Will noticed a third person sitting in an arm-chair in a gloomy corner of the room and recognised Charles Clegg, a business friend of his father's and with whom he was often to be found in the smoking room of the White Hart.

Herbert took up his favourite position in front of the roaring fire, thumbs in the pockets of his waistcoat and addressed the room.

'Children,' he said, 'you know my friend Mr Clegg with whom I have done business for some years, and you have now met his daughter, Mrs Martha Tattershall, and his grand-daughter Miss Amy Tattershall. You will remember perhaps that Mrs Martha was widowed early last year . . .'

Martha took out her handkerchief and dramatically wiped away a non-existent tear from her cheek.

'. . . This very sad event is now perhaps brightened by the news of her daughter Amy's forthcoming marriage, which will be announced this very evening. We shall be just one, big happy family in future and this house will once again have a lady in charge.'

Herbert took Annie's hand and said: 'Not that you haven't done a first class job for your father, Annie; you've been a daughter to be proud of and I know that you'll continue to help your new mother in the house.'

There were no words of praise for Will, but then again, he didn't expect any. He knew his father far too well for that.

72.

It was explained to the children that Herbert proposed to make his announcement once they had drunk the toast to the New Year at midnight and they were sworn to secrecy, departing to the main rooms with uplifted hearts. Amy's sweet personality had come across to them even in this one brief meeting and Will felt that all his prayers had been answered at once. Even Annie managed a sincere smile for Will and they even danced a waltz together, the adults all clapping at their performance.

The evening went on in high spirits, although by this time the issuing of drinks had been placed in other hands and more than once Herbert looked into the scullery at the ever mounting stack of bottles and could be seen making calculations as to the cost of the revelry.

By the time supper was over, everyone was in the best of spirits and awaiting the midnight chimes from the cathedral to herald in the New Year. Although it was a sharp, frosty night, Herbert stood by the windows with his watch in hand and, at a few seconds to midnight, opened them. The bells chimed and the year 1888 was born.

Everyone kissed everyone else and wished them a 'Happy New Year' and Josiah Otter, having consumed rather more than his fair share of port, tried to kiss Mrs Tattershall and missed, crashing into the table and falling onto the carpet in a heap. There was cheering galore at this and someone muttered that Josiah must either be very brave or very drunk to want to kiss Martha when there were so many other eligible females in the room.

By popular consent, Will was sent out into Burton Road and given a piece of coal, a piece of bread and sixpence to bring in the New Year. He entered the door and, in the hushed room, presented them to his father and said: 'Father, may this New Year be a happy and prosperous one for this house and for all our guests this evening.'

There was a great cheer at this and Will found that he had suddenly acquired another sixpence and two pennies. He decided that if this was what happened, no wonder grown-ups were always going to parties.

Herbert stood on a footstool, raised his glass and wished everyone a Happy New Year. Everyone raised their glasses and responded. Then he clapped his hands for silence and spoke again.

'New Year is a time for resolutions, as we all know. We also know that such resolutions are easily broken. Why, Josiah here resolved in the White Hart last New Year's Eve that he would never touch another drop of port in his life, and that resolution lasted for fully ten minutes ...'

There was a dutiful laugh.

Herbert continued: 'However, be that as it may, the New Year is also a time for looking ahead and putting things in order, deciding which way our lives are to go, so to speak. This is a good time to be planning ahead and what better place to announce our plans than here, amongst our friends?'

Josiah uttered a loud 'Hear! Hear!' and an even louder hiccup.

When the laughter had died down, Herbert called for Miss Amy Tattershall to come forward.

Annie came across to Will's side and, to his surprise, held his hand. Will looked at the young girl standing by his father's side. She obviously knew what was coming and was blushing heavily and looking at the floor. As she fidgeted with her handkerchief Will thought that he had never seen anyone so beautiful in his whole life and that, if his true mother had been as lovely as his future step-mother, then she must have been lovely indeed.

'My good friend, Charles Clegg, over there has asked me to make a most important announcement regarding his granddaughter, Amy. She is to be married in the summer of this year.'

Will and Annie looked at each other expectantly as the room buzzed with excitement.

'She is to be married' continued Herbert 'to a gentleman you all know . . . Mr James Baxter of Gainsborough, who cannot be with us tonight due to the unfortunate illness of his father.'

Will felt as if he had been poleaxed. His future mother and his dreams evaporated in one swift instant of time.

'Who is it, then?' whispered Annie in his ear. 'Who is father going to marry?'

'I don't know,' said Will, looking around the room in some concern. People were gathering around Amy, shaking her hand and wishing her luck, the ladies hugging and kissing her and chattering like magpies. Herbert called for silence again.

'But that isn't the only important announcement I have to make' he said. 'As you know, my own dear wife, Sarah Jane, died these twelve years gone, and it is a long time since this house had the presence of a lady to grace it. My daughter, Annie is growing up and is at that age when a mother's guidance is greatly needed, whilst my son, Will, would undoubtedly benefit from such a presence.'

Will looked in horror at the lady who was moving slowly, but surely to be at his father's side.

'I have therefore asked Charles Clegg's permission to marry his daughter, Mrs Martha Tattershall. He has given his permission and Martha has accepted my proposal!'

There was a moment's stunned silence. Martha was at least twelve years Herbert's senior and there had been no indication even in the market gossip that such a move was forthcoming.

As a fresh round of cheering broke out, Will and Annie sat side by side on a sofa and looked at each other. In the whole of their lives they were to feel close to each other only on half a dozen occasions, and this was one of them.

Josiah Otter, glass in hand, sat by them and patted them each on the head.

'Why, Mr Otter? Why?' asked Annie.

'Young lady' he said, 'Your father is a joiner, funeral director and cabinet maker. He's a shrewd business man as well. Martha is Charles Clegg's only child. Mr Clegg is a sick man – you'll notice that he has sat quietly in his chair most of the evening – and he also owns the biggest timber yard in Lincolnshire.'

Mr Otter tapped the side of his nose and looked quizically at them both. 'You figure it out' he said. 'You figure it out.

During the early part of that year Mr Clegg and his daughter

Martha were frequent visitors to the Everton household. Mr Clegg was obviously very weak and even dismounting from his carriage seemed to make him out of breath. In the main he contributed little to the conversation and, if it went on too long, was quite liable to drop off to sleep in his armchair. It was then only a matter of time before he would lapse into a stentorian thunder of snoring when Martha would immediately rouse him and chide him for his ill manners.

On one occasion, after indulging over-freely in the port bottle, Mr Clegg went off to sleep, snored, and, when Martha awoke him, broke wind with an earth-shattering explosion. Martha went brilliant red, Annie looked horrified and Will hid under the dining room table to conceal his laughter. Herbert, three sheets to the wind, swayed against the mantel piece and reassured his future father-in-law.

'Don't concern yourself, sir, don't concern yourself' he said as poor Mr Clegg sought to redeem his actions with profuse apologies. 'As you well know, there is a tombstone in Newport cemetery which explains to us all the necessity to heed the warnings of nature and not to bottle up the worst vapours of our constitution, less it bring us harm. If my memory serves me, the inscription on the stone is as follows.'

He tottered a little, screwed up his brow as if searching his memory and then pronounced his advice for healthy living as recommended on the tombstone:
'Where e'er you be, let your wind go free,
For 'twas want of a fart that did for me!'
Martha went white, Annie uttered an astounded 'Father!' and Will howled with laughter and was promptly sent to bed with no supper and would have received a hefty whack over the head if Herbert had not been too intoxicated to aim straight. Subsequently, Will spent many hours looking for the tombstone but never found it.

Amy Tattershall came only infrequently for she was too much engaged in the preparations for her own marriage, but when she did come, Will found himself looking at her with great longing. He was sure that she was the perfect woman and he could but envy the fortunate Mr James Baxter of Gainsborough. When Amy was in the room it seemed to come alive. Her tinkling laughter and ready smile were infectious and even Martha would occasionally give a half-hearted smile at her quips and jokes. She could wrap her grandfather around the proverbial little finger and it was very obvious that Charles Clegg idolised her in the manner of grandfathers since time immemorial. Herbert himself was obviously very taken with her but, permanently under the eagle scrutiny of his future bride, did little but nod approvingly at the right moments.

As winter turned to spring and the wedding day drew nearer, Will tried desperately to like his future stepmother. He kept telling himself that no one could help their appearance and tried to convince himself that the marriage would give him the affection and love for which he craved. But, try as he would, he could not shake off the feeling that all would not be well. Martha hardly spoke a word to him, largely perhaps because Herbert invariably directed her attention towards Annie, and Annie, not slow to sense any situation which might jeopardise her favoured position with her father never lost an opportunity to strengthen her own situation. She brought Martha tea, put her feet on a footstool and sometimes read to her whilst Herbert pretended to listen and lost himself in a haze of claret and cigar smoke.

As the June wedding day drew nearer, Will withdrew into his shell and even Clink found it hard to cheer him. One day after work, Will was sitting in the cosy kitchen in Gordon Road, indulging in one of Ma Carrot's delicious pasties, when Henry Carrot asked him how he thought he would like his future mother. Will stammered the usual words, but even Henry saw that the boy had a sense of foreboding about the whole affair.

'Take my word for it, Little Will,' said Henry. 'Nature made us all different and an ugly woman can make just as good a mother as a pretty 'un! It's what's down here that matters, here in your soul, not what you look like.' He tapped his chest with a huge fist and then, not really quite sure where his soul might be, tapped himself on the head to make sure.

Clink had already given his parents a graphic description of Martha Tattershall before they had seen her riding up High Street with her father.

'Honestly,' he had said, 'she's just like a witch; dressed all in black, she is, great big teeth and a 'ook nose!'

'It'll match 'erbert's' said Henry. 'Two big conks together, I reckon!'

'Poor Little Will' said Mrs Carrot.

The wedding took place as planned a few days after Will's thirteenth birthday. As both bride and groom had been widowed it was not thought fitting by Herbert to have an elaborate ceremony (it was also much cheaper not to) and the affair was therefore restricted to close relatives and friends. However, Will did get a real new suit this time, but only because Martha insisted that he was not to attend her wedding looking like someone from the workhouse.

'We live near enough to it, Herbert Everton,' she had said. 'We don't have to look as if we live in it!'

After a small reception, Herbert and Martha went off to Mablethorpe for a honeymoon, leaving Will and Annie in the charge of the ubiquitous Mrs Brundage who had been given strict instructions as to how the house was to be prepared for their return. Will quite enjoyed having Mrs Brundage in charge of the house. At least he went to work each day with a good cooked breakfast inside him and returned to a good meal in the evening. She brooked no favouritism either and Annie was not allowed to rule the roost as she did when Herbert was at home.

As the day for his parents' return drew nearer, Will became withdrawn again and one day, when he was sitting on an upturned coffin having his lunch with old Walter, he confided his fears in the old man. Walter considered his answers very carefully. He liked Will and had always felt sorry for him. Sometimes he saw in the boy's eyes that same flash of fire that he had seen in Sarah Jane's all those years ago and this brought the memories flooding back.

'Sometimes when I'm troubled, Will, I go to the Cathedral,' he said, 'and I just sit there in the quiet and the peace of it all and look about me. I ask myself how many thousands of troubled souls have sat there before me and tried to figure out all their problems. I look up at the angels and ask myself how many millions and millions of prayers they've heard over the centuries, and I look at the stone floor and try to work out how many feet have worn those stones smooth . . . must have been tens of thousands of millions, I think.'

Walter carefully folded up his sandwich wrappings and put them back in his tin lunch box. Will made as if to speak, but Walter put up his hand for silence as he took out his old pipe, cupped the bowl in his hand and lit it with a great inhaling of breath. Then he blew out a pungent cloud of smoke, tamped the tobacco down with a gnarled finger end that seemed impervious to the heat, and continued.

'I'm not much with words, Will,' he said, 'I reckon what skill God gave me is in these old hands of mine, not in this empty, old head, but anyone can have doubts and worries. But when I sit in that cathedral and think of all the worries it must have heard over the centuries, then somehow mine seem very small, very small indeed. I just wish that I could light up this old pipe then I really would feel that God understood me, but, of course, I wouldn't light up in church any more than I'd drink a pint of ale there.'

He paused for another drag at the pipe, a far away look in his eyes as a cloud of grey smoke rose to the workshop ceiling.

'I remember the most troubled day of my life, Will, long before you were born. I went into that cathedral before most of Lincoln was at work and I didn't come out until night was falling. I didn't find the answer to my worries then and there, but bless my soul, after a couple of pints and a cheese and pickle sandwich at the Harlequin on the way home, I felt that I could face up to them.'

He looked the boy straight in the eyes.

'Will,' he said, 'I don't think God ever intended life to be easy for such as you and me and maybe there's a purpose in all that. If you listen to the parson he'll tell you that we have to endure things on this earth to make us better for the next world after we die. I don't believe that.'

Will looked astounded. This was tantamount to sacrilege in his young eyes. He had no doubt that everyone went to another place after they died. The good people went to Heaven and the bad ones went to Hell. It was as simple as that.

'What I believes,' continued Walter, 'is that all this nonsense was thought up by them as employs us. For folks like me, ordinary working folk, life can be bloody awful. There's some good things, but it's never easy and as you get older you get worried about what's going to happen to you. No, I think that all this religion was thought up by them at the top. They get us to work like the devil whilst we're here, pay us next to nowt and the only thing we've got to look forward to is to going somewhere better when we're dead! Who's ever come back to tell us what it's like when you're dead? Have you ever seen anyone who died last week standing in the market place and telling us what it's like on the other side? Load of rubbish I calls it!'

He drew heavily on his pipe and then, seeing the concern on Will's face, added: 'Well, perhaps there's something in it after all, but all as I'm saying is that no one ever proved it!'

Will thought a lot about this during the afternoon and when they finished work late in the afternoon he went home by a slightly different route and found himself in front of the Cathedral. He had never been in there on his own and was a little hesitant about entering.

As he went through the great Norman portals at the west end he took off his cap and stood for a moment. It was cool inside and he almost felt a chill run through his veins. The light through the traceried window at the far end was soft and gentle at this time of the day and the bright colours of the stained glass seemed to dominate the whole interior, fading away to shadows in the dimness of the great, high roof.

Slowly he advanced inside. No one was about. It was that quiet hour at the end of the day's work when everyone was hurrying home to their loved ones or stopping off at one of the many hostelries for a relaxing pint of ale. Will thought that Mrs Carrot would by now be bustling over her oven, cooking up a nourishing and tasty meal for her brood. He remembered that Mrs Brundage would be doing the same for him this day and was almost tempted to turn round and go home for he was very hungry after his hard day's work.

The temptation resisted, he walked a little further and sat down at the end of one of the pews. He knelt down and said a little prayer to himself, remembering the mother he never knew and asking God to make sure that she was happy in Heaven. He never thought of his mother without a lump came to his throat and he pulled out a grubby handkerchief to wipe away the telltale tear that ran down his cheek.

A hand fell on his shoulder and he looked up to see a grey haired gentleman standing by him and he made to get up.

'Don't do that,' said the man. 'Budge up a bit and let me sit beside you, young fellow. Are you very sad that you're crying?'

'No, sir,' sniffed Will, 'I was remembering my mother. She died not long after I was born. I wasn't doing any harm here, honestly, sir. I was only sitting and thinking, I wasn't touching anything, honest I wasn't!'

'I'm sure you weren't,' said the man. 'My name is Mr Young, what's yours?'

'William Everton, sir,' said Will: 'People sometimes call me Little Will because I'm not very big.'

'Well, Little Will, it's a grand place just to sit down and think of those we love, isn't it?'

Without waiting for an answer, Mr Young continued to chat to him and gradually Will relaxed a little and told his new friend about himself and about his family.

Mr Young nodded. He knew Herbert Everton by reputation if not in person and felt a great liking for the boy. The sense of unease which Will felt at the return of his father and his new mother was obviously preying on the boy's mind and he did his best to reassure him that all would be well. They sat together, side by side, in complete silence for a few minutes, then Mr Young said:

'How would you like to see the organ, Will?'

Will said that he would like that very much and together they walked down the cathedral towards the Angel Choir.

The great organ soon towered above them, lofty pipes ascending towards the roof.

'Sit on the seat, Will,' said Mr Young. 'It might be a bit high for you, but you might as well sit on it whilst you're here.'

Will was a little nervous and looked around to see who might be watching. He made as if to sit down and then asked: 'Won't anyone mind, Mr Young? I don't think we're supposed to be here, really, you know.'

Mr Young laughed and said, 'I don't think anyone will bother, Will, they're all used to seeing me here. You see, I'm the cathedral organist and I often come here to practice during this quiet hour. Would you like to watch . . . or perhaps you play?'

Before Will could answer, Mr Young disappeared behind the organ and emerged with a cushion which he placed on the seat so that Will could reach the keys. He lifted him onto the seat and then sat beside him.

He asked again: 'Do you play, Will?'

'A little, Mr. Young. Well, that is I can pick up one or two tunes on the piano at home, not very well, mind. I've never had anyone teach me. I asked my father if I could have lessons once, but he said we didn't have money to waste on such nonsense.'

Mr Young didn't answer, but ran his feet gently across the pedals as his fingers picked out a simple melody. The very power of the great organ left Will almost speechless as the sweet notes tumbled over each other in joyous abandon.

'Your turn, now, Will,' he said. 'Come on, it won't bite you. I'll work the pedals if you can't reach them and you play something for me. Just play the bottom row of keys, the one you can reach and don't bother about the others. Don't be frightened by all the other keys and stops, I'll look after them.'

Will smiled nervously. 'I can't play as well as you,' he said. 'This tune is one I like, but I can't play it very well and you might not like it.'

83.

He shuffled a little on the seat and then warily picked out the notes, Mr Young manipulating the stops into a simple harmony.

The notes were faltering and the melody stilted and Will needed not a little help as he stretched across the keys, but slowly and surely the hymn emerged and he and Mr Young hummed the words together:

> 'Loving shepherd of thy sheep,
>   Keep thy lamb, in safety keep;
> Nothing can thy power withstand
>   None can pluck me from thy hand.'

'For a first time that was very good,' said John Young. 'This mighty organ is not really meant for short arms and small fingers, and I doubt if I could have done any better at your age.'

He patted Will on the back and said again: 'Well done Little Will, very well done indeed!'

Will blushed a little and shuffled his feet, only to find that they were still dangling above the pedals and that he had nothing on which to shuffle them.

'Mr. Young,' he said, 'I always heard that my mother loved "Abide With Me". Mrs Brundage said she used to sing it as she worked in the house and our vicar says that on Sundays you could hear her sweet voice rising up to Heaven above everyone else. Would you play it for me, sir, please sir?'

Will moved over and John Young sat before the organ. He closed his eyes and bowed his head as his fingers ran over the keys, the notes emerging clear and bell-like, the great organ sounding as gentle and sweet as the cathedral had ever heard. By now a small group of passers-by, attracted by the sound, had entered the cathedral and gathered around the Angel Choir. One by one, they joined in the words, Mr Young playing very softly so that he did not drown out their singing.

The wonderful and moving words rose into the high roof and echoed gently down again:

'Abide with me, fast falls the eventide . . . '

84.

When it came to the last verse, John Young brought in the full majesty of the mighty organ. To Will it seemed that trumpets and cymbals crashed around his very ears and that the whole building reverberated with the wonderful music which, like magic, his new found friend drew from the keys. It was both joyous and exciting and as the final chords fell back to earth and the organ was silent he was speechless and quite overwhelmed with the occasion.

For a moment there was absolute quiet as John Young sat with his arm around the boys shoulder. Then behind them they heard a murmur and the small gathering dispersed as a gentle voice said: 'Now then, Mr Young, is there a funeral in the Cathedral today, then?'

They turned round to see a gentleman in gaiters, a large gold cross hanging across his purple front, smiling at them both. Will shot to his feet and would have run down the length of the Cathedral and out of the door if Mr Young had not gently restrained him.

'No, my Lord Bishop,' he said. 'It is just my usual afternoon practice and this young man has been so kind as to help me. Considering that he has had no tuition, he shows great interest and, I venture to add, perhaps even a little promise.'

Edward King, later often described as 'the saintly Bishop King', looked at them both over the top of his glasses. He both knew and respected John Young and his fondness for waifs and strays and was not really surprised to find that he had taken yet another one under his wing.

Looking at Will, he saw a small boy whom he judged to be perhaps ten years of age. He was shabbily dressed and his hands and face bore the grime of a hard day's work. His boots were scuffed, his jumper had a hole in it and his tousled hair had not seen brush or comb all day. His cheeks had a white channel on each side where tears had recently run down them and Bishop King deduced that he had before him a very unhappy child.

'Come here, young man,' said the Bishop: 'Tell me your name and where you live.'

Will stumbled down and stood before the Bishop, screwing his cap in his hands, his eyes on the floor and the words came pouring out in a breathless flood.'

'Please, sir, my name is William Everton and I live on Burton Road and my father is a cabinet maker and I work for him in the workshop at Motherby Lane and I'm just thirteen years old although I don't look it and I wasn't doing any harm and if I've got Mr Young into trouble I'm sorry and I didn't mean to and . . . '

'Whoa, whoa!' laughed the Bishop: 'Draw a breath, boy. No one says that you've done anything wrong and as for Mr Young . . . well, I think that he can take care of himself.'

The Bishop sat at the end of one of the choir stalls and indicated to Will to come and sit next to him.

'Why have you been crying, William?' asked the Bishop. 'It seems to me that you've been crying a great deal.' He ruffled his hands gently through the boy's hair as Mr Young turned his back on them and busied himself with his sheets of music.

The words came slowly at first, but then Will told the Bishop the whole story of his father's second marriage and his apprehension at the return of his parents from their honeymoon. He even told the Bishop of Martha's forbidding appearance, always dressed in dark clothes and never smiling, even at the funniest things.

'Why, sir,' he finished, 'she looks just like . . . like . . . like she doesn't want to be happy, not at any price!'

Bishop King hid a smile.

'William,' he said, 'where would we all be if we judged people just by their appearances? I look like a dry, old clergyman, boring as old sticks and . . . '

'But you're the Bishop!' interrupted Will. 'You're the Bishop and you live in this great church and . . . '

'Yes, yes, I'm the Bishop,' was the reply, 'but do you know what I always wanted to be when I was a boy? I always wanted to be a poacher, yes, I wanted to be a poacher. Out in the still, moonlit night, setting my nets for the rabbits or soaking raisins in a drop of rum for the pheasants. Then down to the river to catch a fish or two, that's the life for me, a poacher!'

A careful observer might have noticed John Young's shoulders shaking with silent laughter as he turned the sheets of his music.

'So you see, William, here I am. You look at me and see a bishop, but all the time I wanted to be a poacher . . . but that's a secret, a secret between you and me and Mr Young and it must never be retold, promise me that, young William!'

Will promised with great sincerity.

'But there's one other person knows, William. God knows. When he sees me kneeling down saying my prayers and hears me preaching in the pulpit, God says to Himself: 'There he is! There's that Bishop who really wants to be a poacher, the old fraud! I'd better keep a sharp eye on him.' So you see, William, God knows us for what we are and not what we pretend to be. Certainly, He'll know your stepmother for what she is, not what she looks like, and you must be the same and judge her for what she is, not by her outward appearance. Do you understand?'

Will said that he thought he understood.

'Look at it another way,' said the Bishop: 'When Jesus walked this earth, He paid no heed to what people looked like. He must have seen some dreadful looking people, the sick and poor, the lame and the deformed, people in filthy rags, blind people in the gutter covered in dirt. Think of the lepers, William. They looked so hideous, poor souls, that they had to walk through the streets ringing a bell to tell people to keep away from them. They looked so terrible that some places threw them out and they had to live in caves in the hills. But Jesus didn't see lepers, He saw people. He saw men and women and little children and He held out His arms to them all. They all looked at Him in wonder, William, no one had ever done that before. Here He was, saying "Come unto Me" and meaning it with all his heart and soul. Perhaps if you held out your arms to your mother, or just told her how glad you were that she was coming to live with you, perhaps that would make all the difference. Why not try, William, why not try?'

Will thought for a moment.

'Will it work, sir? Will she love me like my real mother did?'
he said.

The Bishop sighed and responded: 'There's no guarantees in
this life, William, but you must try. You really must try to accept
this lady into your life. Perhaps she also feels lonely and a little
bit afraid. Just promise me that you'll try.'

Will promised.

'Now it must be tea time,' said the Bishop, 'I must be off.
Perhaps Mr Young will let you play the organ again if you ask
him. Let's say a little prayer before we all go home, shall we?'

They knelt in prayer, the Bishop reciting a simple plea that
everyone in the world would learn to understand everyone else
and with a particular plea for Will, that he might find the happiness he so desperately sought.

As Will walked home he realised that this was twice someone
had told him not to judge people on their appearance. First there
was Henry Carrot, a very simple and uneducated man, and secondly there was Bishop King himself, just the opposite. He resolved to make every effort to like his new mother and to see beyond her outwardly stern appearance.

When Herbert and Martha returned from Mablethorpe,
Martha had her ankle bandaged and was walking with the aid of
a stick.

In the enthusiasm of the holiday spirit, Martha had insisted
that Herbert allow her to go on a donkey ride along the sands. A
suitably docile beast had been found and, with a great many ex-
hortations to the donkeyman to take care, had set off along the
sands at a leisurely pace.

All would have been well if a sudden breeze from the sea had
not blown a portion of Martha's long skirt across the donkey's
eyes, causing it to panic, rear up, and throw Martha flat on her
dignity on the beach.

When Will returned home that evening she sat in a corner of
the room, a glass of brandy at her elbow and her bandaged right
ankle supported on a footstool. A stick which she now needed for
support rested against the chair arm. Will remembered his con-

versation with the Bishop and approached her.

'Mother,' he began, 'I . . . '

Martha cracked him across the back of his legs with the stick with such force that it was a full three weeks before the bruise disappeared.

'Don't you ever call me Mother,' she hissed. 'Never, do you hear?'

Chapter Three

A Winter's Tale

THE BRUISE ON HIS LEG disappeared, but the mark on his mind remained forever. Will had taken the advice given to him by both Henry Carrot and the Bishop and had resolved to love and cherish his new mother only to find that she had not the slightest intention of returning the affection. If anything, she was even quicker to raise her hand than his father and even more biased against him.

When Will had first shown the bruise to the Carrot family, Henry had risen ponderously from his chair, buckled on his heaviest leather belt and expressed the intention of giving Will's father the hiding of a lifetime for allowing his son to be so mis-used. It had taken all the persuasion his wife could muster to stop him leaving the house and it was only with her firm bidding that he had eventually sat down again in his armchair like a quenched volcano. He bit into the stem of his pipe and ground his teeth in his anger.

'Why,' he said, 'much as I love and cherish Mrs Carrot, if she was to 'arm these little children of mine, why, I'd give 'er a good hidin' and no mistake. If any man was to 'arm any one of 'em, I'd tie his windpipe in a knot so tight he'd go blue and black in the face!'

Henry screwed his huge hands together until his knuckles cracked and Will had a mental picture of Martha suspended from them and turning a bright shade of purple. Strangely, it didn't upset him one bit.

Herbert was kept very busy with his new wife. Martha was a sharp business woman who had acted as her father's bookkeeper for many years. She knew profit and loss like the back of her hand and whilst Herbert made the deals in the bar of the White Hart, she costed them out and maximised the profit level in no uncertain terms. She was no man's slave and had insisted that if she was to work for Herbert, then she would draw her wages like anyone else.

She had only been returned from Mablethorpe for a few days when she had descended on the Motherby Street workshop in time to see old Walter giving away some odds and ends of timber, much of it rotted and of no practical use. Every Friday evening for years Walter had gathered together these bits in tidying the workshop and had given them for firewood to the poorer families in the area. Even Herbert had never objected.

With a blow of her cane Martha had knocked the pieces from Walter's hands and asked him what he was doing. When Walter explained that this had been the practice of the Everton workshop for many a long year, Martha stopped his unfinished sentence with a wave of her hands.

'Then it isn't the practice any more,' she said, 'You Will, bind these sticks into bundles. They are to be sold, not given away. We are not in business to give away our hard earned profit to idlers who won't work. In future, Mr Smeed, you will give me an accounting every Monday morning of how many bundles of sticks have been sold. If I catch you giving away any more. then the price will be stopped out of your wages. If I catch you a second time, then you'll be given the sack. Do I make myself clear?'

'Ay, missus, that you do,' said Walter. 'Clear as a bell.'

Then Martha went into the workshop, going from one object to another, table to bench to chair and asking the same question every time.

'What do we use this for? Do we use it at all?'

When the answer was in the negative she had Will and Walter lift the unwanted item into the workyard until a small pile of old chairs, a battered sawhorse, a three-legged table and various other odds and ends had been assembled.

'Are these to be burned, Missus?' asked old Walter.

'Burned? Burned?' said Martha with a note of incredulity in her voice.

'No, Mr Smeed, they are to be SOLD. They are hanging

around here taking up valuable space and earning nothing. You will repair them all until they look like new and place an advertisement in the *Lincoln Gazette and Times* offering them for sale. I will tell you what you are to ask for each item, and you are not to take a penny piece less. Everything in this workshop must earn its keep, and that applies to you two as well.'

She walked along the line of junk, tapping each piece with her stick and saying, 'Ninepence! A shilling! Fourpence halfpenny!'

Walter interrupted her once to say 'Ninepence for that old chair, Missus? It's got one leg missing, there's worm in the back and a great chunk knocked out of the seat. It isn't worth repairing, the wood will cost more than ninepence, in fact it'll cost twice that!'

Martha smiled grimly and said 'Not if you use some of that wood you were so keen on giving away for nothing, Mr Smeed. It's sinful to waste, Mr Smeed.'

'Half that wood's rotten,' said Walter, 'I wouldn't sell it to my worst enemy it's so useless. Anyone with half an eye will see that!'

'Then don't sell it to someone with half an eye, sell it to someone who's blind!' snapped Martha. 'If you don't want to work here, then take your money and clear off. Otherwise, you'll do as you're told! A bit of stain and varnish can do wonders for old bits and pieces. You're a craftsman, Mr Smeed, use your skills to good effect instead of making excuses to be idle and wasteful.'

Walter went a bright shade of red. He appeared to be about to say something, but thought better of it and touched his forelock as Martha went out of the yard and back to her carriage.

The combination of Clegg's timberyard and the Everton workshop soon resulted in an increase in business and this was further enhanced by Herbert's connections with the board of guardians of the workhouse. Many of these gentlemen were retired and now devoted their attention to performing the compulsory good works expected of those upon whom fortune had smiled. Several of them sat on the boards of more than one workhouse in the county and the workshop turned out many a table or cupboard for workhouses as far afield as Gainsborough, Sleaford or Grantham. This meant that Herbert was kept busy socialising in the White Hart and Saracen's Head far more than ever before. Guests were invited to the house from time to time and Martha proved herself to be as parsimonious in the kitchen as she had been that day at the workshop.

Although Herbert was a good businessman, she had an exceptional organising ability which turned it to good advantage. Two new craftsmen were soon taken on in the workshop and there was no longer a reliance on the cheap casual labour which Herbert had always used in busy times.

Will found himself taking the pony and cart on many a journey that autumn and winter and, whilst the weather remained tolerable, he rather welcomed the change and the chance to get out of both workshop and home.

By now the Carrot family wealth had gone and Henry Carrot found that his reputation had preceded him. Work was hard to find and he survived mainly by odd labouring jobs. Herbert sometimes employed him to unload timber and to do the general humping and carrying when there was furniture to be delivered far afield. Herbert figured that Henry was so strong that he would do the work of two men and, as he only paid him a bare half of the normal wage, he reckoned that he was getting a bargain. He salved his conscience by telling his friends that no one would employ a jailbird, but he, Herbert Everton, was not prejudiced. Henry had paid his debt to society and was as deserving of a second chance as the next man. Herbert was heard to say this on many an occasion. As for Henry, he had little option but to accept. He had a family to feed and no one else would employ him.

Mrs Carrot carried on with her laundry and cleaning work, whilst Clink appeared to do very little, but always managed to contribute a few shillings to the family housekeeping.

As Christmas drew nigh, thoughts inevitably turned to the previous year when, thanks to Lucy Matchbox, the Carrot household had had a Christmas to remember. Will looked back to that magical Christmas Day when it had seemed that all was set fair for a new life until his father had remarried and life had again taken a turn for the worse. The December was remarkably mild and as the festive season drew near Will remarked to old Walter that it didn't seem a bit like Christmas was just around the corner.

'Funny month is December,' said Walter, 'I've seen it almost as warm at midday as in the Springtime and then again, I've seen 'em ice skating on the first of the month! You never know what December will do next. I don't trust it at all. Once the first of December is 'ere I wears three vests and two pullovers just to be sure.'

To emphasise the point, he lifted his waiscoat and flannelette shirt and counted the layers of clothing to satisfy himself that he had not forgotten anything when he got dressed that morning. Having tucked his various garments back into his trousers he remarked that he rubbed his chest with goose grease every day once it got to the first of February.

'Never had a cough nor a cold in my life, Little Will,' he said, 'and that's because I keeps me chest well covered and don't let them germs get at it. In February when the worst germs is about, if they do get through my clothes they can't get a grip on my chest because of the goose grease. They just slip off my chest and fall down again.'

'Fall where?' asked Will cheekily. 'If they don't suffocate amongst all those vests and things, they must drop right down your trouser legs into your boots and that's why you get corns! Just think, Walter, your corns are always worst in February and I bet that's why! All those germs fumbling around in your boots and not able to get out, why they must be terribly angry, all smothered in goose grease and slithering around those bony old toes of yours, so they turn themselves into corns, I wouldn't wonder!'

'Cheeky young monkey!' exclaimed Walter taking a playful swipe at the lad with his ruler.

94.

Will had met John Young again in the cathedral early in the autumn and had been invited back to his home on a number of occasions where Mr Young had given him some simple tuition on the piano. He had enjoyed this, but it was on those rare occasions when he had been allowed to play a few notes on the cathedral organ that he had felt himself transformed and his spirit soar to the very rooftops. Truly, he thought, even God must be able to hear that lovely music rising into the high roof and into the evening air. Although he had never seen the Bishop since that first meeting, the Bishop had quietly observed him from afar and from a few judicious enquiries had learnt not a little of the boy's family background. The Bishop was well versed in the ways of hypocrites and one day he called on John Young to ask him about Will.

'He's a quiet, lonely boy,' said John. 'He has this very deep yearning for the mother he never knew and he's desperately unhappy, your Grace. His stepmother came as a bitter disappointment to him and from what he has told me the only friends in the world he has are the Carrot family and old Walter Smeed who works for his father. The only time I see him smile is when we play together, particularly when I let him play a few notes on the organ.'

The Bishop thought for a moment and then asked if the boy had any talent.

'It's difficult to say, your Grace. I barely manage to snatch half an hour with him and then he has to rush off home in case he's missed. Some evenings he never turns up at all because of the work he has to do. He certainly has the enthusiasm and he has a delicate touch. He doesn't just play his few simple notes, he seems to live them. If you watched his face you'd see his spirit fly aloft with his music. Yes, I think that somewhere in that unhappy boy there is a hidden talent, but it can never be brought out into the open unless I can have some hours with him on a regular basis. In fact, it needn't be me. Any competent teacher could do as well.'

Bishop King nodded as if in agreement and between them

they hatched a simple plot.

Herbert and Martha were in their sitting room some days later when there was a knock at the door. Annie came into the room carrying a visiting card and announced excitedly that it was Mr Young, the cathedral organist.

As he went into the hallway to greet his visitor, Herbert's mind was thinking of all the business he might acquire at the cathedral. The work of maintainance and restoration was almost continuous and he had visions of pastures new opening up before him. It was therefore quite a shock to him when this train of thought was brought to an abrupt halt by Mr Young's statement that it was about Will he wished to speak.

'Come into my study, Mr Young,' he said. 'Tell me what mischief he's been up to now. He'll have been helped by that blasted Carrot boy, whatever the trouble is. He's a trial and a tribulation to me is that boy, even though he is my only son. God knows, I've tried to guide him on the paths of righteousness, but it appears that he's possessed of the devil and will go his own way.'

John Young assured Herbert that as far as he knew, Will was in no trouble whatsoever, in fact the reverse. He found Will to be a polite and considerate boy with a great fondness for music.

'And that, Mr Everton, is what I wish to discuss with you.' He continued: 'Will has been to my home once or twice and I have sought to teach him the simple rudiments of the piano and I have also allowed him to play a few notes on the cathedral organ.'

Herbert puffed up in anger as he exploded into a torrent of words. 'Been to your home? Playing the piano? Sitting at the great cathedral organ? No wonder his work has been suffering, Mr Young. Don't you worry, he'll not pester you again. I'll give him such a thrashing as he'll never forget and you can rely on that!'

'Mr Everton, I don't think you heard me correctly, sir. All these things Will has done at my invitation. The Bishop himself has spoken to Will in the cathedral and he is well aware of my attempts to tutor him. Indeed, sir, the Bishop has encouraged me to do so. Are you not aware of your son's love of music?'

John Young watched keenly as the mention of the Bishop deflated Herbert like a punctured balloon. He stammered and stuttered and for once seemed a little unsure of himself.

'Well,' he said, 'of course, I've heard him tinkering about on our piano sometimes and I can recognise some of the tunes he plays, particularly the hymns he seems to like. But he's not cut out to be a musician; he's a carpenter like me, a joiner to work with his hands and make and mend things, not to prattle about playing the piano, there's no money to be earned at that.'

'I believe that Will has some talent, Mr Everton. At the moment he is grasping at straws of knowledge, picking up the odd tune here and there from memory because he has a good ear for a note. He deserves proper tuition and a chance to make something better of his life.'

A steely voice from the doorway said loudly: 'And what's wrong with his life, Mr Young? Doesn't he have a loving mother and father, a good roof over his head and good food on the table? Is he not being taught a skill to his hands and a trade by which to earn his daily bread? I would have thought that to want more would be a sinful vanity!'

Martha stood with hand on hip, pince-nez on the end of her nose and stared at John Young as if he had just crawled out from under the floorboards. She brushed aside Herbert's attempt at introductions and said again: 'And I repeat, Mr Young, what is wrong with Will's life?'

'Madam,' he said diplomatically, 'in terms of the basic needs of life, there is many a lad would gladly swop places with Will. As you say, he has food and shelter and clothing and, even as a boy, he is known as a good craftsman at his trade. But there is more to life than that, Mrs Everton. I believe that God has given Will a gift, the gift of music. It's a great gift for, properly developed, it will give pleasure to his fellows and it should not be ignored.'

Herbert did not take kindly to being dominated by his own wife in his own study. Then again, he was finding out that Martha was even harder than he was and that she had a business head far superior to his own. He guided his wife to a chair, bade Mr Young be seated and took up his inevitable posture in front of the fireplace. He missed the warmth of the fire against his rump, but Martha was cutting down on the household bills and the fire was now never lit except in the evenings. God help us when the winter arrives, he thought.

'Mr Young,' he said, 'I am much impressed by your interest in William and the fact that the Bishop himself has an eye on the boy' – he gave great and deliberate emphasis to the word 'Bishop' as he stared at Martha. 'However, we are a simple family, working hard for our very survival in this harsh world and I feel that there is not time enough in our busy day for Will to study music. And if he did, would he earn his living from it? How much does a musician get paid, Mr Young? What would be the demand for his services and how would he support his family in years to come? You see, Mr Young, we have Will's best interests at heart all the time.'

John Young shook his head as if puzzled by Herbert's attitude.

'Many of your questions I cannot answer, Mr Everton. It would require some months of study before we would know whether Will would be an exceptional musician, capable of commanding good fees and earning a good living. It may be that his talent is merely good and not outstanding, but surely the boy has a right to find out? If this chance is not seized now, then it will be too late and the gifts he has will be lost for ever. Lost to the world, sir, absolutely lost . . . '

Martha stood up.

'Sir, a few yards down this road there is a workhouse and in it you will find all manner of persons who, in their lives, have not seen fit to work hard as God intended. They have no doubt dreamed of earning their daily bread by playing with idle dreams rather than by listening to their betters who have exhorted them to work. That they now have anything to eat is solely due to the charity and good works of such as my husband; that they have shelter from the elements is due to the good works of those in trade in this city who support the workhouse and act as its guardians – without pay, mind you, without pay – and if Will were to set aside his trade for this airy-fairy music of yours, then that's where he would undoubtedly end up.'

How John Young kept his temper he would never know. He felt harsh words coming to his lips, but bit them back and endeavoured to argue reason with this virago of a woman.

'Mrs Everton, I do not suggest that Will should abandon his trade at this stage, neither am I mindless of the many charitable works performed in the city of Lincoln by Mr Everton and his colleagues. All I ask is that you give Will a chance. A few months tuition with any one of several good music teachers in this town.'

He reached into his pocket and pulled out a sheet of paper which he held out towards Herbert.

'Here, Mr Everton, I have drawn up a timetable to cover some three months. Will would have a two hour lesson three times a week. Once a week I would meet him to assess his progress and to help him generally and I would be prepared to come around here each evening to help with his practice, for practice he would need. He would also need a fresh mind, and for this reason I suggest that you grant him time away from the workshop for his three weekly lessons.'

'Now I couldn't agree to that, Mr Young,' said Herbert. 'We have a busy trade now and if I were to release Will I would have to employ another joiner part-time. There just isn't the money, Mr Young, there just isn't the money to spare. We barely make ends meet as it is. I thank you for your interest, but the answer must be no. We can't afford it, can we Mrs Everton?'

Martha shook her head.

'It would cost us at least another fifteen shillings a week to find another joiner, even part-time. And for what? So as Will could get grand ideas above his station in life. Instead of loving us as he does now, he'd be wanting to mix with his musical friends and he'd soon forget us.'

And with these words she swept from the room in a rustling of long skirts and without even the courtesy of a 'Good Day!' to her visitor.

Thus was Will denied any musical training and the conversation with John Young was never related to him unless it put ideas into his head. When the Bishop was told, he shook his head sadly and said: 'It's the times in which we live, Mr Young, the times in which we live. Everyone wants to build up treasures on earth and Heaven can wait. Be kind to the lad, Mr Young, teach him what bits and pieces you can.'

In the Everton household after John Young had departed there brewed a most furious row and Herbert could be heard shouting at the top of his voice, 'Damn you, woman, I will be master in my own house! I'll make the decisions here, not you! In future, keep your place and don't interfere in mens' business!'

However, Martha had the louder and more piercing voice and could be heard further down Burton Road. None of the neighbours was left in any doubt that Herbert had met his match.

In the early evening Herbert announced his intention of taking a walk down to the White Hart. Martha, now apparently subdued and calm again, asked him sweetly what he would like for his supper when he returned. Herbert was in no mood to be placated and, jamming his hat on his head and seizing his silver-topped cane, he responded in one violent word – 'Arseholes!'

Martha almost followed him down Burton Road, hurrying to catch the butcher before he closed. Her request caused the butcher to raise his eyebrows, but he had already learned that it was futile to argue with the new Mrs Everton and her wishes were complied with.

It was after eleven o'clock when Herbert returned. He was a little unsteady on his feet, but stumbled into the dining room where, to his surprise, he found the table laid for his supper, complete with silverware and a single red rose in a silver vase by his plate. He nodded sagely to himself. 'That'll teach her!' he mumbled. 'Women have to be kept in their place! She knows who's master now!'

His wife swept into the room carrying a serving dish which she placed on the table. She poured him a glass of wine, brought him his slippers and asked if he was ready to eat now. He pulled

100.

up his chair to the table, seized his knife and fork and indicated that she should serve the meal.

Even allowing for his alcoholic haze, Herbert found it very difficult to cut the meat but persevered and eventually succeeded in transferring the first forkful to his mouth. The taste was quite revolting and it was like chewing rubber. After several attempts, he spat it out all over the table and roared, 'Damn you, woman, that meat's as tough as arseholes and twice as stringy!'

Martha tossed her head arrogantly.

'Precisely, Herbert, precisely! Arseholes you asked for, arseholes you've got!' And she flounced off to bed whilst Herbert's rantings could be heard all the way to Newport Arch as he seized the plate and threw the whole lot into the road.

For the next few days Herbert spent a lot of time in the workshop at Motherby Road. He had learnt his craft as an apprentice and could wield his tools with the best of them. The shavings flew as he took his temper out of the wood, occasionally muttering to himself: 'Bloody women, I'll show her who's boss!' At lunchtime he disappeared down the High Street to the Black Bull and came back some two hours later in a worse temper than ever. Will and Walter kept out of his way, taking a long lunch break whilst he was absent, but always being hard at work when he returned. As Walter remarked: 'Better 'im working his arse off in 'ere than that bloody woman poking her nose into what don't concern 'er.' At least the temporary rift in the marriage kept Martha away from the workshop and since the incident with the firewood Walter had dreaded seeing her again. Will found it to be almost a blessed relief as his father was so incensed against Martha that he almost ignored him.

Just three days before Christmas his father told Will that he would have to make a journey over to Horncastle. They had made three new tressle tables for the workhouse there and these were to be used on Christmas Day to impress the workhouse guardians who would be putting in their customary appearance at the inmates Christmas dinner. In addition, there was a body to be brought back to Lincoln for burial in Newport cemetery. Normally a pauper's grave in the Horncastle churchyard would have been the unfortunate man's lot, but as he had been a soldier who had fought with some distinction in the Crimean War some thirty five years earlier and had originally hailed from Lincoln, a local benefactor had decreed that he must be buried in the town of his birth and had paid for the burial and all other expenses connected with a decent funeral.

'Silly old devil fell in the River Bain one night,' said Herbert. 'Drowned himself in a foot of water and got jammed under a bridge for a week before they found him. He must have been in a right state when they dragged him out. He's already in a coffin, no doubt some cheap job they bought locally so we've missed that bit of business, but at least we've got the funeral to arrange. When you get there the workhouse master will get a couple of the chaps to put the coffin on the cart and we'll unload it when you get back. Tell you what, take that Carrot boy with you to help and I'll give him a florin for himself.'

Horncastle was some twenty miles away and Will worked out that with the steady pace of the old mare it would take about four hours to get there and the same returning. Allowing for unloading and loading at the workhouse, that meant that if they left at about eight o'clock in the morning, they could be back in Lincoln by about five or six o'clock in the evening.

It was barely light when they left Lincoln the following morning and headed east into the countryside, Will having decided to take a roundabout route to pass the day. The boys were pleased to be out together and they chatted busily as the old mare jogged steadily along the country roads. They made good time and when they stopped to give the horse a breather just outside Branston Booths they were both in high spirits. As they took the road over Potter Hanworth fen, Clink remarked how strangely quiet it was. There was not another living soul to be seen and it was not until they reached Bardney that they saw another human being. They stopped at the village shop and purchased bottles of pop and a bag of broken biscuits which they munched as the horse trotted on towards their destination across the quiet countryside. The sky in the east looked very bright and Clink remarked that this was because they were heading towards the sea.

Will had been to the Horncastle workhouse before and, like all other workhouses, he hated going through its doors. From his earliest days he had heard people speak of the workhouse with dread in their voices, the fear of being forced to enter the grim buildings showing through clearly. It was the last refuge, often the end of a bitter trail of humiliation and degredation, for the poor and the sick, the widow and the orphan. In its dark and gloomy corridors could be found all the rejects of a society which did not hesitate to evict a widow and her children for non-payment of rent and then salved its conscience by giving them shelter in the one place they feared going.

The workhouse had no comforts and few of the basic amenities regarded as essential even in Victorian times. Its inmates earned coppers from menial tasks and lived in surroundings which were cold and cheerless and where the food would not have been thought edible in normal circles. For many the only exit from the workhouse was to the grave, the paupers grave where coffins were often stacked twenty deep one on top of the other. Will had been to many such funerals and on more than one occasion had seen the gravediggers putting their weight on the top coffin to crush coffin and occupant to dust to make room for yet another pauper. As they clattered through the gate a group of ragged children ran around the cart, many of them without shoes and looking blue with cold in the bitter wind which swept across the flat countryside from the North Sea with chilling ferocity. Will and Clink gave them the remains of the bag of biscuits and they fought over this as if they were starving.

The overseer, one Mr Fellowes, was a grim apparition, thought Will. He was tall and thin, stooped at the shoulders, and he wore a high wing collar which threatened to cut his scraggy neck every time he moved his head from side to side which he appeared to do very frequently. He had long dark hair which fell onto his greasy collar and great bushy eyebrows beneath which a pair of slit eyes forever glanced from side to side as if seeking to observe one of the inmates breaking one of the numerous rules with which they were saddled. He walked with a shuffling gait and was forever washing his hands with invisible soap. His voice was high pitched and his conversation full of 'hums' and 'ha's'. As he walked through the building inmates carefully kept out of his way or buried their heads over their alloted tasks with great intentness.

Although Clink had no illusions about workhouses he had never been in one before and as they made their way into the building, assisted in carrying the tressle tables by two of the inmates, he glanced around him as if he could not believe his eyes. The house in Gordon Road was no palace but compared to this place it seemed like Heaven and he could not wait to depart its grim portals and head for home.

The tables safely deposited in the dining hall, Mr Fellowes told them to wait whilst he fetched the key to the workhouse chapel where the body was lying, leaving them in the charge of an elderly man whom he addressed as 'Mr Secretary'.

'You're the secretary here, then, are you?' asked Will, 'Is that a good job?'

The man laughed and shook his head.

'No,' he said, 'I'm not the secretary at all. Once, a long time ago, I was the secretary to a titled gentleman. I had a room in a fine house all to myself, my keep and fifteen pounds a year and met all sorts of famous people. Now I'm just a nobody waiting here to die like everyone else. When Mr Fellowes calls me 'Mr Secretary' he's just being sarcastic. You see, I can read and write with the best of 'em, much better than he can, but he's the master here and he resents that, so he calls me 'Mr Secretary' to get his own back, though I've never done him any harm.'

Clink pondered upon this for a moment and then asked, 'If you're a secretary, like you say, why are you in this place? I wouldn't live here for all the tea in China, I can tell you!' Clink ran his hands through his mop of red hair and visibly shuddered as he looked around him.

Mr Secretary looked at the two boys for a moment and said, 'I wish that I was a lad again with all the wisdom of one who doesn't know anything! I'll tell you why I'm here, lad. It's no credit to me, but if it teaches you a lesson you'll remember and keeps you out of places like this, then it's a job well done.

Like I told you, I was once the secretary to a titled gentleman. I lived in his great hall, drank good wine and ate fine food. I was in charge of his library and that was my pride and joy. He let me read all the books I wanted and never denied me access to them. I love books, always have, and I was as happy as could be. There were more than five thousand books and I could take any one of them back to my room to read and study.

I got my food and my roof for nothing and, being a man of simple needs, I still had money to give to my mother who was living alone not far from where I worked, my father having been dead this many a year. The fact that I could do that kept her out of places like this.

However, I'd always wished that I could give her something better. She told me one day that there was a tiny cottage for sale just by the edge of the green and that it could be had for forty pounds. It had a little bit of land to one side that I could have made into a garden for her and where she could have grown a few vegetables and there were two or three apple trees as well. She could have lived there secure until she died. Anyway, I didn't have forty pounds and couldn't get it neither, but it kept preying on my mind and I couldn't stop thinking about it. My mother was getting on in years and if I could have bought the cottage, I could have lived in it as well and it would have been a place for me when my working days were over.

Just about that time there was a librarian came to the hall. My master had engaged him to catalogue his library. Although I had always kept it in good order, he felt that it ought to be catalogued and this fellow was here to do it. I was told to help him all I could. It was interesting work and I fell to with a will.

One evening we had finished work for the day and the librarian had just left the hall when I noticed that he had left his bag which he carried everywhere with him. I picked it up and ran out of the hall with it and just caught him as he was getting into the carriage. As I handed him the bag, it came open and out onto the drive fell one of the library books. I recognised it at once, for it was one of my favourites and I had often looked at it. It was full of hand-coloured pictures of tropical birds, the like of which you would never see in this country.

It was strictly forbidden to take books out of the house and my master had made that clear to him the day we had started the work. I picked up the book and said that I would have to tell my master. He followed me back into the house, pleading that he would be sent to prison. He said that he had a wife and two children. Then he pressed two sovereigns into my hand and grabbed me by the arm. He told me that in London he could get five pounds for the book and that nobody would have missed it anyway.

I shook off his arm and said that I would have none of it; then he said that at home he had thirty pounds and that he would give it to me if I put the book back and told no one.'

Mr Secretary shook his head as if still bewildered by those events and continued.

'Well, I took the thirty pounds and with a small advance of salary which my master allowed me I bought the cottage. The librarian was long gone and I thought that I had heard the last of it and that my future was secure.

It was a fool's paradise. One of my master's friends was seeking rare volumes in the London dealers and came across two books which he recognised as having belonged to the hall. Needless to say, the librarian had been stealing from everyone and he was soon caught. He told everything trying to save himself and said that I had sold him a number of books for thirty pounds. Well, people put two and two together. Where had I got the money to buy the cottage, they asked? Of course, I couldn't account for it.

They sent me to prison for two years. They took the cottage from my mother and sold it to repay my master. She was thrown out and put in the workhouse. She died there – of shame, I wouldn't wonder.

When I came out of prison, no one would employ me. You've paid your debt to society, they said, make a new start. Make a new start! That's a laugh and no mistake! Who would give me a reference? And so here I am, gentlemen, 'Mr Secretary', I am; I do a bit of the bookwork for the workhouse, but that's all the secretary I am, or ever will be.'

He grabbed Clink by the collar and looked him straight in the face.

'Take my word for it, young sir, no one ever forgives you in this world. It takes just a few minutes foolishness and you're damned in this world and probably in the next as well!'

The conversation was cut short by the reappearance of Mr Fellowes, large key dangling from his fingers. He beckoned with a boney finger, indicating that they should follow him, and they entered a side door of the chapel, winding their way up a spiral staircase to a gloomy little room above.

As they entered the room, they were overwhelmed by a strong and repulsive odour.

'Cor, stuff a duck!' was Clink's reaction, whilst Will held his nose and Mr Secretary took out a grubby handkerchief which he held to his nostrils. Mr Fellowes appeared to be totally unaffected.

As their eyes pierced the gloom they saw a plain coffin resting on two trestles in the middle of the room. The winter light struggling through the one grubby window like rice pudding through a sieve revealed very little and Will went forward to light the two candles which he had noticed on a small table. He was stopped at once by Mr Fellowes.

'There's enough light from the window, young Mr Everton,' he said: 'To waste the candles is . . . er . . . hum . . . sinful.'

'No wonder it pongs,' said Clink, 'The coffin lid isn't properly down.'

'No,' said Mr Fellowes, 'He was in the water for some time, I fear, and has become somewhat . . . er . . . hum . . . ha . . . distended is the word, I believe; yes, that's it . . . distended.'

He brushed a non-existent fly from his lapel and then said: 'As we only bought the coffin locally and they were not to be allowed to carry out the burial they . . . er . . . ha . . . hum . . . took offence, I believe; yes, took offence, and wouldn't secure the . . . er hum . . . ha . . . lid. Just dumped him in it, plonked the lid on top and . . . er . . . ha . . . hum . . . made off!

I shall leave you, now, gentleman,' said Mr Fellowes, 'I am sure that Mr Secretary here will . . . er . . . ha . . . hum . . . assist you, yes, assist you; he was a friend of the deceased and should be glad to . . . um . . . er . . . help.' And with these words he shuffled off down the spiral staircase, his lean frame bent more than ever to avoid scraping his head on the low ceiling.

Will looked at the coffin, lid standing some six inches agape on one side, and considered the situation. To Mr Secretary it seemed quite obscene that a thirteen year old boy had been left in charge of this situation, but to Will it was all part of the day's work. The sight of a cadaver held no terrors for him. Coffins, winding sheets, and funerals had been part of the household as long as he could remember. He knew exactly what to do and had seen both his father and old Walter do the same on more than one occasion.

'Right, now,' he said, 'The first job is to put the coffin on the floor. Me and Clink will take one end and you the other, sir.'

They took up their positions and on Will's 'One! Two! Three – Heave!' put the coffin on the floor. As they did so, the lid dropped off with a clatter and the occupant lay revealed. He was clad in a simple white gown, his stomach hugely swollen so that it pulled the shirt up from round his ankles which were of a greeny blue colour. Someone had had the decency to place a linen cloth around the deceased's head and this was tied around his neck with a piece of string so that his face was not revealed. Above the cloth was a mop of long, white hair, strangely beautiful even in death as it curled down around the dead man's shoulders.

Will took the lid and rested it squarely on top of the coffin edge, pushing down to ensure that the screw holes aligned with those in the coffin rim. He placed a long wood screw in each, put two or three spare ones between his teeth and put his screwdriver close to hand. Then he took his pocket knife out, opened the blade and knelt down by the coffin, knife poised.

'You're not going to . . . ?' started Clink. The phrase and the idea seeming almost too obscene to put into words.

'I know what I'm going to do,' said Will, temporarily removing the screws from his mouth, 'You just pay attention to what I tell you to do and do it quickly when I give the word.'

He placed them one on each side of the coffin, one towards the head and the other towards the foot, kneeling down with their backs to the receptacle.

'Now then, when I say "Go!" you jump back quickly and sit on the lid with all your might and don't move until I tell you to. If we don't get it screwed down the first time it'll be a terrible job the second time. Are you both ready?' he asked, knife poised.

There was little to choose between the shades of green revealed in the faces of man and boy as they awaited Will's word of command.

'One! Two! Three – GO!' yelled Will, at the same time lunging forward with the blade of his knife with all his might.

As Clink and Mr Secretary plumped themselves firmly on the lid, a blast of foul air hissed violently from the coffin. If there had been a smell in the room before, there was now a stench so vile that it was impossible to describe. As Will danced around the coffin driving home the screws, Clink coughed and spluttered, whilst Mr Secretary gagged and heaved, eventually running into a corner of the room where he threw up on to the floor. Will drove home the last screw and mopped his brow. Despite the coldness of the room, his brow was running with sweat and his face quite red.

Mr Secretary threw open the window and an icy draught shivered around the room.

Will felt in his pocket and drew out a ball of linseed putty which he used to seal the lid edges. He had seen corpses found in a river before and had come prepared.

'There,' he said, 'that'll keep the gasses from getting out!'

'Dear God, boy!' said Mr Secretary. 'Have you no feelings for the dead? I knew that man, he was my friend!'

'I'm sorry about that, sir,' said Will, 'but he wouldn't feel anything. When you die your soul flies out of your body and goes off to Heaven that very moment. In fact, as your soul flies off it can look down at you lying there dead. Funny, that must be, I think. Anyway, what's left is just your empty shell. It's not really you, it's just a sort of bag that's been carrying your soul around all those years. My father told me that the first time I saw a dead body and I've never been afraid of one since and that's a fact! I must have seen a hundred since then.'

The man looked at this boy, no higher than his shoulder, and wondered what sort of a father could have sent him out on this grisly errand. Then he turned to Clink.

'And what about you, Carrot Top,' he said, 'don't you have any respect for the dead either?'

'I don't like dead bodies,' said Clink with some conviction, 'but Will's my friend and I promised to help him. Besides, I get two shillings for helping and we need the money. If Will says it's the right thing to do, then that's good enough for me. But the sooner this job's over the better. I'll not be sorry to get home tonight.'

Mr Secretary shook his head in bewilderment.

'Nathaniel Bostock, he was. He was a soldier all his life. Joined as a drummer boy from the poorhouse. Never knew no parents or family except his friends in the army.'

He shook his head again and drew out a battered pipe from his ragged waistcoat. Finding that his pouch was empty, he contented himself with sucking the stem, eyes closed as if he was inhaling clouds of fragrant smoke. Then he spoke again.

'At the battle of the Alma in the Crimea he stood over his wounded officer and fought off them Russians single handed until they were rescued. He killed four of 'em with his bayonet and then clubbed another's brains out. His officer gave him a gold watch chain for that, but that was sold long afore he got into this place.

He fought at Inkermann. My, he told some stories about

that, he did. It was a real soldier's battle, fought out one November night in a thick fog. All hand to hand, it was. 'Twas said that many a soldier cut down his own friend in the confusion of that night and certainly the slaughter was terrible. Nathaniel fought through all that.

At Sebastopol he was noticed by the General himself, right in the thick of it, laying about him like a good 'un! Ay, old Nathaniel sent many a man to Hell in his time.

When he came home they gave him a medal for gallantry. The Old Queen herself pinned it on him at a special parade. Everyone said he was a hero and he had only to appear in the tavern with his uniform and his medals all spick and span and everyone would buy his ale for him. But then he took sick and wouldn't mend, so they discharged him from the army with a pension. He showed me his papers once. Two shillings a week he got. "Worn out through long and arduous service", it said. Fancy, served as a soldier for nearly thirty years, man and boy, and they threw him out with two bob a week!'

'That's terrible,' said Will. 'Why did no one do anything for him?'

'He was hungry one winter and he broke into a house and stole some food and a few shillings he found lying about. He was caught and the magistrates said that as he was a hero they wouldn't send him to prison, but the Army found out and they stopped his pension. After that it was only a matter of time before he found his way in here like the rest of us.'

Mr Secretary tapped the coffin gently with his boot.

'So, Nat, now you'll be in Hell and meeting all the others that you sent there before you. I don't envy you, old friend,' he said, 'though at least you've got shut of this damned place.'

Clink said hotly, 'Heroes don't go to Hell, they go to Heaven!'

The old man looked him squarely in the eye and said: 'Thou shalt not kill, lad, that's what the good book says, thou shalt not kill! It doesn't say anything about whether you're a soldier or not. It just says thou shalt not kill.'

The conversation was cut short by the sound of Mr Fellowes

shouting up the stairs to ask if they intended to be all day about the job. They picked up the coffin to carry it down the difficult, winding stairs, Clink and Will to the fore and Mr Secretary behind. As they raised it there was a distinct moaning sound from inside.

Clink started and almost let go, leaving Will struggling to hold his end of the coffin.

'What the 'ell's that?' he cried. 'I heard him say something!'

'Take hold, Clink, before I drop it,' said Will. 'It's nothing but the air rushing out of the body as we move it. I've heard it do that a thousand times! Get hold, man, afore I drop it!'

And so the little cortege moved slowly down the winding staircase, the boys at the front and Mr Secretary at the back. They were not half way down when Will stumbled against one of the iron bolts on the tread and bounced the coffin heavily against the rail. There was a distinct blast of wind from within.

'I'm off,' yelled Clink. 'If he can fart, he can walk!'

And dropping the coffin he made off down the staircase as if the devil were close behind him, almost knocking Mr Fellowes to the ground as he rushed past him at the foot towards the door.

Will struggled manfully to bear the weight on his own whilst at the other end Mr Secretary kept shouting, 'I can't hold it! I can't hold it!'

Realising the inevitable, Will shouted back to him to let his end drop and did the same himself.

He jumped out of the way as the mortal remains of Nathaniel Bostock, one time soldier of Her Majesty's 63rd Regiment of Foot, bumped majestically down the staircase and came to rest at the feet of Mr Fellowes who had witnessed the whole performance with some displeasure.

Will pursued Clink out into the yard and dragged him back inside. He had a temper akin to his father's and was shouting angrily. Clink was near to tears and became a most unwilling accomplice as they lifted the coffin onto the cart and covered it with old sacks and blankets.

The horse being fed and watered, they set off back towards

Lincoln, but not before Will had pressed his last shilling into the hand of Mr Secretary.

This was the first serious argument that the two boys had had during their friendship and the first part of their journey home was conducted in total silence. Clink glanced frequently behind him at the covered coffin and seemed to be totally immersed in his own thoughts. He did this so often that eventually Will pulled the cart to the side of the road to give the horse a breather and asked his friend what was wrong.

'It's him!' said Clink, pointing to the coffin and visibly shuddering. 'It's him! I heard him move in the coffin, I'm sure I did, Will. He ain't really dead, he's still alive and any minute he's going to jump out of that damned coffin and get the pair of us. You heard what the chap said in the workhouse. He's killed dozens when he was a soldier. It wouldn't take him long to polish us off!'

'Clink Carrot, you're daft!' said Will. 'He's dead and he's been dead this past week or more. He can't harm you nor me nor anyone else.'

Will climbed onto the back of the cart, threw aside the coverings and got out his screwdriver and made as if to unscrew the lid. Clink looked on in terror as Will started on the first screw.

'I'll show you,' he said. 'I'll tip him out of the coffin and show you that he's dead!'

Then he stopped for a moment and said thoughtfully, 'Of course, I won't be able to lift him back on my own and you'll have to help.'

'Don't Will, for God's sake leave him be and let's get back home before it gets dark. Alive or dead, I don't want to be out here with him in the dark. Please, Will, let's go home.'

Will put the coverings back and put the horse back on the road again, whipping him up to a trot. By now it had grown noticeably colder and the air seemed perfectly still, Across the fields they could hear the sounds from the farmhouses and cottages carrying far in the still air. They made good progress and by the time they were leaving Branston Booths Will was congratulating himself that he might even be back in time to see John Young and play a few notes on the Cathedral organ. It was about another ten miles to go, he thought.

It was at that moment that the first tiny flakes of snow flittered down through the still air. The horse pricked up his ears and shook his head as if sensing the change in the weather and noticeably quickened his pace.

Clink looked behind yet again and then grabbed Will's arm.

'Look behind us,' he said. 'What's that?'

Will turned around and looked away across the fen towards the way they had just travelled. A dark cloud seemed to be rolling across the fields towards them. As they watched the wind suddenly whipped up and the snow began to fall a little thicker. The cloud was now advancing rapidly.

'It's snow,' said Will. 'It's a snowstorm blowing in from the sea and it'll be upon us any minute. Wrap yourself up, Clink, turn up your collar and put one of those old blankets round your shoulders. We haven't got too far to go now and we'll soon be there.'

Thus saying, he flicked the horse across the rump with the whip, pulled his cap over his ears and draped a couple of old sacks over his shoulders.

The North Sea blizzard caught up with them before they had gone half a mile, thick snow being driven before a strong wind which eddied and swirled around them with increasing ferocity. They had travelled barely a mile before the snow was nine inches deep, the wind driving it into deep drifts where it gathered in the windward of the high hedges. On the other side of the road it was but three or four inches in depth, the wind sending the snow into great sprays sweeping over the hedge top, and Will tried to keep the horse to that side of the road. This tactic was successful for a while, but as the road bent around and the wind changed direction it became increasingly difficult to make any progress.

It was gloomy and fast becoming almost impossible to see more than a few yards, except when the wind abated for a few seconds sometimes and allowed the snow to fall instead of being driven, but these breaks were few and far between and it became slow progress in many places.

The temperature had dropped several degrees since they had left Horncastle and Clink was soon shivering and complaining that he was cold.

'Take the blankets and sacks off the coffin,' shouted Will above the howl of the wind. 'Wrap some around you and some around me.'

Clink did as he was told and the next time Will looked around at him he was sitting hunched up on the box with only his eyes peeping out from a slit in one of the sacks which he had put over his head. The snow was settling on him and Will remarked that it would not be long before people would mistake him for a snowman.

Within another mile the cold was really biting into both of them. Will's teeth were chattering and it was all he could do to keep hold of the reins in his frozen hands. He kept nudging Clink and shouting at him, but the only response he got was a deep groaning sound. The snow got thicker and thicker and the horse began to falter. His breath was freezing around his nostrils and frozen snow hung heavy around his hooves. At times the cart was barely moving, but Will had the sense to realise that he had to keep the horse on the move.

He shouted above the wind to encourage the beast and cracked the whip as best he was able, but his voice seemed to be torn away by the wind and his hands were so cold that he could hardly move the whip.

Time seemed to stand still. The cold was disappearing and a warm numbness was creeping around his lower limbs. His hands were frozen solid around the reins and it hurt to try to move them, whilst he had long since lost the whip somewhere along the road. Then the numbness crept up into his arms and the cold disappeared. He turned to tell Clink who was now just a snow covered mound, but the words wouldn't come from his lips. He had a ringing noise in his ears and he felt, rather than saw, that the horse had stopped and was not of a mind to go further.

Will was curiously unable to move now and felt very tired. He thought to himself that he would just lie down for a few minutes to regain his strength and then he thought that he would be able to get the horse moving again. He was just about to close his eyes and go to sleep when he fancied that he saw a light approaching them through the darkness.

Yes, there it was, dancing and flickering brightly through the gloom, seeming to grow rapidly nearer. He heard a voice shouting and tried to reply, but was unable to do so.

Soon he made out the figure of a man, carrying a large lantern on a pole.

He seemed to loom suddenly out of the darkness until he stood by the cart and reached up and took the reins from Will's hands, rubbing them in his own. Will blinked wearily down at him. He had never known such tiredness in his life.

The man was very tall and broad. He had long snow-covered hair which hung down onto his shoulders over the cloak he wore. He took the scarf from round his mouth and Will saw that he had a beard and moustache, the latter waxed at the ends into spikes. As the wind blew the cape to one side, Will saw that he wore a scarlet coat with brass buttons and that he had medals dangling from his chest.

But it was his eyes that fascinated Will. Even in the gloom he could see that they were large and deep set. They seemed to glow and flash fiercely as the soldier shook Will and shouted at him to keep awake. He jumped up on the cart and pummelled Clink unmercifully until he gave a deep moan and promised to stay awake.

'Do you know any songs, boy?' asked the soldier. 'Good rousing songs that we can all sing?'

Will fought off the weariness that threatened to send him off to sleep at any moment and replied: 'Yes, sir, I know some good hymns, but I'm so tired I can hardly keep awake to sing them. I think it's the cold, but I don't know 'cause I don't really feel it any more.'

'Don't go to sleep, boy, or you'll not wake up again, at least

117.

not in this world. I've seen men do that many a time when I was serving abroad and in the morning all that was left of 'em was a stiff, frozen corpse! Don't you dare go to sleep, nor your friend either!'

He gave Clink a good thump in the ribs which made him cry out in pain.

The soldier went to the horse's head, rubbed the snow from its mane and, putting his mouth close to its ear, whispered encouragement to the animal.

'Right, boys, 'he shouted, 'I'll lead and you'll sing. If I don't hear you I'll come back there and clout you across the ear so hard that you'll think that you've been kicked by the horse! Right, now, sing, damn you, sing!'

And thus they went through the blizzard, the soldier at the head with his lantern singing lustily and at times seeming to drag the poor horse through the deep snow and the two boys singing wearily above the storm. Every now and then the soldier stopped and listened to see if they were singing and, if he was not satisfied with their efforts, he came back to pummel and shove them into consciousness again. The coffin, by now little more than a snow-covered mound, occasionally slithered on the back of the cart and the soldier used his prodigious strength to push it back again, crossing himself each time as he did so.

How many miles they went like that Will would never know. His later memory was of a never-ending journey, his lapses into sleep always broken by the deep, piercing eyes of the soldier staring him in the face and his lusty voice yelling: 'Sing, damn you, sing!' Clink always said that he remembered nothing after the soldier's first appearance through the storm with his lantern until he woke up before a roaring log fire in a farmhouse kitchen.

The fire was painful as its heat thawed out his frozen limbs, the farmer's lusty wife and daughter rubbing at his naked body with their rough hands and he made a feeble effort to draw around him the blankets with which he was covered. The women laughed at his efforts and chided him at his shyness.

'Now, lad,' said the wife, 'if we don't get the blood flowing through that body of yours again, there's liable to be little bits drop off that you'll miss in later life. You haven't got anything that we haven't all seen before!'

Will had already gone through this painful process and was sitting at the table nursing a great mug of steaming soup in his hands. The colour was slowly seeping back into his face.

The door opened and the farmer came in, almost blown into the room by the gale blowing behind him. He shook the snow from his hair and rubbed his hands in front of the fire.

'That's your horse bedded down nicely,' he said. 'I've rubbed her till she's nigh dry as a bone, she's got straw to lie on and hay to eat and she's in my warm barn where she'll come to no harm. You owe your lives to that horse, boys. God knows how far she's struggled through this storm to bring you here and how she found her way into the farmyard from the road, I'll never know. We're down in a hollow and she certainly couldn't have seen it from the road.'

'It must have been the soldier did it,' said Clink as he looked around the room. 'Where is he?'

'Soldier? What soldier? All as we heard was a feeble little voice singing a hymn during a lull in the wind. When we came out into the yard, there you were, two heaps of snow sitting on a cart and the horse damned nigh dead from exhaustion. What soldier is this that you're talking about?'

The boys both chattered together, telling of the soldier and his appearance in the snow. Will spoke of his glowing eyes and Clink remembered seeing his red coat and his medals. They told how he had led the horse through the storm, practically pulling it through the drifts.

The farmer and his family looked at each other significantly and then the wife said kindly: 'Now then, lads, you've been through quite an experience this day and I think enough is enough. Soldier, indeed. There wasn't no soldier when we came out into that yard, just two boys, a horse, a cart, and a coffin! By the way, Sam, what did you do with the coffin?'

The farmer said that it was still on the cart which he had put in the barn.

When the boys were bundled into a warm bed they were still telling about the soldier and the farmer's wife nodded kindly and said that it would all seem different in the morning.

The storm broke over night and when daylight pushed its way through the white world, the snow had stopped and the wind had died down to barely a murmur. Within an hour or two a pale and watery sun pushed its way through the grey sky, the temperature rose several degrees and the snow started to melt.

The farmer stood at the window and shook his head.

'I've lived in these parts for fifty years, man and boy, and I've never seen anything like it,' he said. 'It's done nought but rain all summer and now we have blizzards and sunshine all in the same winter's day. It's not natural I tells you, it's not natural at all!'

Will and Clink had slept the clock round and, after a hearty farmhouse breakfast, expressed an intention of returning home. Clink knew that his parents would be half out of their minds worrying about him and Will thought that even his father might be concerned what had happened.

After an inspection of the road, which still had some huge drifts at its sides, the farmer took out a great shire horse and hitched it to Will's cart.

'This is Goliath, Will,' he said. 'He's the strongest beast in all this shire and he could pull Lincoln cathedral off its foundations if he's a mind to. He'll take us as far as its possible to go. We'll hitch your horse behind the cart and she can follow us. Put some sacks over that blasted coffin, it fair gives me the willies just to look at it.'

They were no more than three miles from the city and the huge beast seemed to make light work of the melting snow, ploughing his way through it like a steamer at full speed in a calm sea. As they neared the city, the snow was much lighter on the ground and it was obvious that not a flake of snow had fallen on the city itself, the blizzard stopping just short of it. This caused Sam Fletcher to shake his head again and state that it wasn't natural.

120.

They were about a mile out of Lincoln when they saw a carriage coming in the opposite direction. For once Herbert and Henry were united in the same cause, searching for their sons, and there was a joyful reunion amidst the snow.

Herbert seized Sam Fletcher by the hand and insisted that he take three sovereigns as payment for his work. Sam touched his cap and seemed very pleased and said it was a pleasure to meet a gentleman. Henry Carrot appeared embarassed, but held out his great paw to the farmer and shook his hand mightily.

'I've nought to give you but my thanks, master,' said Henry, 'but I do that gladly and ought I can ever do to repay you that's in my power you've only to ask. 'Enry Carrot's my name and I'm damned nigh as strong as this great beast of yours. I'll do any work I can to repay you.'

'Your thanks is payment enough, Henry Carrot,' said Sam Fletcher. 'If I judge it right, you've no work and I've none I can give you this winter. Come spring if you still want work, come out to me and I'll find you plenty.'

Goliath was unhitched and the old mare put back in the shafts. The two boys sat with Herbert in the carriage whilst Henry drove the cart to deposit its sad burden in the workshop at Motherby Lane.

The story of the soldier was told and retold, but produced nothing but shaking of the head, particularly when it came to the part where the soldier had disappeared after guiding the cart to the farm.

The good Mrs Carrot had her own explanation of the phenomenon. 'Stands to reason,' she said. 'Why should this soldier go off into the storm and risk freezing to death when he could have stayed at the farm with you where it was warm and safe? Don't make sense nor reason to do that. No, it was the deliriums. That fellow at the workhouse telling you about that body as was in the coffin and 'ow 'e was a soldier and so on. No it was the dreadful cold and the fright and what not gave you the deliriums and you imagined it! The delirious trimmings the doctors calls it!'

And the good lady went back to her baking and would not

hear any other explanation.

Will and Clink went to the funeral of Nathaniel Bostock in Newport cemetery on Christmas Eve. The old soldier had been saved from the ignominy of a pauper's grave by the kindness of an old officer of his former Regiment who had served with him in the Crimea and had heard of his plight. The chaplain from the barracks in Burton Road conducted the service and spoke of the valour of the old soldier who had received the Distinguished Conduct Medal for his gallantry and the wondrous workings of the Lord that had brought two young mourners who had never seen him in his life to his graveside.

Although a subject of conversation for many a day, the matter might have faded with the passing of the years but for old Walter.

In the early part of 1889 Walter fell ill despite his several layers of clothing and the goose grease. Indeed, Lincoln was overwhelmed with coughs and colds, some of which turned to worse things and carried away a goodly number of its citizens.

The summer of the previous year had been notoriously bad. There had been wet, cold weather with no sunshine for weeks on end. The harvest was the worst within living memory, the corn husks half empty and black. This, followed by an exceptionally mild winter, was the reason for all the sickness which was much higher than in a normal winter.

Old Walter himself had proclaimed that it stood to reason that this was the cause. After all, he had said, it needed a few good frosts and a few feet of snow to kill off all the germs bred by the summer sun and breeding in the hedge bottoms. No frost, no snow and no cold meant the germs were free to fly about in the air and get at everyone. This was plain, common sense, said Walter.

When it was pointed out to him that the previous summer had been almost entirely without sun, Walter merely gritted his teeth and said: 'That proves it, then. The germs is wet weather germs and everyone knows that they're the worst of all!'

The epidemic meant that they were busier than ever with fu-

122.

nerals and Walter was greatly needed in the workshop. Herbert sent Will round to his home one evening to see how he was progressing and to ask when he would be back to work.

Will knocked on the door and a faint voice shouted to him to enter. He lifted the latch and went into the little parlour. Walter sat by a roaring fire, a blanket round his legs. His nose shone redly with his cold and his voice was husky. Around his neck he had an old sock from which oozed a brown liquid. It had seeped from the sock and stained his shirt and the scarf around his neck. The smell in the airless room was quite dreadful.

After enquiring as to his health and Walter's reassurance that he was getting much better, Will could not help asking what was causing the dreadful odour.

'Why, it be the pasty,' said Walter.

'Pasty?' queried Will, 'You're not going to eat something that smells as bad as that, Walter? Whatever's in it to smell like that?'

Walter emitted a throaty laugh and said: 'Why bless you, Will, I ain't goin' to eat it! It's round my neck! It's a cowshit pasty, finest cure I ever knew for a sore throat!'

Will felt slightly sick at the very thought and couldn't wait to get out of the house. He quickly enquired when he thought that he might be back to work.

'I got news for you, Will,' he said. 'I ain't coming back to the shop. This is the first illness I've had for many a year and it makes me realise that I'm not getting any younger. I got a widowed sister lives on the coast at Trusthorpe as you know. Both of us is alone now and we'd be company for each other. I've saved a little bit over the years and she's got a few pounds tucked away. What with that and a bit of joinering work I reckon as we'll get by, lad.

Twas Martha that really did it, that day she came to the workshop and had us sell all that damned rubbish. 'Tain't natural for a woman to be a boss, it ain't 'er role in life and me for one, I ain't goin' to stand for it. No woman's goin' to boss me around. That's what really made me mind up.'

'I'll miss you, Walter,' said Will. 'You've been a real friend to me and I'll not know what to do without you.'

'You're growing into a man now, Will,' he said. 'You'll not be "Little Will" for much longer I'll be bound. You're growing up fast and you'll have plenty of friends. One day you'll meet some pretty young wench and you'll find all the happiness you could want. But remember me and perhaps come to see me one day in the summer. It's nice out at Trusthorpe and we could sit out at the front of the cottage and watch the ships going by and you could tell me all about where they're goin' from them books of yours.

When I'm better, I'm going straight out there. I'm not coming back to the workshop. Your father and me, we don't owe each other anything. He don't pay no one when they're sick and so I've nothing to collect.'

Will took the proferred hand and said goodbye. He was genuinely fond of the old man who had saved him from many a row with his father and who had showed him many a kindness. Walter had taught him how to work wood until he was almost as good as he was and Will knew that he would always be in Walter's debt for that and for his friendship.

He had just lifted the latch when Walter called him back and offered him a package wrapped in brown paper.

'It's a present, Will,' he said. 'Something to remember old Walter by. You see, I'll miss you, lad.'

Will eagerly unwrapped the parcel to reveal a handsome book entitled *Heroes of the Empire*. He put it on the table and eagerly flipped through the pages, which fell open at a full page illustration of a medal bedecked soldier. Will read the caption beneath – 'Private Nathaniel Bostock, D.C.M., Her Majesty's 63rd Regiment of Foot, a Hero of the Crimea.'

The same long hair fell over his shoulders and the same piercing eyes looked out from the page straight at Will. Will would have known him anywhere.

He had last seen him leading the horse through the snow in the blizzard.

124.

Chapter Four

'I Might Become Prime Minister!'

FOLLOWING THE DEPARTURE of old Walter, the workshop became a completely different place in which to work. Walter had relied on the methods and practices he had followed for more than forty years and, like many old people, had been totally averse to any form of change. Hence, he had probably made a wise decision to depart from his place of employment before the niggardly practices imposed by Martha brought the whole situation to a violent conclusion.

Herbert saw Walter's leaving as an act of gross ingratitude and prattled on at great length as to how the Everton family had looked after Walter's welfare as man and boy, only to be rewarded by desertion at a time of need when business was expanding and it needed a wise head and a firm hand to control the small workforce now employed.

'Desertion,' said Herbert, 'is treason! If Walter had been in the army, he would have been shot at dawn in front of the whole regiment. Damn me, I'd do it myself. Ungrateful old bugger!'

Martha snapped quickly back at him.

'Don't talk such nonsense, Herbert. Walter was an old fool and getting past his prime. He wasted both time and materials and both those cost money. His sloppy ways encouraged idleness amongst the men and your own son has been allowed to spend his days sneaking away with that Carrot boy, doing God knows what, and fooling about with that musical nonsense.

Now I'll find a foreman that is a foreman, and that's a promise!'

Martha was as good as her word and before the month was out Simon Groom had been brought from Charles Clegg's timber yard and ensconced as foreman at Motherby Lane He had worked for the Clegg family for some ten years, during which time he had managed to marry and produce three children. The

Groom household was a poor one and the whole family, including his wife's mother and father, occupied three rooms in a cottage on the north bank of the Waterside.

At the moment, the Groom family's life was a living hell.

During a particularly ferocious storm a bolt of lightning had struck the bank only a few yards from where they lived. Apart from the immediate terror it had caused them all, a whole section of the bank had collapsed and the front wall of their home had slowly swayed and bulged outwards in front of their eyes. They had fled in panic to a neighbour who had put them up in her already crowded home, thus making a total of ten persons, including four small children, in one tiny cottage.

Large timber props had been placed against the front of the cottage to hold the bulging wall in place until repairs could be carried out, but this promised to be quite a time as the loss of commerce due to the necessary lowering of the water level to repair the bank was deemed to be of more importance than the comfort of the Groom family.

To add to their plight, they were not allowed back into their home as it was considered unsafe. Thus they had no more than the clothes in which they stood and even with borrowing from their hosts, were woefully short of every necessity you could name. Add to this the fact that the family lived from week to week on Simon's wages and it is not difficult to imagine that every ha'penny had to be counted and considered before it was spent.

Thus, when Martha approached him regarding the job as foreman at the Motherby Lane workshop, it was almost like a prayer answered, even if the penance was severe and binding.

'You're on trial, Simon Groom, and don't you forget it,' said Martha. 'I want to see that workshop run properly. There's to be no slacking by anyone, including you. We can't afford to pay people who won't work and their proper place is in the workhouse, not the Everton workshop.

There's to be nothing given away, nothing at all. We're a business, not a charity. Mr Everton sees to all the charity from this family with his good deeds on the workhouse Board of Guardians. He gets no pay for this, but regards it as his godly duty, good deeds being their own reward. If a workman wants to take home a bundle of sticks to light his fire, then you charge him a ha'penny. If he tries to take them home without paying then you fire him at once for stealing and tell him he's lucky not to be in front of the magistrates. Understand?'

Simon nodded, rather bewildered by the responsibilities being heaped upon him, as Martha continued. She handed him a key.

'This key is to a new cupboard which you will find on the workshop wall. Every worker is to keep his tin mug locked in that cupboard, together with his snap for the day. You will issue the mugs to the men and hand them their lunch at twelve oclock precisely and you will lock the mugs back in the cupboard at a quarter to one. Snap will be eaten in the workshop and there'll be no visiting the alehouse. Beer clouds the mind and the judgement and I want no bad workmanship.

Now, regarding Master Will. He's a worker like anyone else. Understand?'

'Aye, lady, I understand,' said Simon, 'but he's the gaffer's lad, I can't order him about like the rest of 'em. It wouldn't seem right to be doing that.'

'What you will be doing, Mr Groom, will be saving the lad from himself,' said Martha.

Simon screwed up his tattered cap in his hands in embarrassment.

'Mrs Everton, I don't rightly understand you,' he said, 'Will's only fourteen years old and a small lad at that. If what I hear's right, he's a craftsman skilled beyond his years. Now I'm new at this foreman lark, but how can we respect the master when I treat his son no better than an apprentice?'

Martha put an arm around Simon's shoulder, causing him to jump backwards in alarm. She patted him on the back and lowered her voice.

'You're a shrewd fellow and no mistake, Simon Groom, and I shall have to take you into my confidence I see. Mr Everton and I are very worried about Will. He's got into bad company, particularly that Carrot lad, and Walter Smeed was not one to make him work. Will would sneak off many a time, doing Heaven knows what mischief, and Walter would do nothing about it. We don't know where he's been going, nor what he's been doing whilst he's been away.'

Like many another person in Lincoln, Simon knew that Will's wicked wanderings had been no more serious than an afternoon's fishing on the Witham or an hour on the cathedral's organ with John Young. Simon was sorry for Will and his joy at the thought of a better job was now being tinged with a touch of conscience. He fumbled uneasily and groped for the right words.

'What you will be doing is a great service to Mr Everton and me and a great kindness to the boy himself. Will's salvation lies in work. Work is good for the soul, hard work is even better. Give him plenty of work, Mr Groom, and his mind will not have time for evil thoughts and his body will be too tired for evil deeds.'

Simon still hesitated a little.

Martha judged that the time was now right for her to play her trump card.

'Now, Mr Groom, the subject of money has to be discussed. How much was Mr Clegg, my father, paying you at the timber yard?'

'Twenty three shillings, lady,' said Simon and added hastily, 'but if I'd stayed there he would have given me a half crown raise at Christmas.'

'Your wages as foreman will be thirty shillings a week, said Martha, 'You'll get a guinea extra at Christmas and another on New Years Day.'

This was riches indeed, but still Simon's inner nature told him that he would be trading his soul with the devil. He knew Herbert by reputation and had studied Martha in some detail when she had worked as bookkeeper for Charles Clegg. He had known her first husband, Jonathan Tattershall, and had seen him as a kindly man with a shrew of a wife who had made his life a misery.

If Martha had previously played her trump card, she now

played her ace in the hole.

'I hear that you're having trouble with your house, Mr Groom?'

Simon poured forth his woes at great length. Martha listened without interruption until Simon ran out of words.

'Mr Everton has an empty house in Wilson Street. Number twenty-three, I believe, quite nice with two bedrooms and a very nice area in which to live. If I had a word with him, I'm sure he might let you have it for, say, three and sixpence a week, Mr Groom.'

Man can stand only so much temptation and Simon Groom did what many a man has done before and since and sold out his principles for the sake of his pocket and his family.

Not one to believe in wasting time, Martha took him straight down to the workshop, stopping on the way only long enough to buy him a bowler hat at Fox's. Resplendent in this badge of office he was introduced to the workforce, now numbering four, as the new foreman to replace Walter Smeed.

Prodded by Martha, Simon laid down the new methods of work, first of all taking all the mugs and locking them in the cupboard. He told the men that they would now only be issued at twelve o'clock and would be replaced in the cupboard not later than twelve forty-five.

"Ere, wait on,' said one fellow, a newly employed carpenter, 'when I came 'ere I was told an hour for me snap, and an hour I've always 'ad!'

There was a murmuring of assent from his colleagues.

Encouraged, he continued: 'And whats more, I ain't 'eard nothin' about me afternoon tea. We always 'ad a break for a cup o' tea in the afternoon with old Walter. Ain't that right?'

Everyone said that it was indeed right.

'Ow can I 'ave me afternoon tea when me flamin' mug is locked away in yon cupboard? Three quarters of an hour for me dinner and no tea in the afternoon, is that what you're sayin'?'

Simon squared his shoulders.

'That's what I'm sayin' and that's what it is,' he said.

'That ain't fair,' said the talkative one, 'I ain't goin to stand for that, not no 'ow I ain't.'

'Neither am I,' said Martha, 'You're sacked. Pick up your tools and go. Mr Groom, check his tool bass and make sure that he hasn't got anything belonging to us in it.'

She looked the man straight in the face.

'Don't ask for any wages,' she said, 'You're lazy and impertinent and I shan't pay you a penny piece. Get your tools and get out.'

The fellow stood his ground.

'It's Tuesday afternoon, he said, 'and I've worked 'ere since yesterday mornin'. That's a day and a 'arf's money you owes me, missus, and I ain't leavin 'ere without it. Ain't that right?'

His mates, suddenly subdued, mumbled amongst themselves but did nothing. Martha went from one to the other.

'Well, have you anything to say, then? If not, get on with your work or get your tools and clear out.'

They all went back to their work, shamefaced at not supporting their comrade, but badly needing the weekly wage that went with the job.

'Now, you,' said Martha, 'I'll tell you for the last time, take your tools and go. You've no business here any longer, so get out!'

For a moment it seemed as if he would knock Martha to the floor, but realising that he would only bring disaster upon himself, he took up his tools and made for the door, turning as he went out to face Martha.

'My names Ezra Pound', he said, 'and no man, nay nor woman, treats me like that, missus. A day and an 'arf's pay you owes me and such I shall 'ave by one means or another. Mark my words, missus, you ain't 'eard the last of Ezra Pound.'

Will, just entering, was almost knocked down as he met Ezra in the doorway.

'Will,' said Martha, 'Come and meet Mr Groom, the new foreman.'

Will had heard talk of this at home and therefore was not

surprised to find that Walter had been replaced. He held out his hand to Simon Groom. Simon took it and said: 'I'm right glad to meet you, Master Will.'

Martha shook her head.

'Just Will will do,' Mr Groom, she said, 'just Will. He works here like anyone else. And you, Will, see that you do work. Mr Groom will be keeping an eye on you and reporting to me. There'll be no sneaking away in the afternoons now.'

And with this parting shot she flounced out of the workshop, long black skirts rustling, the men touching their caps as she passed by.

Life at Motherby Lane now became positively intolerable to Will. He missed old Walter who had been around as long as he could remember and in particular he missed the chats they would have on quiet afternoons, when Walter would tell him about the mother he never knew. The days seemed long and he loathed the performance involved in the continuing economies of the business. Nails were counted out by Simon Groom, whereas they had previously been in a box handy for all to use. Each piece of wood was measured a dozen times before the saw approached it so that not an inch should be wasted, whilst the scrap pieces and off-cuts were carefully accounted for.

His only meetings with Clink were now after work or on Sundays, although it was often his task to take pony and trap and collect a corpse on the Sabbath, or to deliver a coffin to the home of the bereaved and set up the casket on trestles in the living room so that friends and relatives might pay their last respects to the deceased. Whilst Herbert would take great delight in preaching at the Free Methodist chapel in Saxon Street that the Sabbath was a day of rest, he was quite prepared to make an exception in the case of a death.

'It's not the money, Will,' he would say. 'It's our Christian duty to the family to look after the loved one, Sunday or not. It's Gods work, no less, and we should rejoice in doing it.'

Herbert had always thought that in the world of business he had a brain second to none, but he was more and more inclined to give way to Martha in these matters.

When she had told him of the arrangements she had made with Simon Groom, he had almost exploded.

'Thirty shillings a week? Thirty shillings a week? You're mad, woman. You're chucking money away for no reason. He would have worked for twenty five shillings. And two guineas at Christmas? And the house in Wilson Street? Ye Gods, we're running a charity!'

Martha smiled and talked to him as she might have done to a petulant child.

'We paid Walter Smeed thirty five shillings a week. That means that we have saved five shillings a week. Added to that we get back three shillings and sixpence for the rent of 23 Wilson Street, so that really means that we have saved eight shillings and sixpence a week. Take off the two guineas at Christmas and we have saved something like eighteen pounds a year.'

'But the house?' queried Herbert. 'I could have got four bob a week for that! You've thrown sixpence a week down the drain!'

'Yes, and for sixpence a week we've got a foreman who's tied to us because of the house. If he doesn't do as he's told, then out he goes, and with his brood he won't want to do that. As for the two guineas at Christmas time, well, Christmas is a long way off yet. We may be on hard times by Christmas and then he'll just have to understand that we haven't got two guineas to throw away.'

Her thin lips pursed up in what passed as a smile.

Herbert shook his head in admiration, pushed his thumbs in his waistcoat pockets and said that he hadn't thought of that. He reflected that whilst he had acquired a tartar for a wife, he had gained a very able business partner which more than made up for her shortcomings in the former respect.

The prosperity of the Everton household continued to grow and by the end of the year the workshop employed a further two men. Martha was ruthless in her pursuit of profit and shared with Herbert a total lack of concern for the rest of the world in human terms. Those unable to reach the Everton requirements in terms of work were dismissed as shirkers fit only for the work-house and not worthy to be employed.

Dapper as ever, swinging his silver-topped cane, Herbert would walk down Burton Road and along The Bail to the White Hart. He would raise his beaverskin hat to the ladies and greet his business colleagues with a handshake. Lesser mortals would be acknowledged with a brief nod of the head and a curt: 'Morning, Brown, Morning!'

Once passed, many a workman would spit in the gutter and say: 'Mean old skinflint! He'd rob his mother for a farthing!'

Thus it was little wonder that Herbert caught the eye of the local Liberal party, of which he had been a passive member for some years, and that he came under discussion in a private meeting which took place in the landlord's parlour of the Lion and Snake early in 1890.

'Look,' said the chairman. 'Whatever you think about Everton, he's well known in this ward. He owns property, he employs people, he's a member of the Board of Guardians and he's a rising businessman. He's going to make his mark in this town and, if he doesn't make it with us, then he'll make it with someone else. Mark my words, we have to stick together. Just read your newspapers, gentlemen, those damned Socialists have been preaching against us all over the country. If we don't stick together now, were done for.'

Everyone murmured agreement and there was much nodding of heads.

The secretary added his two penn'orth.

'Socialists, Social Democratic Federationists, call 'em what you like, they're trouble for us. I agree with the chairman, gentlemen. Just remember what happened in the General Election only four years ago. An unemployed mechanic in Nottingham, parading as a Social Democratic Federation candidate, pulled five hundred and ninety eight votes! Just think, almost six hundred votes! And don't forget that he was supported by Tory money just to split the Liberal vote. Aye, don't think that these people are all clodhoppers, there's even an ex-Tory at the head of 'em. Let's grab Everton to us now, and anyone else we can get, too.'

'I know that Everton isn't popular, but I say that doesn't matter,' said the chairman. 'It's mainly the women that he's unpopular with, partly because he's a hard old bastard with the men he employs and partly because he treats his son worse than I treat my dog. The women haven't got a vote, thank God, so they don't matter and once the menfolk get into the polling booth, no amount of nagging by their wives can stop 'em voting for who they like!'

More agreement.

'Now, tell me, if it's not Everton for this by-election, who the hell else have we got? We know he hasn't got a chance, but he'll think he has and he's so full of his own importance that he'll fight like a tiger. After all, its a by-election – damned stupid of old Henry to drop dead like that – and when he loses we just follow up next year with a better candidate.'

Thus it was that Herbert was approached and, following this, called a family gathering at Burton Road. Such gatherings were rare and when Will was told that he was to leave work early, clean himself up and be present, he knew that something important was taking place.

Tea was served on the best china and Martha was the perfect hostess, dancing attendance on everyone and insisting on serving them herself, whilst Herbert rather resembled a highly inflated balloon, just waiting to burst and impart his news upon the assembly.

Will sat next to Annie, who knew as little as he did, and gazed around the table.

There were his grandparents, William and Ann, after whom he and Annie were named. Grandfather William, as he was known, was a master carpenter like so many of the Everton family before him. He specialised in the making of fine tables and many a fine Lincolnshire house boasted a sample of his workmanship. Unlike his son, Herbert, he had no desire for fame and worked alone, turning out only one or two items a month from his cottage workshop in the village of Burton. This gave him all the worldly comforts he needed and he was a contented man. Although he lived only a couple of miles away, he was a rare visitor. Will liked him, for he had a ready smile and when they met by accident in the city, sometimes a half crown passed into his hand.

Grandfather William's wife, Ann, was the perfect match for her husband. Quiet and retiring, she adored and respected him, abided by his every wish, and sought nothing else in life.

Herbert was their eldest child and only son and neither could fathom where he had obtained the hard and callous nature. They often consoled themselves by visiting their three daughters, Herbert's sisters and Will's aunts.

The eldest daughter was Rebecca, aged in her mid-thirties, she was a milliner by trade. Her little shop on Silver Street was barely twelve feet wide, but saw a steady stream of Lincoln society and on race days her hats and bonnets could be seen all over the course. She had married one Benjamin Broad, a grocer, and their only regret was that they had no children to bless the union and at this stage it did not seem likely that they ever would have.

Next to Rebecca sat the second daughter, Fanny. She was shy and timid, blushed whenever anyone spoke to her, and it seemed would never marry. She stayed at home with her parents where she was sheltered by the kindly couple from the worst of the world's cruelties and where her constant stammering produced nothing more than a gentle smile and a kindly patience.

The third daughter was Millicent, aged twenty nine and married for just a year to Arthur Sutton, a railway clerk. Milly was already huge with child and, although Will knew the basic facts of such things, he could not help staring at her enormous belly, protruding over the edge of the table, and wondering however it was possible for such a tremendous lump to leave her body. He and Clink had often discussed such matters but neither of them had reached a sensible conclusion. It seemed likely that Clink's idea that birth was achieved by the doctor slitting open the abdomen from end to end was the most likely and both agreed that if this was the case, it was not to be wondered at that so many women died bearing children. Indeed, it was hard to understand why anyone should ever want to get married at all if they had to endure such a trial.

Having said all that, Clink discussed the matter with a wry grin on his face and, as Will was to find out quite soon, was far from innocent in matters of the flesh.

Six people living in a tiny three room house have few secrets from each other and in such an environment the age of innocence does not last long.

The meal over and the plates cleared away, the ladies made to leave the gathering as was customary, but Herbert bade them stay and be seated.

'This matter concerns us as a family,' he said, 'and therefore we should all be present, even the ladies and the children. Will, get out the brandy and the glasses. Perhaps some port for the ladies?'

Hospitality dispensed, Herbert assumed his usual stance at the fireplace, looked around his family and announced with great pride that he had been approached by THE PARTY! These latter two words he said in a tone of reverence normally reserved for the mention of money or God in that order.

Failing to evoke any response other than glances passing from one to the other, he clarified the matter in rather exasperated tones.

'There is to be a by-election for the Council in this Ward and I have been approached by the party to see if I will stand as their candidate.'

Grandfather William puffed on his pipe, sent a cloud of pungent tobacco smoke around the room and then said calmly, 'Which party?'

'There's only one party, father,' said Herbert. 'The Liberal party, of course, I mean the Liberal party.'

Grandfather took another puff, contemplated the glowing tobacco as he tamped it down into the bowl with a gnarled finger end and said: "Tain't so; there's lots of parties nowadays. There's even an Independent Liberal party, so I hear. Then there's these Socialists and there's even murmurings about women being given

136.

the vote. Of course, we mustn't forget the Conservative Party. No, Herbert, there's other parties than the Liberals.'

'What do you want to be a councillor for anyway,' said Rebecca. 'Haven't you got enough to do as it is? There's no pay for it, you know.'

Herbert conjured an expression meant to indicate hurt surprise. Will thought that it was like the expression you might have assumed with severe constipation.

'Money?' said Herbert. 'When have I ever put money first?'

Knowing glances passed around the room, but everyone was spared the duty of telling Herbert the truth by the intervention of Martha.

She looked defiantly at each one in turn and snapped: 'And what's wrong with money, tell me?'

There was no answer and so Martha turned to Rebecca.

'You didn't seem to think that anything was wrong with money when you came to Herbert to borrow to set up your hat shop. No one else would lend it to you, but your brother did. I didn't see you refuse his money then, did I?'

Rebecca shuffled her feet uneasily, but her husband was not so easily put down.

'Ay,' said Ben. 'We borrowed his money and we never heard the last of it until it was repaid. He charged his own sister interest and was round knocking on the door if we were a day late with the payments. Oh, yes, we know all about Herbert and his money.'

'Ben Broad, you're small minded and you've no head for business. You'll sit and rot in that scruffy corner shop in Mill Row until the day you die because you haven't got the go in you to get any further. You, Beccy, you could get on but he holds you back with his pettiness,' said Martha. 'Of course he charged you interest and of course he asked for his money when it wasn't paid. What difference does it make that you're his sister?'

There was no answer and so Martha continued, 'When Herbert is a councillor we know it won't have any wages with it, but it will mean that your brother will be in a position to be looked up to. I would have thought that would have meant something to you, his family. Instead, all you bother about is money!' And to the amazement of everyone, Martha took out a lace handkerchief and dabbed a few non-existent tears from her cheeks.

As a turnaround of facts, it was a masterstroke. No one was deceived by the theatricals, but it put them in a difficult position to answer.

Will and Annie had listened to all this in amazement, never before having been allowed into the family discussions and never before had they seen Martha look remotely like shedding a tear. It was Annie who broke the deadlock.

'My father is a great man,' she said, 'and I shall support him whatever he does and be proud of him. He'll make a fine councillor and one day he'll be Mayor of Lincoln, perhaps even Prime Minister. We should all help him.'

In the Everton household young ladies of seventeen years of age were meant to be seen but not heard and, although Will had no love for Annie, he cringed as he waited for the inevitable wrath to fall upon her. Martha turned to Annie, her face tight and angry and started to speak in a slow, menacing voice.

'When we need to be told by children . . .' she started, but was cut short by Grandfather William.

'"Out of the mouths of babes . . ."' he quoted. 'Perhaps we can all learn something from the younger members of the family, particularly as they have been allowed into our confidence for the first time. You now, Will, you're fourteen years old and growing to be a man, let's hear what you think about your father being a councillor.'

Martha started to tell Will that nobody was interested in what he had to say when Grandfather William snapped in very sharply indeed and silenced her.

'In my house, lady,' he said, 'the man is the master and I'll not have my word silenced, even in my son's house. You've had your say, now sit down and give that sharp tongue of yours a rest. If you can't do that whilst men speak, then get out of the room and to your housework.'

He stood up, leaning towards Martha as he spoke.

Martha was subdued and stammered, her face white with surpressed shock: 'What I meant, father-in-law, was that . . .'

'No one gives a damn what you meant, woman; sit down and shut up!'

Martha turned towards Herbert for support. He half rose and then changed his mind. A fiery streak of temperament ran in all the Evertons and Herbert was not going to challenge his father, even at the risk of upsetting his wife.

'Right,' said Grandfather, 'now that's settled, let's hear what Little Will has to say. Come on boy, speak up!'

In truth, Will was not the least bit interested in his father's political ambitions. He could not see that a seat in the council chamber for his father would make any difference to his own way of life, certainly not for the better, anyway. However, he liked his grandfather and being asked for his opinion made him feel important for once. He spoke slowly and hesitantly, thinking out every word.

'Please, grandfather, I think that if my father wants to be a councillor, then that's up to him and it's his decision as to whether to fight the election. You all seem to be talking as if he's just going to walk into the town hall, but he might not win the election at all. If he does he will meet a lot of important people and that's bound to be good for the business and for all of us.

He can bring all his councillor friends into your shop, Aunt Rebecca, and they can buy their wives fancy bonnets. Aunt Fanny, you could go to the services at the Cathedral with him and perhaps you would meet a gentleman from the council who would want to marry you.'

Fanny went a bright red and the others smiled.

'Anyway,' continued Will, 'I think it's up to him.'

'Well said, Will,' said Grandfather. "That's the only common sense that's been talked here this day. Herbert, if you stand, then this family will help you.' He looked around the room, his very expression defying anyone to challenge his decision.

Herbert put his arm around Will's shoulder.

'I always knew you had brains, William,' he said. 'Now you've proved it. We must talk about giving you a rise in wages – but not yet,' he added hastily.

More drinks were served and, apart from Martha who was still seething under her rebuke from Grandfather William, there was quite a jolly spirit abroad by the time the gathering broke up in the early evening. Annie went to see a friend from the Sunday school who lived in Rasen Lane. Will was tired but was ordered out of the house by his stepmother and he decided to visit Clink.

He was barely five yards down Burton Road when he heard Martha's pent up anger burst in a fury over his father. His father responded and the resultant row could clearly be heard on the still night air for some considerable distance. It had been a long time since Martha was last put in her place.

When he arrived at Clink's house, he found that the family had just finished their evening meal. Sam Fletcher had been as good as his word and as soon as the winter was over, he had found Henry Carrot work on his farm. It meant rising at the crack of dawn and walking three miles to the farm and then three miles home again in the evening after a hard day's work, but Henry didn't mind that. Sometimes he hitched a ride on a cart coming back into the city in the evening and arrived a little earlier, but it was normally at least eight oclock before he sat down at the table.

When they heard that Herbert would be standing for the local election there was a mixed reaction.

Mrs Carrot accepted it as inevitable.

'Toffs stick together,' she said. 'If it hadn't been this year it would have been next.'

Henry took a deep draught from his tankard and then said: 'All this'll change one day. Even I've got a vote now, I'm what's called an agricultural labourer and so I've got a vote. One day everyone in the country will have a vote and then well see some change. Look at my missus 'ere, works 'er fingers to the bone lookin' after us all and yet she can't have a vote to pick them as rules us. That's not fair by anyones ideas. There'll be change, I tell you.'

Having made this profound statement, Henry perched his brood upon his knees, gave them a great hug in his huge arms and packed them all off to bed.

Clink and Will went down to the Waterside to watch the repair work proceeding on the bank. Even though it was quite late, and the light had almost faded, gangs of men were busy trying to rebuild the waterway. Much of Lincoln's trade came via this means of entry into the city and all possible haste was being used to effect the repairs.

The front of the cottage where Simon Groom had lived had now completely collapsed, leaving just a jagged edge of brickwork level with what had been the door lintel. A faded piece of curtain flapped from the broken window frame and on what remained of the parlour wall one could see a picture of a band of angels, the frame leaning drunkenly to one side.

Clink looked at the remains and said, 'I'll bet that foreman fellow of yours is glad he don't have to live there now. From what I hear, it would have been a blessing if the house had fallen on top of 'im.'

'I don't suppose he's a bad fellow really,' said Will. 'He has to do as he's told like anyone else but when my father or stepmother isn't about, he's not a bad sort at all. Mind you, he is a slave-driver and never gives anyone a minutes rest and I can't get out like I used to. I haven't had a music lesson for more than a month.'

Since they had first met some two years previously they had both filled out considerably. Although Will was still short, he had broad shoulders and a stocky chest. Hard work had made him fit and agile and he could do a day's work with the best of his colleagues. His natural ability with wood was well known, his work often the subject of admiration and he was now a most important member of the workshop team. He could be seen rubbing a piece of wood against his cheek, eyes closed, 'talking to the timber' as the other men used to say. Walter Smeed had been a natural teacher and had taught him well, whilst his father and grandfather, both master joiners, had added their share.

Even at Clegg's timber yard, Will was to be seen examining the timber they were buying.

'No, sir,' he would say to the yard foreman, 'we aren't buying that batch. There's enough knot holes in there to start a rabbit warren . . . and we don't want that elm either. Its as dry as chips and twice as brittle. Hasn't been seasoned, I'll be bound.'

Clink had grown in all directions. He was now as tall as most men, lean and wiry, and his bright red mop could be seen miles away as he pushed his way through the market place on busy days. He had gained partial exemption from school due to the poor circumstances of the family and seemed to fill in a hole in the family budget by doing all sorts of odd jobs. Amongst those who did not know him he could pass for an older person and frequently did.

'Tell you what,' said Clink, 'let's go for a gill in the Labourer's Arms!'

'Go for a gill?' said Will. 'No one'll serve us in any of these pubs, we're both too young. My father says that you'll get your throat cut for twopence in any of them.'

'Load of rubbish,' said Clink, 'I know the landlord at the Labourer's, he's served me before. You can get a sing-song and a hot pie – and a hot girl if you've a mind to as well!'

Will had felt the first disturbed murmurings of interest in girls lately. He found himself watching the tight skirts and bulging blouses and felt the first throbbing surges of manhood, but visiting pubs and picking up hot girls didn't seem right at all, even under the expert guidance of his friend.

'I don't know,' he said, 'Perhaps I ought to be getting home now. Father and Martha were rowing when I left and they're bound to blame me, whatever the row's about.'

'Then if you're going to get into trouble anyway, why not make it worthwhile?' asked Clink.

Thus Will found himself being led by the arm into the tap-room of the Labourer's Arms and peering through the haze of tobacco smoke which enveloped the room.

142.

The landlord greeted Clink like a long lost friend and enquired whether he had 'anything' to part with? Clink answered in the negative but said that he might have something at the weekend. Will's pondering at the significance of this message was pushed into the back of his mind by the landlord's enquiry, 'And who might this fellow be then, Master Carrot? I know! He's a ten foot giant from the circus and he's shrunk in the rain!'

Will turned bright red at the laughter that ran through the room and he turned to push his way outside.

Clink caught him by the collar and hauled him back.

'He's only joking, Will. He's only joking, aren't you, George?'

George said that indeed he was only joking, but if he served midgets then he'd be bound to have the law after him and he'd got no desire to see the inside of the prison on Greetwell Road, being as he was a law abiding citizen.

'Tell you what,' said George, 'come with me and I'll fix you up with a private sitting room.'

He guided them into the kitchen at the rear of the taproom and brought two pewter tankards of ale. At Clink's request, he also got his barmaid to bring them two hot pies.

'If you want,' he said, 'you can sit in the yard at the back. It's a fair evening and you can talk in private like the toffs you both are.'

George carried a small table out into the yard and the barmaid brought out the ale and the pies. She was a buxom girl and Will couldn't help noticing the glances that passed between her and Clink. He also noticed that no money passed between Clink and the landlord for the refreshments and reminded him that he hadn't paid.

Clink grinned.

'I have a sort of exchange arrangement here,' he said. 'I gives 'im things and 'e gives me things like this ale and the pies. I'm always sure of a welcome here and if you're a friend of mine then you'll be welcome as well. Mind you, I wish you'd grow a bit!' And he laughed.

Will went white with anger as the Everton temperament came

to the fore. He clenched his fists and rose from the table.

'Sit down, Will, sit down. I'm only joking,' said Clink, 'I wouldn't care if you were two feet tall or ten feet tall, we're still friends.'

He raised his tankard to Will and said, 'Let's drink to friendship, Will. We'll always be friends, no matter what; nothing can split us up and that's a fact.'

Will took a swig of his ale. He had had the odd sip from time to time and never liked the stuff. He thought it tasted foul, but endeavoured to preserve his manly image by taking a huge swig. The grimace on his face told its own story, but he persisted until he had drained the lot. Two more tankards appeared and were as quickly disposed of. Clink seemed quite unaffected, but the cool evening air seemed to mix strangely with the drink as far as Will was concerned and he had difficulty understanding why the whitewashed walls of the yard were suddenly moving from side to side.

Somehow he found himself being guided out of the yard and down the side of the canal. His legs felt like rubber and he seemed totally unable to walk in a straight line, bouncing off the walls like a rubber ball. His speech, too, was slurred and he made Clink laugh with everything he said.

They reached Witham Street and Clink knocked gently on a door. It was softly opened and they were ushered inside by a young lady. The room was illuminated by a single gas light on the wall. Despite the fact that it was a warm night there was a fire burning in the grate. The room was poorly furnished, the main item being a rather large and battered sofa which seemed to dominate the place. Two kitchen chairs fought for space against the far wall and the mantel shelf was tightly crammed with ornaments and family photographs. The carpet was distinctly threadbare in a number of places and Will thought that the whole room smelt rather stale as if the windows had not been opened for years.

Clink introduced the young lady to Will as Ruby.

'Ruby's eighteen, like me, Will,' he said, with a sly wink.

144.

Although Will's fuddled brain realised that Clink was not eighteen at all, he politely shook the girls hand and said he was pleased to meet her, not wondering why Clink should want to be any older than he really was. He was now very hot and feeling somewhat sick, and, without being invited, slumped down on the sofa. Clink helped him off with his jacket and explained to Ruby that Will was not a drinking man, being newly introduced to the dubious pleasures of alcohol.

There was the fumbling of a key in the lock and another girl entered. She was introduced as Polly, Ruby's elder sister, and Will recognised her as the barmaid from the Labourer's Arms.

'Will's not quite as old as me', said Clink, 'He's only sixteen.'

"E dont look sixteen', said Polly, 'Aint 'e the one they calls Little Will, then?'

"That's 'im,' said Clink, 'The best little fellow in the whole of Lincoln and the finest carpenter you ever did see. Size ain't got nothing to do with it, it's quality what counts!'

Polly laughed. 'Don't know as that's right,' she remarked and with a grin at Ruby, added: 'In some matters size is VERY important!'

Everyone else laughed, so Will laughed, although he could not really see that it was a very funny joke and didn't really understand it.

Clink put his arm around Polly and said that they had to go into the other room to transact some business.

'Dont you worry, Will,' he said, 'Ruby'll look after you right well. You'll feel like a new man afterwards!'

Will reflected that he could do with feeling like a new man. His queezy stomach was now running riot with him and the perspiration was running down his face in tiny rivulets. He took out his handkerchief and mopped his brow, trying to get to his feet as the couple went off into the other room. Ruby pushed him back down onto the sofa.

She sat beside him and there they stayed in silence for some seconds until she said: 'Well, then?'

'Well then, what?' said Will.

'Well then, 'ave you got the 'arf a crown?'

'Half a crown?' said Will, delving in his pocket. 'Yes, I've got half a crown. Here it is!'

Ruby snatched it from his fingers and dropped it into a vase on the mantel shelf. At that moment there was a loud giggling came from the next room, followed by a resounding crash and a muffled curse from Clink.

"E's a one, that Clink is,' said Ruby, 'I bet that's the leg fallen off the bed again! 'E broke it last time 'e was 'ere and 'ad to stay and mend it.'

Through the alcoholic haze, Will watched as Ruby stood up and peeled off her woollen jumper, then her blouse, revealing a cotton vest thrust forward by her ample bosom. He felt sensibility slowly returning and started to get to his feet, swaying rather unsteadily, his eyes riveted on the girl. With one swift movement the vest was taken off and flung on the floor and Will found himself staring at the first woman's breasts he had ever seen. They were full and round, the nipples showing brown against the pale flesh.

'Cor!' he muttered, jolted by shock into near sobriety, his face burning and his veins coursing as Ruby came towards him, breasts trembling with the motion of her movements. Her nostrils were flared and her moist lips open wide as she put her arms round his neck and kissed him full on the lips, the twin orbs thrusting against his chest.

By now he was fully aroused and returned the kiss in a fumbling, inexpert way.

Ruby stood to her feet, panting heavily, and divested herself of bloomers and skirt. Hands on hips, she stood in front of Will, stark naked. He gazed mesmerised at the great bush of black hair and yelped in shock as she grabbed at him through his trousers.

'Well!' she said, 'There's some parts of you ain't small!'

Will threw up all over her, a mixture of ale and meat pie cascading down the fair young flesh, grabbed his jacket and crashed his way through the door and into the street, bouncing off the door jamb and falling over in his haste. As he picked himself up and made off as fast as he could go, Ruby's shrieking voice followed him and an empty jamjar whistled past his ear and shattered on the cobbles.

'Ungrateful little sod!' she yelled. 'Come back 'ere and I'll cut it off for you!'

Will had no doubts as to which part of his anatomy she intended to deprive him of and he put on an extra spurt as he turned the corner into Saltergate. By the time he got to High Street he was drawing his breath in great, heaving gasps and vomited again into the gutter. Feeling that he was now safe from pursuit, he made his way down St. Martin's Lane and Motherby Lane, every now and then casting a fearful glance over his shoulder just to make sure. He felt dreadful.

On the other hand, at that precise moment Herbert felt quite wonderful.

Following the row with Martha he had gone down to the White Hart where, in the gentlemen's smoking room, he had revealed to his cronies that he would be standing at the council by-election. Half a bottle of port later he was telling all who cared to listen of the loyalty of his family and in particular of his daughter's comments that he might even become Prime Minister.

'Would you like to be Prime Minister, Herbert?' asked the wag of the assembly with a straight face.

Herbert said that he really hadn't ever considered a career in politics, but that if it was his duty, then he would go where fate might lead him.

'Damn me,' said the comedian, 'I knew when I walked past your house that I knew the gent in the posh carriage and pair . . . Why, I can remember now whose coat of arms was on the carriage door. Oh, Bert, I should have told you when I first came in, you'll have missed him for sure, now!'

'Who? Who was he?' urged Herbert: 'Coat of arms? What coat of arms? Why didn't you tell me earlier? Quick man, who was he?'

The wag drew the last ounce of tension, looking with deadpan expression from one to the other as they all waited for him to apply the coup de grace.

'Why, Bert, it was the Marquess of Salisbury come all the way from London to offer you his job!'

The room erupted in a gale of laughter as Herbert turned white with rage. He hated to be made a fool of by anyone.

'Look here, Bert,' said one as the laughter subsided, 'we're all very pleased for you, but you've got to face it, you haven't got a cat in hell's chance of winning. The last councillor for this ward, Henry Tate, was old and sick. He'd done nothing but go to sleep at council meetings and gorge himself with food at the banquets for the last five years. He did nothing for this ward and he spoke out very loudly against the plans to make the workhouse a better place to live in.

All in all, he's given you a legacy. Now we know that you're new to this game and you'll be up against James Preston for certain. He's just taken on ten more workers in the foundry, all from your patch, and he's put running water into almost every house he rents out. Face up to it, Herbert, you're beaten before you start!'

Herbert beckoned to the waiter to bring his cane and coat. He threw the last dregs from his glass down his throat and made for the door.

'Now then, don't take on so!' said his critic. 'I only meant . . .'

Herbert's eyes flashed angrily.

'Think they're making a fool of me, do you? Haven't got a chance, haven't I? I'll show you who hasn't got a bloody chance! If I do anything I do it to win and by Christ I intend to win this election. Next time I come in this room I'll make you all laugh on the other side of your face and you, Walter, next time I buy my screws and nails from your shop you'll drop sodding dead with the shock! Haven't got a chance? I'll make you all rue the day you said that!'

And with those words he swept out of the room into the corridor like a whirlwind.

'Good night, Mr Everton,' said the manager standing in the hallway. 'I hope that everything was to your satisfaction?'

'Sod off!' said Herbert. 'Your hotel's too bloody hot and your claret's too bloody expensive!'

Pausing only long enough to jam his hat onto his head he swept out through the door and onto The Bail, eyes flashing, his face as red as a turkey cock and murmuring to himself about the loyalty of friends.

'Friends! Who bloody well needs 'em?' he asked himself.

As he reached the junction of Westgate and Union Road he espied a familiar figure leaning against the wall. It was Will. Neck agape, breeches stained with vomit and his shirt tail hanging out, he made a sorry spectacle. Herbert surveyed this apparition with horror which rapidly became concern as the boy staggered and fell down on to his knees.

Herbert ran up the road and lifted the boy to his feet.

'Will, lad,' he cried, 'Whatever's the matter with you? Are you ill? Have you been set upon?' Then he smelt the drink. 'Damn you, boy!' he roared, 'you're drunk! Drunk, I say! Where the hell have you been? Have you no shame?'

He took a mighty swipe at Will with his clenched fist which, if it had connected, would have laid him flat on the cobbles and senseless for sure. Unfortunately, just at that moment, Will fell down again and Herbert's fist connected with the brick wall behind him, raking the skin from his knuckles and making him dance with pain. The language which issued forth in a torrent was not what one might have expected from the newly appointed candidate for the ward. Brandishing his cane, he pursued Will around in circles, every now and then taking an almighty swipe at him with the stick. Had Will been his normal self and running away in the normal manner, it is quite probable that most of the blows would have connected. However, in his intoxicated state he weaved from side to side without pattern and not a single blow landed, Herbert's voice becoming louder with every miss.

Understandably, a small crowd was now collecting about them and encircled them like the spectators at a prizefight.

'Watch out, Will! He nearly knocked your 'ead off that time!'

'Go on, Mr Everton, imagine 'e's got a sovereign on his 'ead,

150.

then you'll 'it 'im!'

In the midst of all this there was the sound of an upstairs window being raised and an almighty bellow which drowned every other sound.

'Can't a man get any sleep in his own house? I 'ave to go to work at four in the mornin'! Take that you noisy buggers!'

The contents of a chamber pot swished through the air, quickly followed by the chamber pot itself. It was unfortunate that it was at this precise moment that Constable Peasgood, attracted by the commotion, pushed his way to the front of the crowd and received the contents of the chamber pot all over his helmet and shoulders. If the constable was unfortunate then Herbert was doubly so, for the pot itself hit him square on the head and knocked him to the floor where he lay moaning softly.

Constable Peasgood stood motionless, the brim of his helmet dripping slowly onto his uniform. His face had gone a deathly white and the crowd slowly drew back and grew silent.

Peasgood took off his helmet and wiped his face with a red spotted handkerchief. Then, slowly and deliberately, he replaced his helmet, fastening the strap securely beneath his chin. Looking up to the window where the perpetrator of this heinous crime stood revealed, he spoke in a loud, clear voice.

'You, up there. Come down at once and open this door!'

'I'm in me nightshirt, I can't come out into the street like this!'

'Go on,' shouted one of the spectators, 'lets be 'avin' a look at your knees, then!'

'If we 'as any comedians in the crowd, let 'em step forward and I'll give 'em something to remember me by,' said the constable. No one seemed anxious to acquire this memento and silence descended again. There was the sound of the front door being unbolted and a young man appeared. He wore a long flanelette nightshirt which came down to his shins and beneath which his toes stuck out like a bunch of knobbly, bleached carrots.

John Peasgood took out his notebook, licked the end of his

pencil and asked, 'Name?'

'Peter Gadsby,' said the unfortunate one.

'Address?'

'Why, I live ere, of course. Can't you see . . . ?'

The constable cut him off short and said again, a hint of menace in his voice: 'Address?'

'Four, Burton Road,' said Mr Gadsby.

Herbert was just dragging himself to his feet, assisted by a couple of onlookers. He was rubbing a swelling the size of a plum on the top of his head and looked distinctly green about the gills. There was a tiny trickle of blood making its way down his forehead.

Peter Gadsby had a premonition as to what might be coming and in a panic, took a wild swing at the constable who avoided it with ease and laid Mr Gadsby flat on the ground with a straight right to the chin.

'Are you alright, Mr Everton?' asked the policeman.

'I think so,' said Herbert, taking a couple of unsteady steps and sitting on a handy window ledge, 'What hit me? What's that all over your uniform, Peasgood? Has it been raining whilst I passed out?'

At this there was an unrestrained roar of laughter. Will seemed to have been rapidly sobered by this chain of events and went to his father's side on the window ledge, dabbing the blood from his forehead with Herbert's spotless white handkerchief and telling his father what had happened.

When the laughter died down the constable asked Herbert if he could walk unaided. Herbert replied that he could. The constable reached into his pocket and removed the brown paper bag from around his sandwiches, carefully replacing the food in his pocket. He passed the bag to Will and said, 'Be a good lad, Will, and collect the pieces of that . . . er . . . receptacle in this bag for me.'

He then put a hand on the shoulder of Mr Peter Gadsby, who by now was being supported on both sides, his eyes chasing each other around in circles as he slowly recovered his senses.

'Peter Gadsby,' he intoned, 'I am arresting you for assaulting Mr Herbert Everton and committing a felonious attack upon an officer of the law, to wit, myself! I shall now take you to the station where you will be charged.'

'I should bloody well think so!' said Herbert.

Peasgood put his other hand upon Herbert's shoulder and said, 'Herbert Everton, I arrest you for causing a breach of the peace and you will likewise be charged.'

Herbert spluttered in fury and raised his cane. The policeman let go of Gadsby and grabbed Herbert's arm in a grip like a vice, causing the stick to drop to the pavement.

'Resisting arrest is a very serious offence, Mr Everton. I shall now let go of your arm and if you attempt to resist me again I shall be compelled to restrain you in the same manner I restrained Mr Gadsby. Do I make myself clear?'

'Will,' fumed Herbert, 'this is all your fault! I'll break your bloody neck when I get you home!'

Herbert and Peter Gadsby were taken to the police station where they were duly charged and released to appear before the magistrates court the following morning.

When he arrived back home, head throbbing and face burning with shame, Herbert laid into Will with his cane with such ferocity that Martha stepped in to avert what might well have been a tragedy. That night, the pain of the bruises stopping him from sleeping, Will first toyed with the idea of running away from home.

The next morning Herbert stood side by side with Peter Gadsby in the dock. Because the two men were essentially charged as a result of the same incident the magistrates had decided that it would save time if they appeared together.

They looked a sorry pair. Herbert was as dapper as ever, but his whole image was spoiled by the huge sticking plaster which covered the crown of his head. In order to make the plaster adhere it had been necessary for Martha to cut off a large part of his hair. Whatever skills she may have had, that of a barber was not amongst them, and spiky tufts of hair stood at all angles around the edge of the plaster, thus making him look like an unkempt monk. His badly grazed knuckles were covered with a spotless white bandage and his arm was in a sling as he had sprained his wrist when Will had dodged his blow and he had hit the wall. His wrist was both swollen and painful and his head ached terribly.

Peter Gadsby had obviously put on his best suit for the occasion. The last time he had worn it was for his daughter's christening and she was now three years old. In the meantime he had put on considerable weight and a ridge of shirt showed below his waistcoat, whilst his jacket pulled at the buttons in a ferocious manner with every slightest movement. His left eye was almost closed and the swelling round about it was now colouring a rich yellow and purple.

Both pleaded not guilty and constable Peasgood was called to give evidence.

Having given his number, rank, and name and taken the oath he took out his notebook, thumbed back the pages, cleared his throat and at a nod from the chairman commenced to read. The panel of three magistrates looked bored as he went on to describe hearing 'an affray which was a serious threat to the peace and at once proceeding to investigate.

The chairman, Mr Ezrah Postle, had dined and wined too long and too well at the Freemason's dinner the previous evening and his digestion was troubling him. Claud Otter, a distant and elderly relative to the solicitor of the same name, was well renowned for hearing most of his cases with his eyes closed. Unkind critics said that he slept throughout and was not fit to be a magistrate, but he maintained that closing his eyes enabled him to concentrate without distraction upon what was being said. Joshua Flood was only newly appointed to the bench and had yet to be assessed by the public at large.

Constable Peasgood had now reached the point where he was describing pushing his way through the crowd surrounding the disturbance.

'As I reached the offending parties I felt an obnoxious fluid descend upon my 'elmet, whereupon it dripped down upon my

154.

uniform which must now be cleaned at a cost of ninepence – which is why I am in my second best uniform this mornin', your worships – and I then . . .'

'Just a moment, constable,' said Mr Postle. 'What do you mean, an "obnoxious fluid"? And where did this "obnoxious fluid" come from?'

Constable Peasgood had spent a long time concocting that phrase to describe his mishap and did not take kindly to being asked to describe it in a more readily understandable manner.

'Why, your worship, from the chamber pot. The obnoxious fluid was what was in the chamber pot before it fell out on my 'ead. It was that sort of an obnoxious fluid.'

This sounded a bit more interesting and a giggle ran around the courtroom.

'Chamber pot?' said Mr Postle. 'What chamber pot was this?'

Constable Peasgood delved deep into his pockets and brought out a brown paper bag from which he allowed the earthenware pieces to fall upon the witness stand.

'It was that chamber pot, sir', he said, 'At least it was a chamber pot until it 'it Mr Everton upon the 'ead!'

Amidst laughter the clerk solemnly picked up the pieces and placed them on the bench in front of the magistrates. Joshua Flood, feeling that he ought to be doing something to justify his presence, picked up what remained of the receptacle and examined it closely, his nose wrinkling in distaste.

'Constable,' he said, 'Where did the chamber pot come from?'

Peasgood thumbed the pages of his notebook and said in a hurt voice, 'I was just comin to that, sir.'

The chairman nodded to him and he continued to read.

'I then perceived a chamber pot of floral pattern flyin' through the air in my direction. Unfortunately this hit Mr Everton, although it was then that I realised that the contents thereof had fallen upon my person.'

The clerk called for order several times amidst the laughter as the constable described how Peter Gadsby had thrown the offending missile from his bedroom window.

'One moment,' said the chairman, interrupting yet again, 'Gadbsy, did you throw this chamber pot at the constable, or, indeed, at Mr Everton or anyone else in that crowd? Couldn't you just have shouted from the window and asked them to make less noise?'

'No, your worship, I did not,' he said in a loud voice, 'I pulled up the window and was about to say: "Now then what about a bit of piece and quiet, then, for a working man?" when my elbow caught the chamber pot, which was on the window ledge, and sent it flying through the air into the street! A total accident it was, sir, a total accident!'

Claud Otter opened one eye.

'Peasgood, read that bit again about what he shouted from the window,' he said.

The constable turned to the appropriate page and repeated . . . 'I observed a malefactor at the window and he shouted "I can't get to sleep in my own house. I 'ave to go to work at four in the morning. Take that, you noisy buggers!" I then espied . . .'

'Yes, yes,' said Mr Postle, 'let me guess! The flying chamber pot!'

He turned wearily to the clerk and amidst laughter asked, 'Mr Smithers, do we have any record of flying chamber pots in the Burton Road area?'

'Why do you keep your chamber pot on the window ledge?' interrupted Mr Flood, 'Why don't you keep it under the bed, or in a bedside cupboard like anyone else?'

Peter Gadsby screwed up his eyes as the laughter died down and one could almost hear his brain whirring as he sought to justify the statement. Suddenly his face lit up.

'Tis for reasons of health, sir, reasons of health. Some time ago my wife was sick and a medical person told me about the noxious vapours what rises from them things . . . '

'You mean, they smell!' said the chairman.

'Very likely, your worship,' said Gadsby, 'but that's not the worst of it. Them noxious vapours carries all sorts of diseases. Keep the pot under the bed and you'll get 'em for sure. So we keeps ours on the window ledge with the window open, winter and summer alike. There's a fair old breeze whips down off the castle walls during the night and it carries the noxious vapours right up the far end of Burton Road and away from the house!'

The chairman placed his head in his hands. Then he looked up at the accused.

'Gadsby, the court is obliged to you for your learned and erudite dissertation upon the subject of the . . . er . . . noxious vapours! I shall have the clerk to the court send out a letter to all the residents in the area asking them to take extra care when your bedroom window is open during the night!'

This sarcastic comment brought a roar of laughter from everyone, but Gadsby positively beamed and said 'God bless your 'onour!'

The rest of the constable's evidence was heard with only a few twitters except when he was describing how Gadsby had tried to strike him and explained that 'he became of a quieter nature when my fist made contact with his eye!'

'Mr Everton,' said Mr Postle, 'I find it hard to understand how a man of your standing can have been responsible for starting all this commotion. What have you to say to the court?'

'May it please your worships,' said Herbert, 'it was all my son's fault. He had been set upon by ruffians down by the Waterside, beaten almost senseless. When I found him at the end of Burton Road, he was so distressed he didn't even recognise me. As I tried to take him home to send for the doctor he went wild and struck out at me. I was very upset at this and I did chase him to try to catch him and it is true that I was shouting and causing a disturbance, but only because I was concerned about him.'

'The constable has said that the boy reeked of drink,' said Mr Flood. 'Is that true? Were you angry with him because he was drunk?'

'Drunk? My Will, drunk? Never, sir! The ruffians who set upon him were carrying flagons of ale and in the struggle as the boy sought to give an account of himself the ale was spilled all over him. No drop of drink has ever passed his lips.'

'How is the boy now, Mr Everton?' asked Mr Postle. 'How is he this morning? I trust he feels better.'

'Indeed he does,' responded Herbert. 'He has a few bruises from his encounter (that part at least was true!) and is feeling sorry for himself, but he'll be at work as usual. Knowing my Will I feel sure that he'll be at work. Thank you for your concern, gentlemen.

I apologise to the court for the inconvenience I've caused and I would like to say that I hold no ill will towards Mr Gadsby, despite the injury he has caused me. It must be quite dreadful to be woken up when you have to be early to work. I hope that your worships will not be hard upon him. He has already lost the best part of his day's pay by attending this court and I would not wish him to suffer further upon my account.'

The three magisterial heads went into a huddle for a few moments. Then Claud Otter closed his eyes again and the chairman pronounced judgement.

'Herbert Everton. Although you are technically guilty of the charge, the court realises that you were beside yourself because of worry about your son. We also take into account your very Christian attitude towards Gadsby, even though he hit you with the . . . er . . . missile. The case against you is dismissed.'

He then turned towards Peter Gadsby.

'Gadsby, until this incident I have never seen you in this courtroom and it appears that you are of good character. Taking this into account, and bearing in mind that your victim has taken the unusual step of speaking in your defence, the charge of assaulting Mr Everton is dismissed.'

'Thank you, sir,' said Peter Gadsby and would have stepped down from the dock.

'Stay where you are!' said the chairman. 'There is still the matter of the assault on constable Peasgood. From what you shouted from the window . . . "Take that, you buggers!" . . . there is no doubt in our minds that you did throw the chamber pot, although we have been highly entertained by your medical knowledge in denying it. The constable was doing his duty when you caused this filthy mess, noxious odours and all, to be thrown all over him, and then you tried to strike him, although from the look of your eye you came off the worst.

We cannot have the law flouted and it was our first thought to send you to prison.'

Gadsby turned pale and gulped.

'However, the court will be lenient on this occasion, but heaven help you if ever you appear before me again. You will be fined one pound for the assault and you will also pay ninepence for the cleaning of the constable's uniform.'

'A pound, sir,' said Gadsby. 'That's darned nigh a week's wages. I haven't got a pound.'

'Then you will go to prison for fourteen days!'

The bailiff was about to seize his arm, when Herbert spoke up.

'If your worships will permit,' he said, 'I will be glad to pay this man's fine. It is partly because of me that he got into this trouble.'

Thus did Herbert assure himself of at least one vote in the forthcoming election and in many a public house that night it was said that old Everton wasn't as bad as people made out.

Like the proverbial snowball, the story gathered as it was told from mouth to mouth and by the time the election campaign started it was definitely a point in Herbert's favour.

True to his word Grandfather William rallied and chivied the family to support Herbert. Grandfather himself rode around the town in a smart carriage and pair accompanied by his wife. Ann was a great campaigner, although she would have denied it. She had to do no more than be her natural kind and charming self to win over the confidence of her listeners. Naturally shy, she had a natural gift of listening and understanding. She made no false promises and never raised her voice even when some of Herbert's critics, not recognising this sweet lady as his mother, were harsh in their opinions of him. 'Nay,' said one fellow, hawking up a great gob of spittle into the gutter, 'I ain't got no time for that

Everton fellow, missus, but I'd vote for you any day if they'd let me!'

Rebecca, Fanny and Milly took turns to deliver leaflets along with Will, although Fanny was forbidden to knock on doors due to the fact that with her stammer she would never have got very far even if she could have summoned up the courage to raise the knocker. The gentle tactics of Grandfather William and his daughters resulted in a slow rash of 'Vote for Everton' posters appearing in the ward and by the time the campaign was ten days old even the elders of the party were beginning to think that Herbert at least wouldn't disgrace them. He would poll a few votes at least to keep the interest alive for the next election.

Then there came an incident which swung the whole campaign around in a different direction.

Herbert had booked the school hall for a meeting and before a modest attendance had acquitted himself rather well. The chairman of the party himself was sitting on the platform with him and as Herbert gave tough and straight from the shoulder answers his respect for him increased.

'What are you going to do about all them cesspits and dungheaps?' asked one questioner. 'There's a hell of a lot of 'em hidden behind some of them posh houses. One outside lavatory between six and seven families. It's neither decent nor healthy. It's landlords like you as does nothin about it. You just rake in the rents and do nothin.'

'I know very little about dungheaps and cesspits,' said Herbert, 'but I'm willing to learn. Indeed, I learned about what goes into 'em just a short while ago!' And he rubbed the ragged hair on the bald patch on top of his pate to a roar of laughter.

'What about shops?' asked another. 'My Flora works six days a week in a grocer's for seventeen and sixpence. She don't finish work until ten o'clock on a Saturday and she starts at half past seven in a mornin'. An 'orse pullin a muckcart don't work as 'ard as that – what do you say about that, Herbert Everton?'

'A disgrace, madam, a disgrace!' responded Herbert. 'We could do with more enlightened employers like Mr Collingham,

160.

the draper. He gave his assistants a half day holiday each Saturday some years ago. You grumble about your daughter working until ten o'clock at night. Don't forget that it wasn't that long ago she was working till eleven! You see, things are getting better. Its only a year or two back that most shops started closing at four o'clock of a Wednesday. Why, I doubt that there's any shop assistant works more than sixty five hours a week now and things are getting better all the time!

Mind you, there's much to be done still, but when I'm elected I shall encourage everyone to have more thought for the working man.'

'Does that include your missus?' asked a voice from the back of the hall.

'Since my good lady took over the administration of our workshop we've taken on four new workers and there's another one to be taken on soon. That's five new jobs my lady has given to the working men of this city, sir, and with her hard work there'll be more to come. It's a pity she's not here to tell you about it.'

'Nay, it's a bloody good job!' said another, turning to the questioner. 'If she were 'ere now she'd give thee a bloody thick ear for bein' so cheeky!'

The meeting over, Herbert chatted for a few minutes with his supporters and then made his way home up Burton Road. The meeting had gone on longer than intended and it was now growing dark. The streets were quite deserted.

As he drew level with the junction with Turner Street he sensed that he was being followed although he had heard nothing and, turning around, found himself face to face with two roughly dressed men. He raised his walking stick at them and demanded: 'Who are you? What do you want?'

'I want six shillings and twopence, mister,' said the taller of the two. 'My names Ezra Pound and I worked for you until a short time ago. Your missus gave me the sack and she wouldn't give me the day and an' 'arfs wages due to me.'

'Look, mister Everton,' said the shorter of the two, 'I'm Ezra's brother. He don't want any trouble, but he can't get work and he's desperate short of money. Just give him the six and twopence you rightly owe him and we'll go away peaceful.'

Herbert was aware of the beer-laden breath and the stout stick with which Ezra kept smacking the palm of his hand. He looked up and down the road but there was no one in sight.

'It's no good lookin around,' said Ezra. 'There's narry a soul about can 'elp you. Just give us me money and well be off, I promise you. You owe it me, mister.'

'If you were fired, you were fired,' said Herbert, 'and that means that you aren't entitled to any money. Look, here's a shilling, now take your hook before I call the constable.'

'You rotten old bastard!' yelled Pound. 'You've asked for it!'

Before his brother could stop him, Ezra lashed out at Herbert with the cudgel. Herbert ducked and the cudgel smashed against his walking stick which he had raised to protect himself. Herbert was no coward and realised that there was now no reasoning with his assailant and no time for finesse. As he stumbled against the wall he raised his pointed boot high, catching Pound in the groin and making him yell with pain.

The second man launched a blow at Herbert and caught him in the ribs, half winding him, and making him grasp his side where the blow had landed. His walking stick fell to the floor and rolled into the gutter, but he grabbed Ezra's cudgel from his hands, smashed it first into his brother's face and then laid Ezra flat on the floor with a blow to the temple.

The brother, blood pouring from his flattened nose, lashed out with a heavy boot and caught Herbert just below the kneecap. The pain was agonising and he staggered backwards into the wall, banging his head against the brickwork. He felt himself losing consciousness as he perceived the attacker closing in for the kill.

He lunged the heavy stick straight out in front of him as hard as he could and straight into the solar plexus, swinging his other hand round into a hooked blow into the villain's adams apple. There was a muffled gurgle and he sank to the floor. Herbert, back against the wall, slid slowly to the ground and blissful obliv-

162.

ion.

The chain of events which followed left only vague memories on Herbert's mind. He remembered hearing voices and someone lifting him from the pavement as the clatter of hooves announced the arrival of the police wagon. Before he swooned into unconsciousness he had a distinct recollection of Ezra Pound struggling with three policemen and being flung shouting and screaming into the back of the van.

He awoke the following morning aching in every limb, his head bandaged and his knee sending stabs of pain from one end of his leg to the other. His exploring fingers found a large bruise across the left side of his ribs and when he tried to move even the effort of sitting up in bed made him feel faint and he sunk back again into the pillows.

The doctor was sitting on a chair at his bedside and put a restraining hand on his shoulder.

'Gently does it, Mr Everton,' he said. 'You've had quite a beating and you're in no fit state to do anything but rest at the moment.'

'God, what happened to me?' groaned Herbert, 'I feel as if I've been run over by a steam engine. More important, what happened to those two sods that waylaid me?'

'You laid 'em both out, Mr Everton! Put paid to both of 'em! Ezra Pound is in the hospital with a severe concussion and his brother is in a police cell with a broken nose and a bruised larynx. He can't say a word; you must have caught him a right clout in the throat and no mistake.'

Will came into the room and enquired how he felt.

'God, boy, how do you think I feel?' asked Herbert. 'I'm full of fun and ready to dance round the maypole! Damned silly question! How do I feel? Bloody awful!'

'Your father's a lucky man, Will,' said the doctor, 'If that boot had been just an inch higher it would probably have shattered your father's kneecap and crippled him for life. As it is, he's full of bumps and bruises, but he'll live. He's a very tough and very brave man.'

163.

'Horseshit!' said Herbert. 'No man knocks me about!'

There was the sound of hurried footsteps on the stairs and Martha came into the room waving a copy of the local paper.

'Look, Herbert, look!' she said, her thin face flushed with excitement. 'Look what the paper says about you!'

Herbert focussed his eyes on the paper as Martha danced up and down in excitement.

'For Gods sake keep it still, woman,' he roared. 'How the hell can I read it when you're jogging up and down like a fart in a colander?'

His eyes ran up and down the columns, murmuring the words: ' . . . Mr Herbert Everton, respected cabinet maker of this city, was attacked in Burton Road by two villainous footpads . . . although unarmed Mr Everton resisted their attempts to relieve him of his purse . . . bloody and battered he fought back and refused to give in . . . finally disabling both his assailants despite fearful wounds . . . police had an easy job in conveying both miscreants to the station . . . Mr Everton is believed to be recovering from his wounds at home . . . undoubtedly he will not be able to continue what was proving to be an interesting attempt to win the local by-election . . .'

'Won't be able to continue?' bellowed Herbert. 'Will, quickly, bring me my best boots and see that they shine like a brass button on a sweep's arse! Martha, see that the carriage and pair is turned out and I want those horses looking like they're ready to pull the royal coach! Annie, lots of ribbons and colours on the carriage and some big 'Vote for Everton' posters on the sides. Ezra Pound, by God, you've helped me to win this election!'

Thus saying, he got out of bed and collapsed on the floor as his injured leg refused to bear his weight.

'Mr Everton,' said the doctor, 'the only place for you is in bed. You can't possibly go electioneering in your condition.'

Herbert seized the doctor by his lapels, his eyes blazing.

'Doctor,' he said, 'you strap this leg up so's I can't damage it any worse. Then give me something to help with the damned pain . . . and don't say me no, or I'll not pay your bloody bill!

164.

Martha, help me get dressed. Will, go out into the road and find two strong chaps to carry me down into the carriage. Here, give them a shilling each. Finished, am I? I'll show 'em!'

By the time Herbert was dressed, Will had found two burly street sweepers to carry his father down the stairs and into the carriage. Bedecked with bandages, but sporting his beaverskin hat perched atop the dressings on his head, Herbert looked pale and drawn, but his eyes shone almost as brightly as his diamond stickpin.

'Where to, sir?' asked the coachman.

'Down the hill and into town,' said Herbert. 'Anywhere there's people lad, anywhere there's people! Just drive round and round till I either pass out or stop at the Saracen's Head!'

Herbert's passage around the city was a roaring success.

Those who had read the paper shouted and cheered. Those who had not asked their friends what the fuss was about and were soon quick to join in the cheering. Herbert raised his hat and acknowledged the cheers but even his iron constitution had had enough by the time he passed the Saracen's Head for the third time. Two men from the crowd carried him into the lounge where eager people pressed so many drinks on him that by the time he got home his wounds were quite painless and he snored the rest of the day away on the sofa, waking so stiff and painful that his curses were dreadful to hear.

The party, realising that public opinion was swinging behind Herbert, suddenly threw help into the ward and it was acknowledged by all and sundry that never had an election caused such a furore in the city of Lincoln.

By the time election day came around all agreed that it was going to be a very tight result. Herbert's opponent, James Preston, refused to be flustered and fought a dignified campaign and whilst Herbert had gained a great deal of support by his courage there were still many who knew him for a hard and unsympathetic employer and would never have voted for him.

Election day itself was a turmoil from start to finish.

From early in the morning Will found himself chasing voters, knocking on doors and chivying people to the polling booth. Even he could not help but admire his father's tenacity and he found himself at the count that evening with baited breath.

The returning officer announced dramatically . . .

'Herbert Albert Everton, four hundred and eighty-nine votes! James Whitely Fletcher Preston . . . four hundred and eighty-nine votes!'

A hum of excitement ran around the room. No one could remember that there had ever been a tie in living memory.

'Well,' said Herbert, 'what do we do now?'

'Is either of you willing to concede to the other?' asked the returning officer.

Both shook their heads.

'Then we spin a coin,' he said, drawing a sovereign from his pocket and handing it to James Preston. 'You, Mr Preston, will spin the coin. You, Mr Everton, will call!'

Herbert called 'heads!'

It was tails.

The whole family sat around the fire in Burton Road. There was not much to say.

Fanny kept dabbing a handkerchief to her eyes. Grandfather William patted his son on the shoulder. 'Never mind, boy,' he said, 'next time, next time for sure!'

Martha kept saying how stupid it was. All that effort decided on the spin of a coin. They might just as well have spun the coin in the first place. Eventually Grandfather told her to shut up.

Will went up to his father.

'Father,' he said, 'I'm sorry that you lost. Truly, I'm sorry.'

For a fleeting moment there was a bond between father and son as Herbert put his hand on the boy's shoulder and said: 'I thank you Will, I thank you, son.'

'Are you allowed to vote for yourself in an election, father?' asked Annie.

There was a ghastly silence.

'Jesus Christ!' said Herbert. 'I never voted!'

166.

CHAPTER FIVE

BOSTON.

A BOUT OF FISTICUFFS . . . AND A JOURNEY TO BOSTON

FOLLOWING THE DISAPPOINTMENT of the election Herbert became quite ill. The physical effects of the injuries suffered at the hands of the Pound brothers, together with the energy he had spent in the last few days of the campaign, combined with the disappointment to send him to his bed for a few days. At times he ran a high fever and the blow which he had received on his leg caused it to stiffen and require frequent treatment. By the time he was fit to give evidence against his attackers he looked very pale and drawn.

Ezra Pound was sentenced to a year with hard labour and was dragged screaming from the dock, vowing vengeance against Herbert, whilst Ezra's brother, Caleb, was held to be less guilty and received only six months. He accepted the sentence quietly and walked slowly out of the dock to the cells beneath.

As Herbert was about to leave the court he was told that Caleb had asked to see him before he was taken away to prison.

Caleb came to the point very quickly.

'I'm sorry that you haven't been very well, Mr Everton,' he said, 'and I'm sorry that Ezra and me did you over, though God knows you gave as good as you got. 'Owever, I reckon as you still owes Ezra his day and an 'arf's pay. His missus'll need every penny she can get while Ezra's inside. She's got three young 'uns to look after and naught comin' in now. It's only coppers to you, Mr Everton, but it means a lot to 'er.'

Herbert mopped the rivulets of sweat from his forehead and flexed his stiff leg, his brow furrowed with the pain. He looked Caleb straight in the eye, hunching forward slightly, deep-set eyes flashing and the proud Roman nose looking for all the world like the beak of a predatory bird. He spoke very slowly and clearly, venom in every word.

'You can go to hell; you, your brother and all your brood. And think on this, Caleb Pound, to keep you company inside your iron bars. When you come out, there'll be no work for either of you in Lincoln, nay, nor for twenty miles round about. When your wives come to the gates of the workhouse, they'll be turned away, them and all your brats with 'em. If you want to live, then you'll live elsewhere. Damn the bloody lot of you!'

It took three constables to drag Caleb away. There was no more God-fearing man than Herbert Everton whose favourite passage in the Bible concerned exacting an eye for an eye and a tooth for a tooth. If he could get two eyes and two teeth, so much the better.

Herbert's pain made him take his temper out on everyone and even Martha kept out of his way, whilst Annie was several times reduced to tears by rough words such as her father had never used to her before. Will received more than his usual quota of blows and did his best to keep out of his father's way. The workshop bore the brunt of his anger and one carpenter lost his job for taking two minutes more than the stipulated lunch break.

At the White Hart Herbert drank more than his fair share and his cronies grew tired of his bad tempers and bad manners to the waiters. Had Herbert but known it, it was this which cost him the chance to fight the ward again, for the Party had been truly impressed by his spirited performance. However, this evil side of his nature, now revealed for all to see, was not what was expected of a potential councillor. He could be as wicked as he liked in private, but his public image must be on a higher plane. It was to be in a new century before Herbert Everton's name again appeared on a ballot paper.

Because of the incident with Ruby, Will's relationship with Clink became quite strained. Will felt that he had been made to look foolish and for several days had been quite convinced that everyone was laughing at him. He had refused to go out with Clink and they had quarrelled for the first time. Thereafter he had dodged meeting Clink on every occasion, but one evening as he was walking home from work he met Clink's father at the bottom end of Burton Road. Will would have passed him by with a short 'Good evening, Mr Carrot', but the giant of a man stood firmly in his way.

'Will,' he said, 'you an' our Clink 'ave been mates for a long time now; good mates, that is. Now me an' Mrs Carrot, we've noticed this last week or two that there's something amiss between you. That's sad, Master Will, for good friends is 'ard to come by for all of us. I know as 'ow my lad's upset over it all, an' I reckon you're none too pleased either. It's not for such as me to interfere, but Mrs Carrot an' me would be very pleased to see you both friends again.'

The big man shuffled his feet in embarrassment and put a giant hand on Will's shoulder.

'Will, lad, I'm not much with words and I ain't 'ad much schooling so it's 'ard for me to tell it right, but Mrs Carrot cries over this an' that's somethin' I don't like to see. No matter what you fell out over, it can't be that bad, now can it?'

Will had a vision of the good Mrs Carrot, shoulders heaving as she sobbed, whilst Henry Carrot stood by not knowing what to do to comfort her. He remembered that very first Christmas when his world had seemed to be full of misery and how she had taken him into her arms and made him one of her own. He felt a lump in his throat and fought to keep back a tear.

'I wouldn't do anything to hurt you or Mrs Carrot,' he said. 'Clink's the only proper friend I've got . . . that is, apart from you, of course, and Mrs Carrot. I'm sorry that we quarrelled and I'm sorry that it upset Mrs Carrot.'

'Tell you what, then,' said Henry, 'the Fair's in Monks Road. When you've 'ad your tea, why not come down and go to the Fair with Clink? I'll give you both a thre'penny Joey, then after the Fair you can come back to our 'ouse an' Mrs Carrot will 'ave a fine pie ready for supper!'

Thus was the rift healed, and that evening they found themselves at the fairground. It was a great pageant of noise and music, each of the new great steam organs seeking to drown out the rest.   Cymbals crashed, the newly-invented traction engines chugged away and the showmen shouted out their attractions. Young men in their Sunday best sought to impress young ladies with their skill at knocking down coconuts or winning prizes on the stalls.   Pennies were rolled down chutes and there were cries of excitement from the winners and groans from the losers.   Great gallopers whizzed round and round whilst the girls screamed in mock terror and the lads feigned indifference and showed off by holding on with one hand.

But to Will it was the smells that attracted him.

Over everything hung the pungent smell of hot oil and steam. Now and then came the sickly sweet whiff of toffee from one of the many toffee apple stalls and the savoury aroma of Grantham brandy snap.   The smell from the pie stalls was quite mouth-watering and to two young lads absolutely irresistible.   They stood in the crowd at the foot of the helter-skelter, pies in hand, cheering with the rest as the participants came whizzing down the chute, the girls screaming as usual, clutching their skirts around their ankles.

'Why do girls always have to scream?' asked Will. 'Every year they go on the rides and scream their heads off.   If they're frightened, why do they go on the things in the first place?'

'Very clever is girls,' said Clink.   'They ain't really frightened at all, you see, but if they pretend they are, then it's alright for the lads to put their arms round 'em to protect 'em.   If their mothers is watchin', they won't shout at 'em so much as if they did it in the street.'

Having delivered this piece of wisdom, Clink bit deep into his pie and sought to get a glimpse of ankle as the girls slid down onto the mat at the bottom.

At the bottom end of the fairground were the fortune tellers' booths.   At the entrance to gaily coloured tents stood a selection of ladies and gentlemen, swarthy in appearance with scarves around their heads and large, dangling earrings flashing in the lights.   They wore open-necked silk blouses and even the men seemed to be dripping with gold jewellery.

170.

'The one and only Gypsy Smith!' proclaimed one banner. 'The future revealed!'

'The original Donna Teresa, descendant of the Spanish Royal Family, will tell your fortune!' said another.

'My grandfather says that if that chap is the one and only Gypsy Smith, then he must be two hundred years old,' said Will, "cos he was here when my grandfather's grandfather was a lad!'

Clink took a closer look at the original Donna Teresa, standing at the entrance to her tent in a proud hand-on-hip pose, head tossed back at an angle, wheedling voice tempting passers-by to learn what fate had in store for them.

'I knew it!' said Clink. 'Underneath all that muck on 'er face, it's Sally Potter from the butcher's shop in Orchard Street!'

The regal lady squealed in anger and, leaping forward, caught Clink a resounding clout across the ear and sent him staggering into the crowd.

'Take that, you 'orrid little bleeder!' shouted the descendant of the Spanish Royal Family. 'An' if you come back, I'll give you some more of the same!'

Clink beat a hasty retreat, rubbing his ear, whilst the crowd laughed as 'Donna Teresa' resumed her royal stance as if nothing had happened. Even Will was laughing as they ran through the fairground and when they reached the far end, they both sat on an upturned barrel and laughed until their sides were splitting.

'Let's go back!' said Clink, 'We can 'ave a bit of fun with Sally and she'll never catch us.'

So back they went, sneaking around the back of the tents to take 'Donna Teresa' by surprise. However, in the noise and confusion they finished up at the next tent down, that of Madame Rosa, 'Foreteller of the future to Kings and Queens'. They were about to sneak round the back again when a bony hand descended upon Will's shoulder.

Will turned around to find himself gazing into the deepest, brownest eyes he had ever seen. Madame Rosa was as skinny as an old crow and as brown as a berry. Whisps of straggly, black hair protruded from beneath the coloured scarf she wore on her

171.

head and she had a pair of gold hoop earrings which Clink later swore were as big as bicycle wheels.

'Come inside, young master,' she said, 'I can see as you're a gent and no mistake, just as I can see that your friend's a villain and booked for the hangman! Come inside and let old Rosa tell your future. Hear about what lies ahead for you and how you'll make your fortune. You've a lucky face for sure, not like that red-headed rogue that's with you.'

'Thank you very much', said Will, 'but I'm not sure that I want to know what lies ahead. What's gone behind hasn't been all that good!'

'Go on,' said Clink, 'listen to what the old crow has to say. It's all a load of nonsense and she tells everyone the same thing. Learnt it all off by heart, she 'as. It'll be a good laugh.' Will went reluctantly into the tent, but when Clink went to follow, Madame Rosa barred his way.

'A man's future is his own,' she said. 'It's not for you to listen to!' And she rushed the curtain across the doorway, pausing only to hang a notice on the tent pole — 'Madame Rosa is in consultation'.

Will found himself seated at a small table. An oil lamp hung from the roof of the tent, one side being blacked out, so that all the light fell on him and Madame Rosa stayed in the gloom. He jumped as something brushed across his legs and sighed with relief when he saw that it was nothing more sinister than a black cat.

'There, see,' said Rosa. 'Black cats for luck! Old Drake likes you, and he knows, does Drake!'

He bent down to stroke the cat, which promptly scratched his hand, drawing blood.

Will snatched his hand away, looking with dismay at the three scratches which now ran down the back of his hand, the surface of the skin just broken and blood running in the furrows.

Rosa grasped his hand and examined the scratches carefully, shaking her head and muttering to herself as she turned his hand this way and that. 'That's strange,' she murmured, 'that's strange, indeed. Drake's drawn blood, but Drake has no claws!'

'No claws?' gulped Will. 'A cat with no claws?'

'Drake is very old, very old indeed. I call him Drake because he sailed the Spanish Main with the great sailor himself . . . aye, three hundred years ago, it was . . . three hundred years ago when my forefather was taken prisoner by El Draco, just off Tortuga, and he grabbed that cat just before Drake sent his galley to the bottom and a hundred souls with her!'

A slight breeze made the lamp flicker and Drake jumped onto the table, eyes sparkling in the gloom and his shadow looming large on the side of the tent. Will felt a chill run up his spine and the hair on the back of his neck prickle as the cat arched his back and purred loudly.

'That's not true,' he said. 'No cat lives to that age. It never sailed with Francis Drake, that's impossible!'

Rosa shook her head, sighed, and pushed Drake to the ground.

'Like the rest of the world, young master,' she purred, 'you believe only what you see. But beyond what you can see is what you can feel and beyond what you can feel is what you know is there, but can't feel! Your path through life is guided by the spirit world and Drake is part of my spirit life, always guiding me. He was old when I was young, and he'll be old when I'm long dead, and even when your bones are turned to dust, young Will.'

'How do you know my name?' asked Will.

Rosa smiled and turned his hand palm uppermost.

'Cross the gypsy's palm with silver and the future shall be revealed,' she said.

Will found a silver threepence which he put into her wrinkled hand. Rosa didn't even look at it as she placed it into her pocket. She stared hard at his palm, her scrawny fingers tracing the lines across it, back and forth, over and over again.

'Aren't you going to look in the crystal ball?' asked Will.

'Your future is mapped clear in your hand, young master,' she said, fingers moving back and forth across his palm. 'Never have I seen a hand with the lines so clear and determined.'

She raised her hand and stared deep into his eyes until he felt that she was looking into his very soul and searching out all his secrets. He felt a shudder go up his spine in case she could see the episode with Ruby and the way he had run off down the road with Ruby shouting after him.

'You will shortly make a journey,' she whispered and Will had to lean forward and strain to hear her. 'It will be the first of two journeys before the year is out and your life will change, slowly but surely your life will change.'

She paused and with brow furrowed traced one line across his palm with great pressure.

'You carry the mark,' she whispered. 'There it is, hidden beneath the others, but there it is.'

'What mark?' said Will, grabbing his hand back and staring at it, 'I can't see any mark.'

The mark is there, but you will never see it, my lad, for only those who have the sight can see such things. Before you are one and twenty you will meet one who will see the mark, a fair lady to be sure and one who has the gift. She will see in you what I have seen and she will stay by your side all the years of your life. But you will use her cruelly and not until you are very old will you realise her worth to you.'

'That's all nonsense,' said Will. 'How could you possibly know that? I don't believe you a bit!'

The gypsy sighed.

'I know because it's written in your hand,' she said, 'just like I know that you're a carpenter, that you're not happy at home and that you have a cruel father and mother . . . and I know that that red-headed villain outside is your only friend. I also know that you like music and that you had an old man who was a friend and that he's gone now . . . perhaps he's died or perhaps he's gone away, but he's gone, of that I'm certain.'

Will gasped in astonishment.

'Old Walter,' he murmured, 'you know about old Walter? How do you know all those things? Wait, let me fetch Clink!'

He rushed outside and dragged Clink protesting into the tent.

'Here,' he said, putting Clink's hand flat on the table in front of the fortune teller, 'Tell Clink about himself, just like you told me.'

Rosa leaned forward and looked at the hand, then she pushed it away and said: 'No, I won't read that hand. Never!' A visible shudder ran through her slender frame and she said again: 'Never!'

The cat jumped onto the table, arched his back and spat angrily at Clink. Rosa held the animal back and put a hand wearily to her forehead as if she was very tired.

'Go away, lads. Go away and leave old Rosa in peace,' she said.

'But what about Clink?' persevered Will. 'Tell him about the future like you told me. He's my best friend, just like you said, you've got to tell him!'

'That's right,' said Clink, 'You read my fortune. If you can, that is, 'cos I think it's all a load of old rubbish and you don't really know anything about the future at all! You're a cheat!'

Rosa half rose from her seat. She was very angry and the boys moved towards the door.

'This much I will tell you,' she hissed, 'only death will end your friendship. Now get out. Come back again and I'll put the curse on you for sure!'

As she took a step towards them they ran out of the tent, pushing each other aside in their fear.

They decided to postpone the baiting of 'Donna Teresa' until another day and moved off down the fairground towards the sideshows, debating whether Rosa really could see the future. Will was not as sceptical as Clink. He told him about the prediction that he would make two journeys before he was twenty-one.

'You'll do that tomorrow!' said Clink.

'Tomorrow?' said Will. 'You can't prophesy the future!'

'That I can,' he said. 'You'll make two journeys tomorrow for sure. One down to the workshop in Motherby Lane and one t'other way goin' 'ome again!'

By this time they were passing the boxing booth.

On the platform outside the booth stood a nattily dressed gent in a bowler hat. He wore no jacket and his waistcoat was of a bright floral pattern. His bright blue trousers were sharply creased and his highly polished shoes were topped by a pair of white spats. He had a heavy walking stick topped by a large silver knob and with which he rapped on his rostrum to gain attention. Either side of him stood a man in boxing kit. Both of them had flattened noses and cauliflower ears and the taller of the two was distinctly cross-eyed. They jogged up and down, every now and then shooting out fearsome punches at imaginary opponents as they ducked and weaved.

A large banner atop the tent proclaimed that this was 'Captain Jack's Gymnasium — the Home of World Champions!' and the flags of all nations fluttered in the light breeze above their heads.

'Roll up, roll up!' shouted Captain Jack through his megaphone. 'Gather round now and survey two of the finest boxers ever seen in the ring. For a modest copper or two come inside and witness the finest exhibition of the noble art of fisticuffs ever seen in this fair city of Lincoln! It's a man's sport, nay friends, it's a GENTLEMAN's sport, patronised by all the crowned 'eads of Europe throughout the ages!

Roll up! Roll up! Come closer and shake the 'and of two fine exponents of self-defence.

'Ere, on my right, the 'eavyweight champion (he pronounced it "Champ . . . eee . . . en") of all America, Canada and the Rocky Mountains the one and only . . . QUICKDROP McGINTY!' And he threw out his hand in a dramatic gesture towards the big, cross-eyed man on his right.

The boxer turned his back to the crowd to reveal the back of his robe emblazoned with the words 'Champion of America!' then turned to face them, throwing off the garment to reveal a great hairy chest and a not insignificant paunch which wobbled as he threw out a couple of mighty punches towards those nearest to the rostrum, his eyes rolling to the middle of his head as he did so.

176.

There was a roar of laughter from the crowd, quickly quelled by a shout from Captain Jack.

. 'It's easy to laugh, friends, very easy indeed. But which of you would like to come up on this platform and go five rounds with McGinty? Come on, now, all you what laughs, step up 'ere, don't be shy. They calls 'im Quickdrop because 'e drops opponents quicker than you can count the 'airs on a bald man's 'ead!'

'Aye,' shouted someone from the crowd, 'that's because they can't see who 'e's lookin' at!'

The two boys roared with laughter along with the rest whilst Quickdrop McGinty put on what was meant to be a terrifying expression and lashed out wildly towards the crowd who instinctively backed away. When the tumult died down Captain Jack turned to the boxer on his left and roared through his megaphone.

'And on my left, my lords, ladies and gentlemen, I give you the one and only crowned champion of the Orient, favourite of the King of China and admired by the Emperor of Japan . . . loved by the little brown men in Burma and raved about by the dusky ladies of Borneo . . . feared by opponents throughout the realms of the East . . . KING COBRA!'

The boxer turned his back to the crowd to reveal a brightly coloured snake embroidered on the back of his gown. It was coiled to strike and its forked tongue was plain to see. A large 'Oooh!' went up from the audience as the gown was thrown onto the platform and the boxer revealed a similar design apparently tattooed on his hairless chest.

He was a well-muscled young man who bobbed about lightly, ducking and weaving and throwing out punches at lightening speed. There was not an ounce of flab to be seen on him and his deep-set eyes were cold and hard. He had a tuckered scar running down the right side of his chest from shoulder almost to waist and this appeared to make him lean slightly to the right, almost as if the stitching of the wound had pulled him to one side. King Cobra turned to his left and raised his arm so that the scar pulled red and angry for all to see.

'Yes', shouted Captain Jack, 'look at that scar . . . did ever you see such a fearsome wound? The Cobra got that defending the King of China from a band of assassins intent on murderin' 'im! 'E pushed 'is Majesty out of the way and received a fearsome blow from a sword that cut 'im open from one end to the other! Inside the tent you will see on display a solid gold medal weighing a good 'arf pound and given to 'im in gratitude, together with numerous other awards won by these two fine exponents of the art of fisticuffs.

My lords, ladies and gentlemen, can you afford to miss this wonderful display? And all you young gents, anxious to impress your lady friends, I'll give you the chance to win a gold sovereign!'

'And 'ow do we do that?' shouted a voice from the crowd. 'Ask the King of China for a loan?'

'Empty pots makes the most noise!' responded Captain Jack. 'To win a gold sovereign all you 'ave to do is go one round with either of these two sportsmen. First of all they'll give you a fine exhibition and a few 'ints on the noble art. Then they'll issue the challenge to all comers. Last just one round, about three minutes, and still be on your feet at the end and there's a gold sovereign for you!

Roll up! Roll Up! I'm openin' the gymnasium now, admission is just two pennies, two pennies for a fine entertainment and the chance to win a sovereign. Can you afford to miss this, I asks you, can you afford not to come inside?'

Captain Jack went to the table at the entrance to the tent and, flanked by the two pugilists, commenced to admit the eager crowd, the copper coins rattling into a tin box as he shouted into his megaphone: 'Thank you, sir, thank you. – Go on, madam, feel 'is muscles, 'e won't mind — thank you, thank you, sir!'

By this time Will was down to a penny and was ruefully turning out his pockets in the hope of finding another. Clink grabbed him by the arm and propelled him towards the entrance.

'Come on,' he said, 'I've got fourpence!'

Inside the tent the benches were arranged in tiers around the ring in the centre. The crowd jostled for a glimpse of the solid gold medal inside the display case on a table in front of the ring. It was as broad as a saucepan lid and indeed shone like gold, the curling dragon in the centre standing out in high relief.

Will and Clink pushed their way to the front of the crowd and Will gazed open-mouthed at the huge medal.

Clink looked much more closely and then pronounced to Will that it wasn't gold.

'It's gold plated,' he said, 'Look at that edge, you can see the plating liftin' off a bit. Solid gold, my eye!'

As Captain Jack went into the ring there was a scramble for the seats at the front and an expectant hush settled on the crowd as the two boxers entered the ring and went to opposite corners where they were fanned with towels by seconds.

'My lords, ladies and gentlemen,' bellowed Captain Jack, 'This is a demonstration bout of the noble art of boxin', given by two champions. They will first of all demonstrate the basic movements and this will then be followed by three rounds of boxing.

Introducin', on my right, the champ . . . eee . . . en of all America, Canada, and the Rocky Mountains . . . QUICKDROP McGINTY!'

Quickdrop came out of his corner to the centre of the ring, hands clasped above his head, and jogged up and down to a mixture of cheers and boos before returning to his corner.

Captain Jack turned towards the other boxer.

'Introducin', on my left, the champ . . . eee . . . on of all the Orient. Beloved by the King of China 'ose life 'e saved . . . quick as a strikin' reptile! I give you . . . KING COBRA!'

King Cobra slid into the centre of the ring, fists flashing in all directions, then danced up and down on the spot, fists clasped above his head. This time the noise was mainly boos. There was something slightly menacing about the cold eyes and emotionless expression which did not endear him to the crowd.

The timekeeper rang his bell and the two boxers came to Captain Jack in the middle of the ring and squared up to each other.

'We shall now demonstrate the basic blows and tactics,'

179.

shouted Captain Jack. 'Watch carefully, you young gentlemen, for what you learn 'ere tonight may well stand you in good stead!'

'The straight right!'

King Cobra made a slow-motion punch to the jaw of Quick-drop McGinty who rocked backwards in mock shock, his eyes rolling in all directions. Then he made a series of full speed jabs at the air.

'Note the action of the arm, straight from shoulder to fist and 'ittin' 'ome like a ramrod,' continued the tuition.

'The left 'ook! Note how Cobra gets inside McGinty's guard with a straight right and then whistles 'is left 'and upwards in a 'ookin' manner and gets 'im on the jaw! 'Ence, it is called the left 'ook!'

Once again the punch was thrown in slow motion, but somehow as McGinty rolled on the end of the fist, he managed to get his nose on the end of Cobra's right hand and let out a yelp which could be heard clearly all over the tent. There was a huge roar of laughter which Captain Jack endeavoured to explain away as: 'A little 'umour 'elps you remember the lesson!'

'Now, it is as important to be able to avoid a blow as to give one, and we shall now show you 'ow to block a punch.'

This time McGinty was the aggressor and as King Cobra held his open glove defensively in front of his face, McGinty shot his fist into it several times in slow motion.

The crowd was now getting a little restless with the slow motion and was anxious to get on with the real fisticuffs.

'Go on now, Mary McGinty!' yelled Clink, ''It 'im with your feather-duster!'

The audience screamed with laughter, but McGinty went purple and in all the excitement shot a full powered blow straight into King Cobra's chest and knocked him flat on his back, taking Captain Jack with him to the canvas. This met with a roar of approval and, as Cobra came up from the floor, Captain Jack had to restrain him from turning the demonstration into a full-blooded battle.

The timekeeper rang his bell frantically in an endeavour to

restore order, but it was quite a while before the two boxers went back to their corners and Captain Jack recovered his equilibrium sufficiently to announce that the contest would now begin.

The introductions were made all over again, together with the attendant cheers and boos and the two boxers touched gloves and were exhorted to: 'Make it a good, clean fight, accordin' to the rules. Now go to your corners and come out fightin'!'

From the outset it was obvious that the two boxers were as different in style and skill as chalk and cheese.

King Cobra danced lightly about on the balls of his feet, right hand tucked firmly against his chin and his elbow into his side, whilst his left hand shot out again and again towards McGinty's face. McGinty stood more or less on the same spot in the centre of the ring, shuffling round and round to keep facing King Cobra. Now and then he lunged forward and let rip a mighty swing towards his opponent, the 'Whush' of its passage through the air being plain to hear and it was obvious that if such a blow ever landed, that would be the end of the contest.

Round two followed much the same pattern with the crowd getting restless and shouting for action until, one minute from the end, a blow from King Cobra struck McGinty on the end of the nose. He put his glove to the injury and to the crowd's surprise, blood spurted from between his fingers in a most alarming fashion.

As King Cobra danced around him, McGinty looked at the blood on his gloves and let out a bellow of rage. Like a traction engine under full power, he steamed forth from his spot in the centre of the ring, mighty arms swinging like flails as he pursued his adversary around the ring, Cobra's jabs bouncing off him like peas off a rhinoceros.

This was more like it and the crowd was now on its feet and roaring for more.

Finally, by sheer bulk, McGinty trapped Cobra in a corner and made contact on the side of his head with an almighty wallop. Cobra went down as if poleaxed whilst the crowd roared with delight.

'One! Two! Three!' counted Captain Jack.

'Four! Five! Six!' yelled the crowd.

'Seven! Eight! Nine!' counted Captain Jack, commencing to raise his hand to signal the end of the contest. Then the bell sounded for the end of the round and the crowd groaned with disappointment as the seconds dragged King Cobra back to his corner, where there was much splashing of water and slapping of his cheeks.

When the bell went for the final round King Cobra appeared to be unable to come from his corner, twice getting to his feet and then slumping back again. McGinty hovered over him like a mountain, eager for the kill, but Captain Jack held him back until a rubbery-legged Cobra swayed from the stool into the ring, arms sagging at his sides and a vacant look on his face.

McGinty shuffled towards him, arm raised as if measuring his distance, and then released a mighty punch which, had it connected, seemed sure to have taken his opponent's head from his shoulders.

As the crowd yelled, King Cobra suffered a miraculous revival, swaying to one side as the blow whistled past his head, arms suddenly reverting into the usual posture, feet dancing merrily on the canvas as he got around behind McGinty, who stood looking vacantly to one side for his opponent.

To the crowd's delight, Cobra tapped him on the shoulder and, as he turned round, released a shower of blows into McGinty's midriff. The joy was short-lived as McGinty delivered a blow which was not in any boxing manual. Clenching his sizeable fist, he thumped it down like a hammer straight on the top of Cobra's head and floored him.

Cobra got up at the count of eight and once again demonstrated his remarkable powers of recovery, staggering out of harm's way for a full thirty seconds and shaking his head like a terrier just emerged from the river. Then he launched a frenzied attack on McGinty, culminating in a straight right to the jaw.

Incredibly, the huge man swayed and faltered, eyes rolling into the middle of his head. Caught by a left hook, he tottered once more and then, like some felled oak tree, dropped both arms to his sides and crashed backwards to the canvas where he was duly counted 'Out!' by Captain Jack and dragged back to his corner by his seconds.

Cobra danced around the centre of the ring, hands clasped above his head, as Captain Jack pronounced him the winner and the audience applauded. Then the customary round of applause for the loser was called for and the crowd cheered as Quickdrop McGinty, by now incredibly recovered, came to the centre of the ring and shook hands first with Captain Jack and then with King Cobra.

'My word', said Will, 'what a scrap!'

'I've seen better', said Clink. 'but then again, I've seen worse.'

The timekeeper rang his bell several times and as silence descended again, Captain Jack announced that King Cobra now extended a challenge against all comers to stand against him for one round of three minutes.

'Come on now, my lucky lads,' he exhorted. 'Who'll be the first to try his hand? What about you, sir? Yes, you with the pretty young lady on your arm. Come up 'ere and show 'er what a man you are!'

'He'll do that after the Fair, behind the gasworks!' yelled someone as the young man went pale and the girl blushed a furious red as the crowd laughed with delight.

'And a very witty young gentleman you are,' responded the Captain, 'but will you accept the challenge? No? Are there no brave lads in Lincoln, then?'

Stung by the challenge, a young soldier jumped into the ring. He made a fair showing, but was no boxer and within two minutes had been floored twice and declared himself unwilling to continue. He left the ring to groans, a large swelling appearing on his jaw.

'That didn't take long!' shouted the Captain, holding a gold sovereign in the air for all to see, 'Come on, now, my lucky lads. Is there no one in Lincoln wants to win a sovereign?'

The crowd booed loudly and young ladies tried to push forward reluctant young men, but it appeared that no one in Lincoln really did want to win a week's wages for going one round with King Cobra. Suddenly the boos turned to cheers and Will was horrified to see that Clink was in the ring, throwing off his jacket and shirt and flexing his muscles.

The Captain took him by the arm and said: 'Now then, young fella my lad, I acknowledges that you're a brave chap, but I can't permit no juniors to engage in the noble art. It's just too risky for you. Come back in a year or two and try again.'

'I ain't no junior,' shouted Clink, 'I'm nineteen years of age and old enough to join the army and fight the 'eathens, so I'm sure I'm old enough to fight 'im. 'E may be able to beat the others but 'e won't floor me, I can tell you!'

There was a great bout of cheering and shouts of: 'Let the lad 'ave a go! What are you afraid of? We all heard 'im say 'e's nineteen. Go on, let 'im 'ave a go!'

'Very well' said Captain Jack, 'Sit on a stool in that corner whilst I announce you in the proper manner . . . what's your name, lad? And who's your second?'

'My second's my friend, Will Everton, down there. Come on up, Will! My name is . . . ' and he whispered in the Captain's ear as Will climbed into the ring. Will didn't really know what to do, but he fanned Clink with a towel whilst Captain Jack made his announcement.

'My lords, ladies and gentlemen! A contest of one round between . . . on my left, the champ . . . eee . . . en of the Orient, King Cobra (resounding boos) and the challenger on my right . . . "QUICKSILVER JOHN"!' As the cheers nearly raised the roof of the tent Will looked at his friend in amazement.

'Quicksilver John?' he whispered, 'Where did you get that name?'

'It was in a Penny Dreadful last week,' was the reply, 'and he won against the world champion!'

Quicksilver John's pugilistic debut was a brief one.

He managed to steer clear of King Cobra for a few seconds, using his height to pop out a few unskilled jabs, but fancying he saw an opening swung a mighty punch at the champion of the Orient, who promptly ducked and landed the straight right he had been demonstrating earlier high on Clink's cheek bone. Clink went down onto the canvas and struggled to his feet at the count of seven, but the Captain stood in front of him and refused to let him go on, saying that he had proved his courage to everyone and that common sense said that he must not go any further.

King Cobra took hold of Clink's hand and held it high in the air.

'He's a brave lad, ladies and gentlemen, but I won't fight him any further, it wouldn't be fair on 'im!' he shouted.

The crowd murmured and became restless and Captain Jack sensed that he had to do something to retrieve the situation.

'We all appreciate a good loser,' he shouted. 'Here, young Quicksilver John, here's a crown for you. A silver five shilling piece carrying the effigy of our beloved Queen, God bless 'er. She'd 'ave been proud of you tonight an' no mistake!'

And he held the large silver coin high for all to see before placing it into Clink's hand. Clink, a large red patch rapidly appearing beneath his eye, perused the coin with glee and showed it to Will. The murmurs turned to applause and a shower of coppers came flying into the ring. The two lads gathered the coins into Will's cap and, picking up Clink's jacket and shirt, left the ring to shouts of: 'Well done, young fellow! Well done!'

As they sat back on the bench Will put his arms around Clink's shoulder and laughed with glee as they counted the coins. Their calculations were disturbed by a mighty cheer and they looked up to see John Peasgood, dressed in his Sunday best, climbing into the ring. He spoke to no one, but went to the vacant corner where he carefully handed his jacket to a spectator, took off his waistcoat complete with gold watch and albert, and carefully undid front and back collar studs to remove his white, starched collar. Then he took off his flannelette shirt which he carefully folded and hung over the ropes. Putting his braces back over his bare shoulders he nodded to Captain Jack and said: 'I'm ready!'

He may have been ready, but Captain Jack certainly wasn't. After a whispered consultation with King Cobra, he held up his hands for silence. He remembered Peasgood from previous visits to Lincoln and was not anxious to add the loss of a further sovereign to that of the crown with which he had already parted. Anyone in the crowd who lived in the Burton Road area also knew the huge constable and a buzz of excitement went around the tent. 'King Cobra is upset at 'avin' 'urt the lad and 'as announced that 'e is retirin' for the rest of the evenin'. He feels that . . . '

The crowd was never to know what the boxer felt, for the rest of the announcement was drowned in a series of catcalls. However, Captain Jack had been a showman for many years and was quick to sense the mood of the crowd which was turning quite ugly.

"Owever,' he yelled above the din, "owever, Quickdrop McGinty will take his place!'

Mr McGinty was quickly pushed back into the ring, grumbling that he had taken the challengers last night and that it wasn't his turn. There was still another performance to go that evening and he wasn't keen to risk an encounter with anyone as large as John Peasgood, but he was left with little choice.

The bell sounded and McGinty took his usual shuffling stance in the middle of the ring, whilst Peasgood danced quickly around him, guard held high. However, the moment he dropped his guard, McGinty caught him with a blow to the body which almost winded him and then followed it with a wild swing to the side of the head. Peasgood saw it coming and weaved away, the blow catching him a painful glance on the ear. To the roar of the crowd, he rubbed his ear, then spat on both hands and rubbed them together.

Sensing what was to come, McGinty backed away as Peasgood came forward, but was too slow to avoid him. For a moment the two men stood toe to toe slugging it out, then McGinty was seen quite clearly to wobble on his feet.

'Come on, John!' was the roar, and Captain Jack looked anxiously towards the timekeeper who, despite the fact that less than two minutes had elapsed, raised his hand to sound the bell for the end of the round. This he was prevented from doing by a burly pair of gentlemen who suddenly appeared on either side of him, their large, flat feet proclaiming their calling.

At two minutes and forty-five seconds John Peasgood was distinctly in control of the bout and at two minutes and forty-six seconds he hit McGinty straight on the button with a mighty right hand that laid him flat on the floor of the ring. There was tumult as Captain Jack, a forced smile on his face, handed over the sovereign which John Peasgood put carefully into his waistcoat pocket.

As the crowd left the tent Captain Jack was already up on his rostrum drumming up business for the final performance of the evening. King Cobra was with him, but of Quickdrop McGinty there was no sign.

Will and Clink now had a further two shillings and twopence ha'penny to add to the crown which Clink had won. However, Clink had declared that he would keep the crown for ever. He declared that never in his life had he felt so important and that if he could get the cheers and five shillings every time for a black eye, he would gladly submit to being punched around a boxing ring every day.

'Just think, Will,' he exclaimed, 'all those people were cheering for me, every one of 'em. I felt like a king up there, particularly those first few minutes when he couldn't lay a finger on me. I didn't feel so grand when he flattened me, but even then they were cheerin' me on an' I would have 'ad another go if they'd have let me. Another few seconds and I'd have 'ad him for sure!'

'Another few seconds and he'd have knocked your head straight off your shoulders, more like!' responded his friend, avoiding a friendly swing at his own head.

They used the money from the boxing ring to have rides on the Gallopers and the Helter Skelter in between various confections for which they both had a prodigious appetite. They had just emerged for the fifth time from the chute of the Helter Skelter when Clink suddenly said: 'Well, would you believe that!' and pointed in the direction of the beer tent. There at a table outside sat Constable Peasgood, King Cobra and Quickdraw McGinty surrounded by a host of empty tankards and acknowledging the plaudits of the crowds, now wending their way home as the fairground started to close down for the night.

King Cobra spotted Clink and beckoned him over, bidding him sit down at the table with them.

'Well now', he mocked, 'if it isn't Quicksilver John, complete with a fine black eye from his defence of the title!'

'If I hadn't been stopped, I'd 'ave won,' said Clink, 'But your gaffer could see that and so he stopped me. I ain't no coward and I'll fight you again any time you like.'

'No one's calling you a coward, lad,' said John Peasgood. 'You had a lot of spirit to stand up like that against a professional boxer.'

'Sure, I'm only joking,' said the pugilist, 'You put up a good show, but there's a bit more to boxing than dancing about and thrashing your fists in the air. It has to be learned like any other trade. Ain't that so, Percy?' 'It is,' responded Quickdrop McGinty. 'And from the state of my face, I ain't learnt very much so far!'

As they all laughed Will asked him why they called him Percy.

'Because Percy's my name,' he answered. 'In fact to tell it in full, my proper name is Percival Sovereigns Bishop, Esq!'

'Cor!' said Clink.

'My Ma called me Percy because she liked it; Sovereigns so as I'd never be without money (tho' that ain't been very successful!); and Bishop 'cos anyone except the Bishop might have been me father!'

'I've been thinking,' said Will, looking closely at Percy. 'When you got hit on the nose there was blood all over the place, but there isn't a mark on your face now. Your nose isn't even swollen and it certainly hasn't been bleeding. How did it get mended so quickly?'

The three men looked at each other and laughed.

'Well,' said Percy, 'the crowd loves a bit o' blood. If someone ain't bleedin' they ain't 'appy, so we does our best to oblige the payin' customers. When I goes into the ring, I 'as this little bag of ox blood taped on the inside of my glove. Now, at the point that we've agreed, e' 'its me on the snout. I puts me glove to me nose an' yells out an' at the same time I bursts the little bag of blood all over the place — a little bit of blood goes a long way, looks like it's 'alf a pint!'

'That's cheating!' said Will.

'Well, it is an' it isn't,' said King Cobra. 'If 'im an' me bashed 'ell out of each other, night after night, then we'd both be on the slab before the end of the Fair. This way, we gives the crowd what they wants and we don't get 'urt too bad. Everyone's 'appy! You enjoyed the fight, didn't you?'

'Yes, I did', said Will, 'but if it's all faked up, why did you give Clink a black eye?'

The boxer rubbed the end of his nose with his hand and gave a sly grin to his friends.

'Because as soon as 'e came out of 'is corner, I could see as 'e 'ad the makings of a fighter. He crouched low, 'is 'ands never still, weavin' and duckin' like a pro and very 'ard to follow. Sam, I says to myself, if you don't put that lad away quick, then 'e'll 'ave you for sure! Then I thought as 'ow 'e'd 'ad the courage to come up in the ring when all the grown men wouldn't and as 'ow it'd be a shame to really 'urt 'im after that. So I put 'im down quick, rather than drag the fight over a full round. After all, I'd 'ave 'ad to defend myself. If 'e'd knocked me out, that'd be me finished for sure. Captain Jack would 'ave thrown me kitbag out and sent me on my way.'

Clink was almost speechless with pride at this tribute to his ability, which was supported by both Percy Bishop and John Peasgood and for once he had nothing to say.

Seeing his embarrassment, King Cobra held out his hand to Clink.

'Samuel Parfitt's the name, young Quicksilver John, an' I'm proud to make your acquaintance,' he said.

'What about this "King Cobra" name, then,' said Will, 'I suppose all that's made up as well?'

Samuel Parfitt shrugged his shoulders.

'I was in the Orient,' he said, 'I was in the Navy, out on the China station. I was the fleet champion. Then one day we sent a landin' party on shore. Them Chinese was running riot. They'd chopped the 'eads off two German missionaries an' 'ad lots more they'd taken prisoner. They 'ad 'em all in a little church what the missionaries 'ad built and was threatenin' to set the 'ole bloomin' lot on fire.

Well, we couldn't 'ave that, so in we went to get 'em out.

My God, them Chinese was fierce fighters. They 'ad old muskets an' 'alf of 'em blew up in their faces, they was so rusty. Then they came at us with swords an' axes and spears. We dragged the reverent gentlemen out o' that church in double quick time.

I 'ad 'old of an old gent. 'E 'ad white hair and a white beard an' 'e kept mumbling at me in a foreign tongue as I tried to 'urry 'im along through the garden that was round the church.

We'd just got near the wall when this 'orrid little Chinese, no 'igher than twopennorth o' coppers, jumped over the wall an' chopped the old chap over the 'ead with an axe all in one go.

'E was a gonner for sure, an' as I dropped 'im I ran me cutlass straight in one side of that Chinese fella's ribs an' out the other. Shrieked somethin' 'orrible 'e did, and that's when one of 'is mates sneaked up behind me an' tried to do for me.

I 'eard 'im comin' and turned round just in time to duck 'is sword loppin' me 'ead off, but 'e slashed me wide open. The pain was somethin' dreadful, but I knocked the sword out of 'is 'and with me cutlass an' grabbed 'im round the throat till 'is face was all red an' blue an' I 'eard 'is neck crack. Then I passed out.

When me mates picked me up they reckoned as 'ow they had to lever me 'ands off his throat.

Then they patched me up an' said I weren't fit for duty no more. They chucked me out of the Navy after ten years loyal service!'

Sam Parfitt, alias King Cobra, smiled bitterly.

190.

'Aye, lad, I've been to the Orient an' served me Queen an' country. An' they threw me out. Said I could still work an' gave me a pension of three bob a week. If I tried to lift anything 'eavy that old wound would split open again an' I'd be as dead as a doornail. I can't work, not like other folk, so I does the only other thing I knows, I boxes. But old Percy there, 'e's me mate an' 'e never 'its me on that side.'

Percy smiled and put his huge arm around his friend.

'Don't take on so, Sam,' he said, 'You an' me, we're mates. We look after each other.'

He turned to the boys and said: 'All what 'e's told you is true, lads. It's the ale as makes 'im down in the dumps, but a better fellow never breathed. 'E'd give you 'is last tanner an' never ask for it back.'

Sam took another deep swig from his tankard.

'Tell you what, lads,' he said, 'there's nothin' like being at sea. Just the sky and the water. And when you gets out in the tropics, that's the time. You can sleep on the deck and when you look up, there it is! All God's 'eaven, everywhere, all around you, goin' on for evermore as far as the eye can see.

And the stars! My God, there's a sight for any man! Millions and millions of stars, coverin' all the sky and reflectin' in the water.

An' not a sound, lads, not a sound, save for the ship's bow swishin' through the water. God's 'eaven and God's peace and quiet an' I was as 'appy as any man. Now it's all gone for me!'

He put his head on the table, fell fast asleep and snored.

'Right,' said John Peasgood, 'Let's take 'im 'ome, Percy! We've drunk the best part of Captain Jack's sovereign and you can both lodge with me tonight.'

Will suddenly tumbled to the truth of the matter.

'Why', he said to Clink, 'they fixed it up between themselves to win the sovereign!'

'The Lord 'elps them as 'elps themselves!' said Constable Peasgood: 'Remember that, young Everton, the Lord 'elps them as 'elps themselves and don't rely on anyone else!'

And dragging a mumbling Samuel between them, the constable and the boxer made their way home.

For many days Will found himself dreaming of the star-filled heavens as described by Samuel Parfitt. The description had made a lasting impression upon him that he was never to forget and by the time the autumn came around he had made up his mind to run away to sea.

He had been saving very carefully since the Fair and doing a few odd carpentry jobs in the evening to earn extra money. By October he was ready and the only thing holding him back was whether to take Clink into his confidence.

However, fate took a hand in the matter in that one evening he met a very worried Clink. They sat in their favourite place by the side of the River Witham and Clink poured out his troubles.

Will had long suspected that Clink didn't always get his money the honest way. Often he would have a shilling or two without seeming to have done any work and he now seemed to be known in many of the less desirable taverns in Lincoln. What he was now about to hear would only seem to confirm his own suspicions.

'It was late this afternoon,' said Clink, 'and I was in the Butter Market trying to get a couple of hours work in the clearing up when I noticed this toff at one of the stalls.

"Look 'ere," he says, "I'll 'ave a pound of that best butter and six of your eggs. Mind you don't give me short weight with the butter and the eggs 'ad better be fresh."

Then I noticed this purse lying on the ground behind him. Real fat and bulging, it was, and tied at the neck with a gold cord. Of course, I picked it up an' I was just about to tap 'im on the shoulder and tell 'im that 'e'd dropped it when all of a sudden 'e turns around.

"'Elp, thief!" he shouts. "This villain of a lad 'as picked me pocket and stolen me purse! Look, there it is in 'is 'and!"

Well, I just dropped the purse and ran like 'ell with 'alf the market runnin' after me and every one of 'em shoutin' like the devil. I got away, but some of them folk must 'ave recognised me.

Will, what am I to do? If I go up in front of the beak it'll mean goin' inside for sure and my Ma would never get over that.'

'Did you really find the purse, Clink, or did you take it from his pocket, just like you did that day at the racecourse when Constable Peasgood saved you from being turned in?' asked Will.

'If you don't believe me, then what chance have I got of anyone else listenin' to me? You're supposed to be my best friend,' responded the alleged culprit.

Will replied that it didn't really matter whether he believed him or not, because the magistrate certainly wouldn't. Then he told him about his plan to run away to sea.

'Why go to sea?' asked Clink. 'Why not just run away to another town miles away? You'd be certain to get work, you're such a good carpenter that anyone would take you on.'

'No,' said Will, 'I'm tired of working every hour that God sends for a few bob a week and being knocked about into the bargain. If anyone gets anything good in our house it's always Annie. No one seems to care what happens to me. Besides, I've seen the looks on the faces of our workmen when my father's in one of his tempers. All frightened to death of losing their jobs and wondering where they'll get another. I'll not be a part of it.

What finally did it was that boxer we met at the fair and the way he talked about the sky at night when he was at sea. I've kept dreaming about all those millions of stars up there in the sky and all reflected on the water. I came down here one night when it was fine and I looked up at the sky and the stars, and then I looked at the water. But there wasn't much to be seen. The buildings blot out the stars and most of the reflections in the water, too.

Then I went out to Burton village where Grandfather William lives and I stood in the middle of the biggest field I could find. I could see the stars then, twinkling and shining, even through the trees, and there was hardly a sound until I heard Big Tom chime the hour. Just a breeze rustling through the branches. I stayed there quite a long time and just looked up at the sky. I've often thought that perhaps Heaven didn't exist – old Walter used to say it was something invented by the toffs to keep working men hard at it – but that night I felt I was actually looking at it. I hope there is a Heaven, because if there is, that's where my mother will be, my real mother I mean, and one day I'll actually see her.

But until then, I've got to look at the sea and the stars, just like the boxer described. Imagine, Clink, nothing but stars as far as the eye can see and all around you, just stretching on and on, right out of sight.

That's why I'm going to sea and I'm going in the morning. I shall get the train to Boston and look for work as a ship's carpenter.'

'Let me go with you,' said Clink. 'I don't fancy going to sea, but at least I won't get taken inside and there must be plenty of work in a busy place like Boston.'

Thus was the decision made.

Clink pointed out that it would be better if they went in the evening rather than the morning. As he rightly pointed out, once Will didn't turn in for work in the morning, Simon Groom would send a messenger hot foot round to Burton Road to see where he was. If he didn't go straight home after work, no one would think much about it for several hours and that would give them a head start against anyone bringing them back.

'That is if anyone wants us back!' he added.

The following day Will put a few possessions in a knapsack which he left with Clink and put his savings securely in a leather purse which he tied around his waist with a cord.

The working day seemed to drag interminably and for once he found himself hauled over the coals for his standard of work, for try as he would he could not concentrate.

'Call that a dovetail?' asked Simon Groom, 'It looks more like a duck's arse to me. I don't expect poor work from you, Will, what's the matter with you? You'll have to take off the side of that coffin and do it again. And see that you make good that joint. I don't want to see you using another piece of wood.'

Work over, he went via a roundabout route to the Great Northern Station where he met Clink as arranged and took possession of his knapsack.

They approached the third class ticket office and asked for two tickets to Boston.

'Singles or returns?' asked the clerk.

'Singles,' said Clink, 'we ain't comin' back to Lincoln.'

'One and elevenpence 'a'penny each,' said the ticket clerk. 'That's three and elevenpence. Platform three. The train leaves in ten minutes.'

The journey to Boston was conducted largely in silence. Once the train started to move out of the city and into the countryside Will began to realise the enormity of what he was about to do. He had rarely been outside Lincoln in his life and yet here he was about to voyage to far off lands, and not a soul knowing where he had gone save Clink. The telegraph poles seemed to rush by at an alarming rate and the clicketty clack of the wheels seemed to say over and over again 'I'm not coming back! I'm not coming back!' However, he possessed the Everton streak of stubbornness and his misgivings were soon cast aside.

The journey lasted just over an hour, the slow train stopping at a host of smaller stations, but then Boston Stump came in sight on the horizon and they stood at the window as the train drew slowly through the points and sidings and into Boston.

Occasionally above the houses they could see the tip of a tall ship's mast and on the incoming evening breeze there was a distinct salty tang, mixed with not a little of the odour of fish from the busy fish docks.

Eventually they made their way up West Street into the High Street, then over the Town Bridge and into the Market Place. Here they sat on a wall and discussed what they should do next.

Boston was a busy town and although by now it was dark, there was still plenty of bustle in the streets. The town served as an export base for much of the local produce which found its way into Boston via the River Witham and the various navigable canals. Business was booming and from the various seamen in the streets could be heard a variety of tongues. Some of the foreigners would have come into town on the ships which brought timber, hemp and tar from the Baltic or perhaps on those bringing linseed from the Black Sea area.

The founding of the Boston Deep Sea Fishing Company in 1885 with its fleet of steam trawlers and smaller smacks had stimulated much employment in the town and many a continental boat now docked at Boston and sold its cargo in the busy fish market, French and German tongues adding to the babble in the streets.

Locomotive whistles could be heard from the railway sidings and there was a constant clanking of wagons being shunted which carried clearly on the night air.

Truth to tell, both boys felt rather lost.

In Lincoln at this precise moment Herbert was just sitting down at his favourite table in the White Hart and relishing the thought of that first welcome glass of port which was his favourite libation. The pain from his injuries had now almost disappeared and he had subsided from his mood of positive anger and uncouthness into his normal one of impatience and irritability.

Recognising a business friend entering the bar he nodded and asked after the health of the friend's mother, who was seriously ill.

'No change, I'm afraid, Herbert,' he replied, 'but thank you for asking after her. I've been to Newark to see her today. In fact I'm rather surprised to see you here this evening. I thought that you'd have been on holiday with Will.'

'Holiday with Will?' queried Herbert. 'Will isn't on holiday. Whatever gave you that idea? Whoever goes on holiday in October anyway? It's nippy enough to freeze the hairs off a brass monkey, never mind strolling up the seafront at Mablethorpe.'

'Now you mention it, I suppose it is rather late for holidays,' said his friend, 'but when I got off the train a while ago I felt sure I saw young Will in his best suit getting on the Boston train. He had a knapsack on his back and was with that red haired lad from Gordon Road.'

The mention of Clink was enough to send Herbert, glass untouched, hurtling across the Bail to Gordon Road where he thun-

BOSTON

19

197.

dered on the Carrot household's door, waking the children in bed and putting Henry Carrot in a very bad mood indeed. He was in no mood for Herbert's rantings and was not a bit worried as to Clink's whereabouts.

'My son's got a home to come back to, Mr Everton', was his final remark, 'and come back to it 'e will, just as soon as 'e's ready. It wouldn't surprise me if your lad never comes back, for there's little love for 'im in that cold place of yours.'

And with that he slammed the door in Herbert's face.

Meanwhile Will and Clink were debating what to do next. The night was drawing on and, as Clink pointed out, if Will went wandering around the docks in the dark he was likely either to fall in the water or get his throat cut by the many miscreants said to lurk in such places. They needed a place to stay until morning.

'That'll do!' said Clink, pointing to the Peacock and Royal Inn at the end of Market Place, 'We might as well be swells on what might be our last night out together, 'cos I've made me mind up I ain't going' to sea. I might get drowned! I'll take me chances on dry land.'

'We can't stay there,' said Will, 'We're too young to be staying in a place like that.'

'Don't talk daft,' responded his friend, 'We've got some money, haven't we?' 'I've got some money,' said Will warily, 'I don't know about you!'

Protesting, Will was dragged straight through the front door of the Peacock and Royal and into the dining room, where they sat at a corner table. They made an odd contrast, Will in his best suit, collar and tie and Clink in his usual ragged jumper and shabby trousers, his mop of red hair rendered untidy by the breeze. It was little wonder that every eye in the room turned towards them.

The landlord puffed into the room and, jerking his thumb towards the door, made his instructions quite clear.

'You two — 'op it!'

Will went to rise, but Clink put his hand on his shoulder and pushed him back into his seat. He looked the landlord up and down very slowly before speaking.

'That's no way to speak to Master Everton. When his father finds out you'll really be in trouble. You've heard of Mr Everton of Lincoln, I'll be bound?'

The landlord's puzzled face gave Clink a much needed respite from the effort of aspiration.

'No, I ain't,' said the landlord. 'What's Mr Everton to me, then?'

'He could be a very good customer', said Clink, 'But when he appears here later tonight and finds that you've thrown out his son, I wouldn't like to be in your shoes. He's the biggest cabinet-maker and timber merchant in the whole of Lincolnshire.'

Clink was seized by a brainwave.

'He's down at the docks now, buyin' a whole ship full of timber and he brought Master Will along to learn the trade, so to speak. "Owever' (he quickly corrected himself) – 'However, bein' a gentleman he doesn't let his son roam around the streets at night like a ruffian.

Edgar, he says to me, take my son along to the Peacock and Royal for dinner and book a room for the night. I'm told it's a very fine establishment. This here bargaining may take a bit longer than I thought.'

'However' (by now he was getting quite proud of his 'h's and he said the word again to make sure), 'However, it appears that we are not welcome and must go elsewhere.' He made as if to rise.

The landlord looked doubtful.

'Now wait a minute,' he pondered, 'if 'e's this toff's son, then what's 'e doin' with a scruffy vagabond like you, eh?'

'I'm 'is coachman', said Clink, 'but today we ain't brought the 'orses, we came on the train!'

'I've got some money,' said Will, withdrawing the purse from the recesses of his clothing and putting a sovereign on the table. The remainder of the money in the purse made a heavy sound on the table top as Will threw it down and seemed to put the landlord in a quandary. By now the remainder of the diners were making an interested audience and he had his reputation to think of.

'Tell you what,' he said, 'the little fellow 'ere can sit 'ere and 'ave 'is dinner and I'll get a room ready for 'im and 'is father. But if you're a coachman like you say, then you'll be used to the stables and that's where YOU can eat and sleep!'

And without further ado he grabbed the protesting Clink by the scruff of the neck and dragged him from the room amidst loud laughter. Will got up to join him, but Clink indicated that he would be alright and shouted: 'See you in the morning, Master Will!'

Will enjoyed his dinner and, by paying for his room for the night in advance, got both a good night's sleep and a hearty breakfast. He explained the absence of his father by saying that it was nothing for these negotiations to drag on throughout the night as each tried to haggle the other for the best price.

'After all', he said nonchalantly, 'he is buying a whole ship-ful.'

The landlord didn't believe a word of the story by now, but, as he had been paid for both food and lodging, he saw no reason to protest. As they left the door, he called them back and gave Clink a small brown paper parcel.

''Ere's some sandwiches and a bit of cheese,' he said, 'just in case 'is father gets delayed buyin' any more forests!'

They sat together on a bench outside the door in the warm autumn sunlight.

'Are you sure that you won't come with me?' said Will. 'I'd hate to leave you behind, you're my best friend and I'm sure you'd make a fine sailor.'

'It's not for me, Will,' was the answer. 'I've never really 'ad any thoughts about foreign parts, not serious ones anyway. I might learn to live there, but I couldn't die there. It don't seem right to me to die far away from 'ome in a strange place where you ain't got no family. I'd hate to think that I'd never see the Cathedral towers again or hear Big Tom. No, Will, it isn't for me.'

Will insisted that they share his remaining money between

200.

them and when this was done, he held out his hand. Clink grasped it warmly with both hands and then made his way back into the town as Will turned towards the docks.

He found the docks very busy with ships unloading everywhere. One was taking on coal and Will was showered with black dust as he passed by, much to the amusement of the loaders. He stopped at a nearby horse trough and washed his hands and face with a cloth from his knapsack. Then, as he rounded a corner of the wharf, he saw the most beautiful ship he had ever seen.

The Lucy Jane was a three masted clipper ship, her tall masts and rigging reaching into the sky. Her graceful lines were lovely to behold and Will had no doubt that this was the ship for him. Boldly he marched up the gangplank only to be stopped at the top by a burly seaman who asked what he wanted.

'Please take me to the captain', said Will, 'I want to be a sailor.'

'Sailor?' laughed the seaman. 'You ain't even big enough to make a decent sized bollard! Get along with you, afore I throw you in the drink!'

'Just a moment', said a voice from the deck, 'let the lad aboard, Mr Thompson.'

'Aye, Captain,' said Mr Thompson, touching his cap and beckoning Will to go forward.

Theophilus Orange was a small man, some five feet seven in height. From beneath a gold-rimmed cap, long white hair fell onto his shoulders.

His face was permanently tanned by almost fifty years of wind and weather and his grey eyes were surmounted by the biggest set of eyebrows Will had ever seen. They seemed to swoop outwards from the bridge of his nose and sweep into wings pointing towards his temples. His jacket had polished brass buttons and he wore a spotless white shirt and a black tie.

He had first rounded the Horn in 1845 and had now lost count of the number of countries he had visited. He stood erect, proud of his post as Captain of this lovely craft which was both wife and family to him and had been for twenty years past.

Will touched his cap as he had seen Mr Thompson do and repeated his wish to be a sailor.

'Want to sign on as a cabin boy, eh?' asked Captain Orange.

'No, sir, as ship's carpenter!'

'Ship's carpenter?' said the Captain. 'How old are you? Thirteen at the most, I'd say. And what sort of a carpenter would you be at that age?'

'Please, sir, I'm fifteen, nearly sixteen almost, and I'm one of the best carpenters in Lincoln. Well, I was until I left it,' said Will.

Before the Captain could reply, Will delved into his knapsack and pulled out a small package wrapped in oilskin paper.

'Here's my birth certificate, sir.'

As the Captain perused the certificate Will pulled out a small parcel wrapped in brown paper and tied up with string. He unwrapped the contents and handed them to Theophilus Orange.

'Sir, that's how good a carpenter I am,' he said.

The Captain was holding a miniature five-barred gate. It was no more than eight inches long and six inches high. It was made of polished oak and each joint was perfect. It swung on a gatepost by a pair of gleaming tiny brass hinges and was secured to the other post by a chain and padlock. The padlock was also of shining brass, but the chain was made of wood. It fascinated Captain Orange and he turned it first this way and that muttering under his breath: 'Beautiful! Beautiful!'

'The little chain is made of one solid piece of wood, sir,' said Will. 'Examine it as closely as you like, but you'll not find a joint in it anywhere. Old Walter taught me how to do that. He always said that nothing was more beautiful than a proper five-barred gate.'

'Aye, boy, and I think he was right. Did you really make this yourself without any help?' asked the Captain.

'Yes, sir,' was the reply, 'and I can make you anything you like, as long as it's in wood.'

'Mr Thompson!' bellowed the Captain. 'Fetch me Mr Bellowes!'

When Mr Bellowes was found, the Captain handed him the

model and said: 'Mr Bellowes, how good is that as a piece of woodwork? Could you make it any better?'

Mr Bellowes examined the little gate with great care and then handed it back.

'No, Captain, I couldn't and I doubt as you'd find a man who could,' he said. 'It's as fine a gate as I've ever seen in my life.'

'Lad,' said Captain Orange, 'Mr Bellowes is my carpenter and I never had any cause to complain about him. Mr Bellowes, this lad has made that gate and tells me he's a carpenter and wants to work on the Lucy Jane. Take him below, give him some wood and then come back in an hour and tell me what he can do.'

'Come on, boy, look lively now. Jump to it when the Captain gives an order!' yelled Mr Bellowes as he disappeared into the bowels of the ship, Will running after him dragging his knapsack.

They emerged on deck an hour later.

Mr Bellowes touched his cap to the Captain and said, 'Captain, the boy's every bit as good as he says he is. I've never seen such skill in a lad of his age.'

'Right, boy. What's your name? Well then, Will Everton, a sailor you shall be. You shall be ship's boy and Mr Bellowes shall teach you all about the sort of carpentry we need on board ship. Welcome aboard, Will.' said Theophilus Orange.

Will's joy was short-lived as Herbert clambered breathlessly up on deck followed by two policemen.

'Not so quick, Mr Captain,' said Herbert. 'This lad's my son and I'm taking him back to Lincoln with me. Has he signed any papers yet?'

'No,' said the Captain, 'but if he wants to be a sailor, I don't see as how . . .'

'I don't care what you don't see,' said Herbert. 'He's my lad and you can go to hell!'

Captain Orange bristled and Mr Thompson and Mr Bellowes moved forward awaiting the word from their Captain.

'My name is Theophilus Orange, mister, and you're standing on the deck of the Lucy Jane. I'm her captain and no man stands on my deck and speaks to me like that. You can apologise or you can go over the side, fancy clothes and all, aye, and those two po-licemen with you. This is my kingdom, mister, and you're tres-passing.'

Herbert knew when he was out of order.

'My apologies, Captain,' he said. 'I've been worried out of my mind over the boy all night and his mother has had to have the doctor with the strain of it all. He's a wicked, ungrateful lad and doesn't appreciate his loving family.'

Thus was Will removed from the deck of the Lucy Jane, look-ing wistfully over his shoulder at the ship's graceful outlines as he was marched down to the quayside.

Theophilus Orange shouted down to him from the rail.

'Will, you've forgotten your gate!'

'That's alright, sir', shouted Will, 'please keep it. I can make another.'

'That I will, boy, that I will,' shouted the Captain, 'I shall keep it in my cabin and remember you. Goodbye, shipmate!'

When they got to the railway station they found a dejected Clink in the company of another policeman and both boys were handed into Herbert's care, each policeman being sent on his way with a half-sovereign.

In the sitting room at Burton Road, Martha sat waiting.

'Herbert', she demanded, 'you must give the boy the hiding of his life. The ungrateful little wretch. How could he?'

Herbert went into the sideboard cupboard and took out a thick and heavy belt.

Will went to the fireplace and picked up the brass poker.

'Father, you've brought me home, and if it's your will I sup-pose that I'm stuck here until I'm twenty-one. But I give you my word, strike me with that belt and I'll bend this poker over your head, even though they hang me for it. You've beaten me for the last time.'

He backed into a corner, the poker held high above his head. Ignoring Martha's protests Herbert walked out of the room. He never laid another finger on Will to the day he died.

Back in Gordon Road, Mrs Carrot set a meat pie in front of

Clink and said: 'You must be hungry after your journey. Eat Up!'

When he had finished his pie and a mug of tea she said very casually: 'You've had a visitor, Edgar. Twice he's been here.'

Visions of the law catching up with him ran through Clink's mind and with heart beating overtime he asked, 'Who was it?'

'Didn't leave his name,' said Mrs Carrot, busy washing pots. 'He said someone in the market told him where you lived and that's how he found this place.'

Clink gulped audibly and waited.

'He said that there 'ad been some misunderstanding in the Butter Market,' continued Mrs Carrot, 'something about a lost purse and you not waiting to be thanked. Anyway, this woman in the market saw you pick it up and hand it to him and she told him where you lived.

'Well, he said he was too busy to call again, but he left you five bob for yourself! It's over there on the sideboard!'

Chapter Six

A Lincolnshire Legend

THE TIME IN PRISON hung heavily on Ezra Pound. He rebelled against the discipline, the poor food and the harsh labour. Victorian prisons were meant to punish, not reform, and for those who rebelled against the system a hard life became even harder. Ezra felt that he had been imprisoned unjustly and that if anyone had offended against the law it was Herbert for not paying the wages due to him. As the long days slowly passed he became more sullen and withdrawn, often passing a full day without speaking to a single person.

His hatred of Herbert was common knowledge to both prisoners and staff and he never lost an opportunity to express it when he believed himself to be out of earshot of the warders. The prison governor sent for Ezra's brother, Caleb, and asked him to reason with the man, pointing out that if he went out of prison and harmed Herbert, there would be twenty witnesses who would tell the court of his threats. But thoughts of Herbert dominated Ezra's every waking hour. It was both food and drink to him and fuelled his spirit during the long days of incarceration.

At a staff meeting the chief warder warned his staff to keep a close watch on Ezra.

'That fellow, Pound,' he said, 'I've never seen a man who reminded me more of a barrel of black powder with the fuse lit and ready to blow. He's to be given no leeway. Watch him every minute.'

Things came to a head one day in the dining hall when a fight broke out and Ezra received a blow on the head from a chair.

He lay unconscious for two days and there was some doubt as to whether he would survive. No amount of questioning could ferret out the culprit but there were many who said that the assailant was his own brother, tired of the constant talk of revenge.and knowing the damage that would be done to the whole family if he carried out his threats. However, no member of the staff had actually seen the blow struck and the prison community closed ranks and had nothing to say. No one liked Ezra, and no one would bear witness against Caleb.

Ezra spent several weeks in the care of the visiting physician, recovery being very slow. It was several weeks before he seemed to have got over the effects of the injury. His memory became unreliable except in respect of Herbert, whose name he was often heard to utter in his sleep. His previous moroseness seemed to disappear and he became almost amenable to other human beings, seeking their company whenever the harsh prison regime allowed. For a time he was allowed almost daily visits from his wife in the hope that this might help him to a full recovery, but this was not to be.

The doctor told the governor that in his opinion the blow on the head had badly damaged Ezra's brain, subduing his aggression, and that he no longer saw him as a threat to discipline. He recommended that Ezra be allowed a few simple privileges and that the company of other human beings would aid his recovery, although there was always the danger that the injury would cause him to relapse, or that he might suddenly drop dead due to the pressure caused upon his brain by the frightful blow. Ezra himself seemed sublimely oblivious to the interest he was causing and seemed to get great pleasure from the simplest things.

He became friends with one Abel Vickers.

Vickers was a seaman who had jumped ship at Grimsby and made his way to Lincoln by train. He had got drunk in the Wellington Inn in Broadgate, hit the licensee on the head with a bottle and needed three constables to restrain him. Consequently, he was now undergoing a longer stay in the city of Lincoln than he had originally envisaged.

He held Ezra fascinated with his tales of foreign parts and particularly Australia. Vickers described it as a wide open land where one day there would be opportunities galore for young people wanting to get away from the dirt and grime of Victorian England.

'Mark my words, Ezra,' he would say, 'Australia won't always be wilderness and convicts. It's springing up fast. There's fresh air and a man can breath as God intended. What 'ave we got 'ere? Nothing except damned 'ard work for very little pay and the promise of 'eaven if we behave ourselves until we pops off. Rewards in the next world but bugger all in this except 'ard work slavin' for the toffs!'

Ezra nodded his head.

'I knows all about toffs,' he said, 'one of 'em put me in 'ere and I ain't never goin' to forget that.'

But it was the talk of kangaroos that really impressed Ezra. Like many of his generation, he had never seen in the flesh most of the wild animals pictured in books he had read at school. Lions and tigers were familiar creatures, so were elephants and giraffes, but he could not recall ever hearing of the kangaroo. He would furrow his brow, his whole face a picture of determined concentration, and try to visualise the creature as described by Abel.

'It's as tall as a man, sometimes taller, and in its shape it's a bit like a rabbit. Little feet at the front, sort of 'anging out like a dog beggin' for a bone, and its back feet is enormous. It sits on its back feet. They're sort of joined in the middle, the back 'alf sitting flat on the ground an' it balances on them. My God, you should see its tail! It must be six feet long, pointed at the end and it can break a man's neck with one blow.

At the front it's got a pouch . . . no, Ezra. it ain't on a strap round its neck . . . it's natural, just there, all part of it. That's 'ow it was born, with a pouch at the front of its stomach. The females, they carries the young 'uns in this pouch, you can see their 'eads sticking out sometimes. I don't know what the males carries in their pouches, in fact maybe the males ain't got no pouches for all I know, but it's a mighty beast is the kangaroo.

I was in Melbourne once – that's in Australia – an' I went to a circus where they 'ad this kangaroo that could box. There it was

208.

in the ring, wearin' a pair of bright red pants an' a blue vest, sitting in the corner of the ring as large as life!'

'Go on!' said Ezra. 'You never saw no such thing!'

A warder standing nearby came closer to listen.

'I certainly did,' said Abel. 'This fellow comes into the middle of the ring an' says 'e'll give ten bob to anyone who'll spar a round or two with the animal an' stay on 'is feet. Well, you can imagine, ten bob for dancin' around the ring with an animal! There was such a rush as you've never seen. We all wanted to get the ten bob.

First in the ring was a Jack Tar on shore leave. He was a big chap, great 'airy chest an' muscles like a steam engine.

Well, they fastened the gloves on the kangaroo an' the animal leaps into the middle of the ring, sort of stands up on its tail and belts this matelot such a clout with its back leg that he went straight down, out like a light and didn't come round for a full ten minutes!'

'Never,' said Ezra, 'I don't believe you!'

'As God's my witness, it's true!' said Abel. 'I saw it with me own eyes, so I did! But that wasn't the end of it. That beast, 'e downed four blokes, one after the other, as calm as you please, didn't turn a hair 'e didn't. There wasn't a one got anywhere near the animal; just up 'e goes on that tail an' WHACK with that back leg an' that's another one on the deck! Then up goes this great foreign bloke. Never 'as I seen a bloke so big. I swear 'e blocked out the daylight when 'e got up in that ring. First of all 'e kneels down in the corner and crosses 'is self; then 'e says some sort of prayer in an 'eathen tongue what I couldn't rightly understand. Then 'e faces up to the brute.

Now, I'd been watchin' that animal an' I seen it gettin' madder and madder. It was snortin' and grumblin' to itself like an old man whose been woken up from 'is nap in the armchair. It's eyes was all bright an' it was slaverin' like an angry dog.

Well, God 'ave mercy on the poor bloke! This time the kangaroo rears up on its tail like before, but as the bloke tries to move out of its way it lets go with BOTH legs! They 'it 'im straight under the chin an' the next thing we saw was 'is 'ead flyin' off of 'is shoulders an' sailing through the air! God, it was 'orrible! There was blood everywhere, spattered all over the place it was. 'Is body just fell with a thump, 'is neck all spoutin' blood like a fountain, while 'is 'ead was bouncin' down the street.'

'Jesus!' said the warder. 'How 'orrible! What 'appened next?'

'Well, as you might guess,' continued Abel, 'the place was in uproar. Everyone wanted to do for the beast, but it took one mighty leap on them great back legs, sailed over our 'eads an' was off down the street like a bolt o' lightening. I swear it could leap fifty feet on them great legs.

Then, when it gets to the end of the street, it spies this bloke's 'ead lyin' in the gutter, picks it up in 'is front paws, an' boots it over the rooftops like a football! It kicked 'is 'ead so 'ard that no-one ever found it again!'

'Go on!' said Ezra for a second time, 'I don't believe you!'

'It's true,' protested Abel, 'every single word is true, I swear. That kangaroo made off into the wilderness like the devil was after it; it must 'ave been jumpin' seventy feet at a time, no one could ever 'ave caught it. An' it was laughin'.'

The warder smiled.

'Now then, Vickers,' he said, 'I think that's enough of your tall stories for one day.'

'Sir', said Abel, ''ave you ever seen a kangaroo? Then 'ow do you know it ain't true? I swear they're as big and strong as ten men an' they can leap fifty feet in a go — straight up in the air at that.'

This conversation made a great impression on Ezra and he became a constant companion of Abel Vickers, pressing him over and over again to repeat the story about the boxing kangaroo. One of the warders gave him pencil and paper and he had Abel draw him a picture of the kangaroo.

Abel was no artist and the resulting animal was shown as having a shaggy coat, large pointed ears and back legs which strongly resembled coiled springs. It had glowing eyes and the most enormous tail. Just for a touch of effect, Abel added a pouch at the front from which peeped the head of another beast of similar appearance. From time to time Ezra would abandon his normal mode of walking and spring along in great bounds.

'Look! I'm a kangaroo!' he would shout and inmates and warders alike would laugh and shout at him.

'Come on then, Ezra — let's see you jump over the wall!'

Ezra was released from prison in the early autumn of 1891.

He appeared before the governor and prison chaplain before being let out into the world again. This was a different Ezra Pound to the one who had entered prison the previous year. The sullen and morose man had now become almost childlike in his outlook. Spells of quiet thinking were interspersed with periods of frenzied activity and he was genuinely sorry to be leaving Abel Vickers behind. Their friendship had flourished to their mutual benefit, for Vickers had found a willing audience for his travel stories which other prisoners dismissed as imagination.

'Pound,' said the governor, 'you're going back to your family now and they're going to be a tower of strength to you. It isn't easy coming out of prison, any more than it is coming in. You've paid your debt to society, but you'll find society is slow to forget what you've done.

I'm going to put you in touch with an organisation that helps released prisoners and they'll try to find you work. Now when you go home be kind to your wife who has been loyal to you throughout this dreadful time. She has looked after your children and has worked her fingers to the bone keeping a roof over their heads and staying out of the workhouse. She's a very wonderful woman and you are a lucky man to have her waiting for you.'

The physician gave Ezra a piece of paper.

'From time to time you'll have headaches, Pound, and you'll have to rest for a day or two. Here's the address of a doctor colleague of mine in the city. As soon as you're settled back home you must go to see him and follow his directions. He will give you something to ease the pain. Good luck, Pound.'

Ezra looked around the room, smiled and said, 'Thank you for letting me stay here. It's been wonderful. Can I come back?'

The two men exchanged glances.

. 'No,' said the governor, 'we don't want to see you come back to prison. We want you to go home and keep out of trouble. You'll do that, won't you, Pound?. Now go along with the warder and he'll give you your things and let you out. I don't doubt that your good lady will be waiting outside for you.'

Thus Ezra was released from prison and into the waiting arms of his wife and family. The prison doctor had explained to Mrs Pound that she would find Ezra much changed and that his injury had altered his personality to a marked degree. He was a caring man, often disturbed by the plight of the prisoners, and he could see great difficulties ahead for the Pound family.

In later life Mrs Pound was to remember the next few weeks as the happiest time of her married life.

Although it distressed her to see Ezra's mental state, he was a much easier man to live with than he had been before his troubles. He showed no inclination to violence and was genuinely affectionate towards her and his children, with whom he played constantly when he was at home. One of the favourite games was to balance a broomstick across two buckets and then see who could jump highest over it. Ezra entered into this game with great enthusiasm, always lifting the broomstick higher and trying to achieve impossible leaps. Sometimes he would fall down, but as the children shrieked with laughter he would pick himself up and try again and again.

On only one occasion did Mrs Pound have doubts about Ezra.

The children were at school and that day there was no casual labouring for Ezra, for it was this type of work, found for him by the aid society, which kept body and soul together.

Mrs Pound looked out of the scullery window to see him leap over the broomstick, lose his balance and crash against the yard wall with a mighty thump. He sat on the ground rubbing his head and looking dazed and, as she helped him to his feet, he looked her straight in the eye and said: 'Mother, it was Herbert Everton did that to me. He hurt me. It was Herbert Everton. He was there all the time.'

212.

The worried woman put him to bed where he slept the rest of the day and then woke up as if nothing had happened and she never heard him mention Herbert Everton again.

That Friday, Ezra came home from work and handed his wages over to his wife, still intact in their brown packet. He asked her to give him two shillings to buy something with, something he had seen and wanted very badly. When asked what it was he wanted, he merely smiled and said it was a secret, a secret that he could not share even with his own wife and children. Mrs Pound gave him the two shillings and thanked the Lord that the days when half his wages would have been spent in the pub on his way home had gone for ever. As the minister was prone to say, 'The Lord works in mysterious ways, Mrs Pound!'

Early on Saturday morning Ezra went to a second-hand stall in the New Market and purchased the old fur coat which he had seen the day before. He also bought some strong thread and a packet of needles. The coat was almost threadbare and was not really worth the ninepence asking price, but Ezra smiled and said that he would need it with the winter fast approaching.

In Hungate Place there was a derelict building and it was here that Ezra would spend many an hour. The front wall was almost intact, supported by timber props, and someone had abandoned an old sofa in what was left of the parlour. Hidden from the street outside, Ezra would sit here, drawing pictures of a kangaroo which daily became more bizarre, and it was here that he hid the fur coat, together with two large springs which he had removed from the sofa, a tattered leather cash bag on a strap and a long tasselled cord which had originally helped to drape some fine velvet curtains across a window.

The following week the local constable was patrolling along the Place when he heard a quiet voice singing 'Nearer my God to Thee'. Peering through the gaping window space, he espied Ezra sitting on the old sofa and apparently mending his coat with needle and thread and quietly humming as he worked. Knowing Ezra and seeing no harm in his actions, the constable quietly withdrew without disturbing him.

A week later a drunk was looking for somewhere to sleep off his affliction and entered the derelict house in Hungate Place. It was not quite dark and, as his eyes became accustomed to the gloom, he found himself facing an apparition such as he had never seen even in wildest delirium. He had made his way over to the sofa meaning to lie down for a nap when from behind his intended bed rose what he later described as a monster.

Fully seven feet tall, the head was shapeless and covered with fur. Somewhere behind the two holes must have been eyes, but the drunk could not see them, so deeply were they set. Two floppy pointed ears hung to the sides of the head like a distressed rabbit, whilst its front legs were held in the posture of a dog sitting up to beg. The whole of its body was covered with tatty fur, like a dog with mange.

As the poor fellow stood petrified with fear, the monster bounced over the back of the sofa in one mighty bound and stood facing him, no more than a few feet away. The drunk was later to swear that instead of feet it had springs, but in the twilight he might have been mistaken. Of the fact that it had a long tail with a tassel on the end, he had no doubt at all.

Never was a cure for alcohol so quickly achieved. Now apparently stone cold sober, the fellow ran screaming up Hungate and did not stop yelling until he was pounced upon in St Martin's Lane by two burly constables who promptly conveyed him to the cells in the police station, where he continued to repeat his story over and over again to anyone who would listen to him. Of course, being a well known alcoholic, no one believed him at that time and in the morning he was given bread and cheese and turned out into the street, where he swore to all and sundry that never would another drop of strong drink pass his lips.

The following evening Will and his father were working late in the Motherby Lane workshop and it was dusk before they put the hefty padlock on the gates and turned towards Beaumont Fee to walk home. Since Will's attempt to run away to sea the previous year their relationship had been much less stormy, although it was always strained, and Martha never lost an opportunity to

214.

drive a wedge between them. There was no relaxation of the routine of hard work and Will was working even harder by doing a little carpentry on his own account, the earnings from which he hid carefully away from prying eyes. They had gone but a few yards when Will sensed something behind them and turned round. His gasp of amazement caused Herbert to look back as well.

'Ye gods and little fishes!' he said, 'What's that?'

Peering at them from a doorway was the head of a huge animal, or at least they thought it was at that time. It had floppy rabbit-like ears atop a fur-covered head with deep set eyes. As they peered into the gathering gloom and wished that the gas lamps were lit, the animal emerged from the doorway and made towards them in a series of erratic bounds, dragging a long tail behind it.

'Look!' shouted Will, 'It's got springs on its feet!'

As the beast was almost upon them it turned in the direction of Herbert and with a mighty bound appeared to try to kick him on the chin with both feet at the same time. However, the springs appeared to be carrying it out of control and it shot straight over his shoulders at a height of some six or seven feet. Just at this moment the lamp-lighter appeared round the corner. Before he had time to comprehend what was happening, his pole was seized, cracked across his own head, and the animal disappeared in a series of lop-sided bounds into the distance.

They reported the incident at the police station, the lamp-lighter rubbing his head and swearing that his skull was broken. As the incident had taken but a few seconds, recollections were rather vague, but when the evening shift arrived at the station there was an alert constable who connected the incident with that of the drunk the previous week.

The following day two men were despatched to the derelict house in Hungate Place. Sure enough, they found Ezra sitting on the sofa, Bible in hand and staring into the distance as if he was not aware of their presence.

'Vengeance is mine, sayeth the Lord,' he mumbled, 'How are

the mighty fallen. It is more blessed to give than to receive.'

Of the reported monster there was no sign and when they asked Ezra if he had seen anything unusual he merely shook his head and offered to show them some of his drawings. This offer they declined, although, had they taken advantage of it, they might well have been assisted in their enquiries. The story rapidly spread throughout Lincoln, growing with every telling, until it was the subject of conversation in every teashop and public bar.

In the White Hart, Herbert found himself the centre of attention, which he did not actually dislike, and he repeated the story time and again, suitably fortified with fine claret to withstand the shock of its recollection.

Will discussed the matter with Clink and wondered what sort of creature it could be. The next sighting was by a Mr Fletcher living in East Bight cottages. He had been tidying his small garden of autumn leaves late in the evening and had just lit a bonfire to burn them, when his attention was caught by movement on top of Newport Arch. There in the rapidly fading evening light he saw the monster, crouching and gazing intently in the direction of the Cathedral.

As he peered into the gathering gloom, endeavouring to make out who or what it was, Mrs Fletcher came into the garden and, following his line of gaze, saw the apparition herself. She gave a piercing scream and collapsed into the arms of her husband. When he turned again towards the Arch, the figure had disappeared and he was afterwards to swear that it had bounded some twenty feet from the top of the Arch and away down towards the town centre, although no one else appeared to have seen it do so. Over the next week there were another two sightings, both witnesses telling of the amazing leaps made by the creature.

One swore that it was nothing human, but an animal such as he had seen illustrated in books and to be found in Australia. However, the fact that he had plainly seen a leather cash bag hanging from its shoulders made that theory seem rather ludicrous and the story was put into more scorn by the fact that this same witness also saw that it had a long tail with what appeared to be a velvet tassel on the end. The second witness was of a more sober frame of mind and swore that it was a man, dressed in a costume, and with large springs attached to his feet and which he controlled in his leaping with amazing skill.

'It is no more than some damned silly Spring Heeled Jack!' he declared, and the name stuck, being rapidly picked up by the local press.

The sightings of the creature had some consistency in that they were almost invariably in the Newport area and always at dusk. Ladies did not walk the area once the light started to fade and many a man carried a stout cane for protection. The police put on extra patrols including two constables on horseback so that they might pursue the creature with some chance of catching him, but their quarry proved very cunning in avoiding their movements. Herbert declared that nothing, man nor beast, was going to stop him going about his business and nothing did.

One evening he took Annie to visit a friend who was holding a small supper party at the local college, both of them blissfully unaware that their progress was being observed. Herbert left his daughter at the door with the strict instruction that he would collect her at ten o'clock on his way home and that on no account was she to leave the college before then.

When Herbert departed, a figure detached itself from the shadows and made its way round to the rear of the building, shinning up a drainpipe with amazing ease and onto the roof where it was later found to have prised open a skylight.

The appearance of Spring Heeled Jack at the ladies' supper party was frightening in the extreme.

He opened the door very softly and stood there for a full ten seconds before anyone saw him. Then there was a piercing scream as every head turned towards the door and a mad panic ensued to get to the far end of the room away from him. Within the flash of an eye pandemonium broke out.

Spring Heeled Jack made a mighty leap onto the top of the table and this proved his undoing. His springs slipped and slithered as he shot across the polished table top, scattering plates and cutlery willy nilly as he shot off the far end and through the first floor window with a mighty crash of breaking glass. With remarkable presence of mind he somehow obtained a grip on the window ledge and this broke his fall as he fell heavily to the flower bed beneath.

A couple of the braver spirits ran to the window just in time to see the bizarre figure limp into the shrubbery and disappear.

When Will arrived, having been called from home, he found Annie quite prostrate and her father had to send for the carriage to take her home to bed. She was visited by the doctor who pronounced her to be overcome with shock and recommended that she should spend several days in bed with a diet of beef tea and chicken broth.

Herbert was quite beside himself with anger.

'I'll have that bloody fellow, man or beast, no matter what he is, I'll have him for sure,' he ranted. 'Where's the police that a raving wild animal can break into a young ladies' establishment and threaten to ravish the lot of 'em and get clean away with it?'

Martha's protestations that no one had either been ravished or even threatened with it met with no avail. When Herbert got a bee in his bonnet it was not allowed to fly away.

The following day Ezra Pound woke up with a badly swollen ankle and twisted knee and had to spend a few days off work as he could hardly walk. He answered his wife's enquiries as to the injury by telling her that he had lost his footing in a pothole and twisted his leg in falling.

When Spring Heeled Jack had not been seen for several days, interest began to fade and attention turned to other subjects. Herbert expressed his intention of making a journey to Caistor, some twenty odd miles away. The prime attraction for Herbert was that it had a workhouse containing some two hundred and fifty souls.

Martha was really ahead of her time in her way of thinking, for she was never content to let the business remain static. Always there had to be thoughts for making even more money and she was constantly pressing Herbert to consider the business which was to be found in the neighbouring towns and villages. Workhouses were a particularly good source of revenue in her eyes for there was a constant stream of business for the undertaking profession. Even more attractive was the fact that the accounts were settled by the parish and thus was payment assured.

She argued that if they could establish a small workshop in every town with a workhouse, then the business would expand beyond their wildest dreams. Herbert was of a more cautious nature. Although not averse to making money, he had a great aversion to spending it and had more than once calculated the cost of such a venture.

'Added to all that', he would say, 'there's the plain fact that none of us can be in two places at the same time, let alone half a dozen. That means that you have to trust someone else to run the job. Human nature being as it is that means two bob in our pocket and half a crown in his! Multiply that by these half a dozen workshops you talk about and we'll just be feathering other people's nests, not our own.

Buggered if I'm laying out all that money so that lazy devils can steal it. Think of it! Every year, hundreds of pounds being drained away from us! It's positively terrifying!'

He visibly shuddered.

'We don't do it all at once,' said Martha, 'we do it one at a time. Will could be put in charge of the first one. He's certainly craftsman enough and he's your son, after all.'

Herbert shook his head and said 'I'm not really sure about Will lately. He's become more withdrawn and I'm not sure he'd want to live anywhere else.'

'If you've any sense in your head, you'll make damned sure that Will does as he's told and get's a clout round the head if he doesn't,' snapped back Martha.

Herbert shook his head again.

'Those days have gone,' he said, 'Will's almost a man now and he's already tried to run away from home once. Any more beatings and he'll go again for sure and then we'll never find another joiner to work for the wages we pay him. Will's no fool. He knows he's good at his job and he'd never starve. There's little enough now to keep him here except the roof over his head and his friendship with that Carrot boy. Will's a rare creature, a man that's happy with his own company. He doesn't need other human beings and he could happily live without them, but he'll be true to the few friends he does have.'

However, to keep the peace Herbert agreed to take a trip to Caistor with Martha to examine the possibilities of opening a workshop there.

'Mind you!' he warned her, 'I've not decided anything for certain.'

They arranged their visit for a Saturday, this being market day and Herbert thinking that it would give them a better feel as to the potential in the town to see it when it was busy. As they boarded the train they failed to notice that Ezra Pound was riding in the guard's van, a large sack slung over his shoulder, but would not have attached any significance to it if they had. After all, Ezra was now known as being a bit touched in the head and all his wild threats against Herbert prior to his accident seemed to have come to nothing.

'He'll keep clear of me if he knows what's good for him!' Herbert had boasted on more than one occasion. 'He's got more sense than to have another go at me after the thrashing I gave him last time. Besides, he'd go down for ten years next time and daft as he is, he must know that.'

They were met with pony and trap at Moortown by Jasper French, a workhouse guardian with whom Will had had some previous business dealings and who had expressed an interest in any enterprise Herbert might bring to Caistor. The three mile drive from the station to Caistor was a cold one. The bitter wind scourged the bleak landscape with the icy sleet of the North Sea and despite blankets and scarves all three were chilled to the bone by the time they arrived at the Red Lion in the market place.

Despite the weather, there seemed to be plenty of business about. Rosy-cheeked ladies swaddled in shawls sold the local produce at their stalls, farmers haggled and various tinkers

220.

traded their wares.

As they dismounted from the trap, a watery sun emerged from behind the clouds as if in welcome and the scene seemed suddenly a little warmer and brighter.

Herbert made straight for the parlour and the roaring fire.

'Landlord!' he roared, 'Three large tots of whisky!'

Turning to Martha he snapped 'And don't damn well tell me that women don't drink whisky! We're all frozen to the marrow and need to get our pipes thawed out. Landlord! Don't take all day or you'll have three corpses on your hands, and stiff 'uns at that!'

'Coming, sir, coming!' said the landlord, tray in hand, 'We've been expecting you, Mr Everton. Your lunch will be on the table shortly, as fine a piece of roast beef as you've ever seen and a bottle of our finest claret, compliments of Mr French. I've given you the private room so as you can discuss your business undisturbed.

Should you wish to stay the night, sir, there's our best room at your disposal.'

'Stay the night?' queried Herbert, 'I can't see me staying a minute more than I have to in this God-forsaken hole!'

He was cold. He was in ill temper and he was annoyed that Martha's ideas had dragged him away from Lincoln. When Herbert was bad tempered he took it out on whoever got in his way.

It was indeed a fine lunch, served in a cosy room looking out over the square. The huge slab of beef would have served an army and was cooked to perfection, a thin, red juice sliding down the blade of the sharp knife as the serving girl carved the thin, even slices. The vegetables were fresh, despite the lateness of the season, – "Tis my secret, sir, is the keeping of the vegetables,' said the landlord – and the apple crumble served as a pudding with fresh cream would have melted the heart of Satan himself. The claret was rich, well-aired and free from sediment and the after lunch brandy warmed any tiny corner of Herbert's person which might still have been in need of restoration. Even Martha felt compelled to compliment the house, whilst their host, Mr

French, positively glowed with pride at the spread which had been placed before them.

A room was placed at Martha's disposal that she might rest for a while and the two men sat by the glowing fire with their cigars and port to discuss business.

Jasper French had already found several premises which he thought might well be suited to a joiner's workshop and also had his own ideas for the foundation of a partnership. Thus, as the port mellowed the conversation, the day drew on and the cries from the market place began to diminish in volume as traders packed up. The condensation ran down the window panes as a pale sun began to dip down below the level of the buildings. The old Roman wall cast long shadows across the market place and Caistor's market day began to die for another week.

'Tell me, Mr Everton,' said Jasper French, 'what is this strange tale I hear about this Spring Heeled Jack character? Have you seen him yourself?'

Herbert recounted in great detail how he and Will had been the first people to see the creature and how Spring Heeled Jack had tried to strike him down. He also told of the apparition's appearance at the party attended by Annie.

'Tell me,' said Mr French, 'do you not find it strange that this creature apparently pursued you down the street and then later appeared before your daughter? As I understand it, Spring Heeled Jack has appeared no more than half a dozen times in the city of Lincoln and yet you or your family appear to have been directly involved on at least three of these occasions.'

'I never thought of it like that,' said Herbert, drawing deeply on his cigar and releasing a pungent cloud of smoke into the small room. 'I suppose that it's just coincidence. I have no doubts that it is some maniac seeking to draw attention to himself, but when he's caught he'll pay for what he tried to do to my daughter, you can rest assured of that, Mr French.'

'Forgive me, Mr Everton,' said Mr French, 'but I understood that the creature did no more than give your daughter a rather nasty shock. Surely, he didn't actually . . . er . . . er . . . try to

222.

actually, well . . . you know, Mr Everton . . .'

'No, he didn't actually get anywhere near her, but there's no doubt in my mind what was on his mind . . . he intended to ravish her, sir, ravish her like the animal he undoubtedly is. Mark my words, Mr French, he'll kill someone afore he's done and then he'll finish up swinging on the gallows and good riddance to him, I say!'

The conversation was terminated by the appearance of Martha, who suggested that a leisurely walk around the square might be beneficial, and that at the same time they might perhaps examine the premises suggested by Mr French.

Thus was a reluctant and well mufflered Herbert dragged out into the decidedly chill evening air.

They had barely gone thirty yards beyond the Red Lion when a piercing scream made them turn around in time to see Spring Heeled Jack bounding towards them. Casting great long shadows in the twilight, he appeared to bound prodigious distances on his great springs and there was little doubt that he was heading straight for the trio. His tail bounced on the cobbles behind him, the pouch over his shoulders smacking up and down on its leather strap and his long ears flapping as he bounced towards them.

Martha screamed and turned to run towards the safety of the Red Lion, but so great was her hurry that she tripped over her long skirts and fell headlong into a malodorous pool of cow dung left from the market. Mr French appeared rooted to the spot, jaws agape in disbelief that the subject of their recent conversation should actually have appeared in Caistor and be heading towards him, whilst Herbert brandished his silver-topped cane and shouted for all to hear, 'Right, you heathen bastard, let's be having you!'

As Spring Heeled Jack drew abreast of them, he changed his direction at right angles with amazing dexterity, lashed out with his foot and hit Herbert square on the jaw, knocking him flying onto the cobbles, his cane clattering as it rolled away from him.

People were running from all corners of the market place and a small crowd soon took up pursuit of the monster. Spring Heeled Jack ran down a side street, pursued by the mob who had the strength of numbers to encourage them, and apparently disappeared as the crowd looked here and there.

'My God! There he is!' shouted an old man, pointing upwards, and sure enough there was Spring Heeled Jack on the roof of a row of cottages. Sticks, bottles and stones were thrown at him, but he bounded from roof to roof with an agility which was amazing, his final bound taking him onto the crest of part of the old Roman wall, where he stood defying the crowd with a weird roaring sound which seemed to belong neither to man nor beast. In the rapidly failing light with its long shadows he was a truly horrifying sight.

With a mighty bound of fully twenty feet he bounced from the wall towards the mob which suddenly lost its courage and scattered screaming in all directions as he leaped towards them, the panic being halted only when a local poacher who had been making his way out to the woods suddenly drew a folding shotgun from beneath his voluminous jacket and fired a shot towards the monster. However, his cartridges contained no more than the puff of powder and whiff of dustshot needed to knock a roosting pheasant from its perch and the charge bounced harmlessly from Spring Heeled Jack's covering.

Spring Heeled Jack hesitated and took a step backwards.

Seeing this, the mob suddenly regained its courage and those at the back pushed those at the front forward again as Spring Heeled Jack suddenly turned and ran away, the crowd once more in hot pursuit. Through side streets and alleyways they ran, but Jack had disappeared again, only to reappear on the walls of the New Barracks where a further shot was fired as he disappeared into the gloom.

By now it was dark and all further efforts to find the monster failed and the crowd withdrew home where windows were shuttered and doors barred against the intruder. A few of the braver spirits gathered in the Red Lion and the White Hart to recount their heroic pursuit of Spring Heeled Jack to those who had not been present, but no one went home alone that night in Caistor, nor for many a night afterwards.

In the Red Lion Herbert was recovering from the shock, whilst Martha lay still weeping in the room which Herbert had assured the landlord they would not be needing. Not planning to stay overnight she had not brought a change of clothing and lay shivering beneath the bedclothes as the servant girls strove to wash her clothes and rid them of the evil smelling manure which had soaked them through. Herbert had been knocked senseless by the blow to his jaw and it had taken him some time to recover. By now he was positively ranting and his language was not fit to be heard. His words were promoted partly by the suspicion that it was more than coincidence that his path and Jack's continued to cross.

Ezra Pound walked the long three miles to the railway station alone in the bitter cold, humming as he walked and occasionally changing his heavy bag from shoulder to shoulder. Sometimes he would have a conversation with himself, there being no one else present on the dark country road to hear him.

'You know, Abel, I don't think you told me true about that thing in Australia . . . Spring Heeled Jack hit him right on the chin and 'is 'ead stayed right where it was! I know it did, 'cos I was there; now Abel, you're my friend, but I shall 'ave to come back an' get a bit more information . . . no, I know it's not your fault!'

When he arrived at the station he had two hours to wait for the morning milk train, but a friendly porter stirred the dying embers in the waiting room and brought him a mug of steaming tea, after which he curled himself up on a bench and slept the sleep of the innocent until the arrival of the Lincoln train. By the time Herbert and Martha left their hotel to the peal of the Sunday morning church bells, Ezra was tucked up and fast asleep in Lincoln, denying all attempts by his wife to get him to say where he had been.

The Caistor appearance was reported throughout the county and there was now a genuine apprehension as to where he might appear next. There was not long to wait.

Will finished work early one evening. Simon Groom was out attending to a quotation at a local church and Will took this opportunity to say that he had to go to the ironmongers to order coffin fittings. He left as the early winter dusk was falling, jamming his cap firmly on his head and wrapping his muffler around his neck to keep out the biting cold, and made his way to his mother's grave in Newport Cemetery. He often came here when he felt depressed and thought of what might have been if his mother had lived. During the season he brought bunches of wild flowers, for he had often heard old Walter tell of Sarah Jane's love of flowers, particularly those which she could gather herself from the fields and hedgerows. During the winter months he would content himself with tidying the grave and at Christmas time he would place holly branches on her last resting place.

Early one Sunday morning he had rounded the hedge into the private section of the cemetery and had almost disturbed Herbert, immaculately clad as usual, placing a small bunch of primroses on the grave. Will watched unobserved as Herbert stood for several minutes, head bowed and both hands resting on the silver top of his cane. He stood motionless staring at the ground and then wiped one glove across his eyes, squared his shoulders, lifted his bowed head and walked briskly away.

On this winter evening Will had the cemetery almost to himself. In a far corner the gravediggers were placing their tools on a handcart and as they made their way towards the toolshed they said goodnight to him. Will heard the clatter of the wheels going over the cobbles and the rattle of the doors as they put their tools away, but the sound barely registered; he was so deep in contemplation of what might have been that he neither heard the chattering of the workmen as they made their way home, nor the tolling of the lodge bell which indicated the cemetery gates would shortly be locked. His breath seemed to freeze in clouds on the icy air, but he did not feel the cold, being so deeply engrossed in his own thoughts. It had been raining quite heavily for some days, and as Will stood silently in contemplation the first drops of

226.

a fresh rainfall fell on his bare head.

It was the heavy clanging of the gates in the distance which jerked him from his reverie. He pulled out his silver pocket watch to check the time and this set him on another trail of remembrance regarding Lucy Matchbox as he rounded the hedge, head down, and bumped straight into a tall figure. 'I'm so sorry, sir, I didn't . . . ', he started to say until the fact that he was staring straight into the face of Spring Heeled Jack stunned him into silence.

From the depths of Will's five feet two inches Jack looked enormous. The gathering gloom emphasised his size and the fact that Jack grabbed him with two strong hands was hardly necessary to restrain him. Will was rooted to the spot with terror. The ludicrous head with its floppy ears and hidden eyes loomed above him and the mangy fur covering only served to make the monster look larger then ever. One hand released him and delved into the leather bag where it remained clutching some hidden object.

'I'm sorry about this, Will,' said the monster, 'I've nowt against you and it's a pity that it's come to this. But it's all written in the Bible, you see. Only this morning I was reading my Bible and suddenly there it was, plain for all to see. It's never been meant for me to get your father; it's all written down there, just as the Lord intended me to see it on this very day!'

By now Will was struggling, but the one hand held him firm without effort.

'You see, Will,' continued Jack, 'that's what it says . . . these very words . . . "And the sins of the fathers shall be visited on the sons . . . yea, even unto the fourth generation" . . . it doesn't seem fair, but I can't argue with the good Lord . . . his will be done!'

He relaxed his grip slightly as his other hand started to withdraw from the leather bag. With a mighty effort Will wrenched himself free and ran shouting down the cemetery towards the main gate, his bellowing causing the cemetery keeper to emerge from his lodge just in time to see Spring Heeled Jack bounding after Will amongst the tombstones, his springs causing him some bother amongst the headstones and giving Will the chance to get onto the path. By the time Jack gained the footpath, Will had reached the main gate which was locked, but he knew of a gap in the fence and jumped through into Newport, almost knocking flat a group of men making their way home from work.

'It's him!' Will gabbled as they got to their feet and he pointed to the cemetery. 'It's Spring Heeled Jack, he's after me!!'

Three of the men jumped through the gap in the fence in time to see Spring Heeled Jack bounding down the pathway in great leaps and bounds. There was a pile of broken slabs awaiting removal lying just inside the gate and one hefty fellow picked up a large chunk and hurled it at Jack, catching him a glancing blow on the shoulder and knocking him off his feet. Encouraged by this success, his comrades also bombarded Jack with hefty stones from the pile and suddenly the hunter became the hunted, reversing his direction and bounding back down the pathway, pursued by the workmen and the cemetery keeper, his great leaps taking him ever further into the lead.

Bounding over the wall at the rear of the cemetery with ease, Jack disappeared into the ground beyond, hotly pursued by the workmen who climbed over the wall after him. A spasmodic pursuit by an evergrowing band of men and boys wound its way amongst the shadowy gaslit area around Nettleham Road, but it was not until Jack reached Newport Arch that he was definitely spotted again.

'There he is!' was the cry, and the mob, growing all the time, set off after him down East Bight, but so quickly did he move that only the most fleet of foot could keep him in sight and by the time he reached Eastgate the pursuers were drawn out into a long, straggly line behind him.

The six foot railings around the Cathedral grounds held no fears for Jack, but in the gloom he misjudged his leap and the spikes on top slashed the calf of his left leg, causing him to yell out in pain and giving the pack encouragement. Through the Minster Yard he bounded, leaving a splatter of blood behind him as he skirted St Margaret's burial ground. He left Cathedral Close, keeping in the shadows, and found himself at the top of

229.

Greestone Stairs. They stretched down some two hundred and fifty yards and he hesitated slightly before he commenced the descent, a pool of blood forming on the paving stones and being quickly washed away by the rain which was now falling quite heavily.

He had gone less than halfway down when the springs on his feet took him out of control on the steep slope and he crashed heavily into a lamp post, knocking himself to the ground just as the first of his pursuers arrived at the top of the steps. Jack scrambled up, pulling the springs from his feet and throwing them away into the darkness, his first limping steps causing him to yell out with the pain of his injured leg. Seeming to draw amazing strength, he ran down the remaining stairs and reached New Road, the pursuing crowd shouting that he had lost his feet.

'Now we'll get him for sure,' they yelled, slipping on the wet steps as they thundered after him, hurling anything that came to hand in Jack's general direction.

Jack jumped the four foot wall on the east side of New Road and dropped into the dark shadows of the grassy slopes some ten feet below, biting off the pain as his injured leg jarred with the shock of landing. Crouched in the shadow of the wall he heard them reach the bottom of the stairs and argue which way he had gone, all the time being joined by people attracted to the commotion. By now he was quite wet and the bitter cold, together with the loss of blood which pumped unimpeded from his wound, made him feel quite light-headed. Pulling himself together, he wound a kerchief around his leg.

Two policemen had now arrived and were organising the pursuit. Jack heard them direct sections of the crowd in different directions and instructing them to keep quiet until they saw their quarry, at which time they were all to shout in unison to attract the rest of the crowd. Taking advantage of the situation, Jack kept to the shadows around the edge of the cattle market and moved towards Monks Lane which he crossed unobserved as a line of men began to move down from the slopes below New Road.

Jack crept into the yard of Cooke's Plough Works, but as he

slipped out of the gate at the southern end of the yard he was spotted by a group of men leaving work and their shouting soon brought the whole mob streaming down upon him again. Fear now led wings to his flight and he sped past the Steam Packet Inn on the Waterside, stumbling and splashing through the puddles, seeking the dark shadows of the gloomy terraced houses in Strickson's Yard, Leo Place and Alma Terrace.

As he slipped quietly under the railway bridge which spanned the River Witham he had shaken off his pursuers who were busy combing through the terraces and even into the bars of the Golden Lion and Druids Arms. By now the loss of blood was serious. He felt light headed and his mind was full of confused images which he could not understand. He lay on the bank, near to the edge of the river which was fast flowing due to several days rain, and tried to rally himself. He felt as if he were sliding down towards the river and caught hold of a small bush to steady himself. Over and over again he murmured to himself, 'Oh, Lord, why hast Thou forsaken me?'

There was a shout from behind him as someone spotted a pool of blood in the light of a gaslamp.

'Look!' they shouted, 'He's wounded . . . the blood leads towards the river! After him!'

The fur coat a sodden, heavy mass and, the ludicrous ears running with the rain, Jack made a last effort to get to his feet, but he was bleeding to death and his legs buckled beneath him. He grabbed hold of the bush with both hands and pulled with all his might, straining to get to his feet. In the soggy ground the roots slid slowly free and the half-conscious Spring Heeled Jack slid quietly into the swollen waters of the river, the soaking fur coat pulling him below the surface almost at once.

One of the crowd combing the bank was later to swear that he had heard a quiet voice say 'Into thy hands, O Lord . . . ' but no one else had heard it and the search continued for several hours without success, whilst the story spread around the city that evening, each bar adding a few details of its own. By the time the streets emptied there can hardly have been a citizen of

Lincoln who had not heard at least one version of the pursuit.

As the darkness of night gave way to a cold and miserable dawn, Mrs Pound put out the lamp which she had left all night in the window, wiped the tears from her eyes, and set about clearing out the grate so that the children might come down to a warm room before they went to school.

'No, sir,' said Will as he faced the police inspector that morning, 'he never said a word when he grabbed me, and it was so dark and I was so scared I couldn't see whether he was man nor beast.'

No amount of questioning could budge him from that story.

Later, he put a day and a half's wages into a blank envelope and dropped it through Ezra Pound's letterbox on his way home from work.

CHAPTER SEVEN

GOLD BRINGS SORROW

BY WILL'S SEVENTEENTH BIRTHDAY he had grown to full manhood. He was still no more than five feet three inches in height, but he was sturdy and very fit. His skin was losing its youthful bloom and he now needed to shave every day. This fact was brought home to him when he had to spend part of his meagre wages on the purchase of razor, brush and soap. This caused much good-humoured chafing from the men in the workshop, particularly when he purchased a shaving soap with the enchanting title of '*Roses of Araby – a shaving soap for refined gentlemen*'.

The first morning he used it in his bedroom it caused Martha to remark on its 'very common aroma'. Herbert was more forthright and thought the whole home smelled 'like a house of ill-repute'. This caused Martha to ask Herbert how he knew what a house of ill-repute smelt like and another fine row ensued.

Annie gave a smarmy smile as they sat at breakfast and said, 'That's a nice smell, Will.'

Before Will could express his thanks that someone liked his shaving soap, Annie added a rider to her verdict. 'We used to have a girl at school used that perfume, Will; a very common girl, she was!'

Clink explained that he had no such problem with his shaving.

'A lick of carbolic at the kitchen sink an' a quick up an' down with me Dad's cut-throat; then I shoves me 'ead under the tap an' that's it.'

That year of 1892, the fortunes of the Carrot family were at a low ebb. The financial help which had been given them by Lucy Matchbox was no more than a dim memory now, sometimes talked about when they sat around the fire at night. Henry Carrot had lost his job at the farm, not because his work was unsatisfactory, but because the farmer had purchased a new plough and horses and couldn't afford them and Henry as well.

'God knows, Henry,' he said, 'I reckon you're as strong as any horse, but in these times I can't afford you. Perhaps when the hay making comes around I'll have a few days work for you.'

Although Henry's fracas with the law was now some time in the past, he found that his reputation still hung over him whenever he applied for work.

One day it had seemed that he had obtained a job as a labourer at Clayton and Shuttleworth's, but just as the terms of the job were being put to him, a foreman who knew him came into the office and whispered into the clerk's ear. The clerk shook his head at Henry and he left the office without saying a word, his dreams of a regular Friday wage disappearing into thin air. He walked back into town, calling at a couple of places on the way where he thought that there might be some casual work to be had, but without success.

By the time he reached the Lincoln Arms on the High Street his normal cheery disposition had left him, and his massive frame disposed of three pints of Dawber's best bitter in double quick time. That left him completely broke and when a friend offered him a tot of spirits to cheer him up he was not slow to accept. By the time he staggered towards the Stonebow on his way home for dinner he was weaving in an alarming manner and was inevitably arrested and charged with being drunk and disorderly.

The magistrates were not unsympathetic to Henry. Most of them had seen him before them from time to time and knew that he meant no one harm. On this occasion he was dismissed with a warning and after the hearing one of the bench remarked quietly to the senior police officer in court that if only one of the old brigade like Peasgood had seen Henry he would never have appeared in court at all, but would have been sent home to sleep it off. This did not please the police officer who took any criticism of his men as a personal slight to himself and he mentally marked Henry down as one to watch in the future.

It was only a few days after this that the Carrot's youngest

234.

child, Emily, was taken ill. She complained of headache and soon developed a temperature. Mrs Carrot was not unduly worried at first as colds, chills and fever were part and parcel of the crowded conditions in which they lived. However, when the seven year old became delirious, Clink was sent post haste to fetch the doctor who, looking down the child's throat, saw the tell-tale white spots and diagnosed diptheria. He removed the child to the hospital, but the condition became worse and before the week was out she died. Sick with worry that their other children would contract the disease, the Carrots spent sleepless nights watching them and grieving for little Emily. Henry Carrot seemed to grow old overnight, his massive shoulders slouching under his burden of sadness and worry.

When Herbert opened the door and found Henry Carrot on the step it was a great surprise to him. Henry twisted his cap in his hands as he asked to have a word with Herbert in private. Even Herbert's heart was temporarily softened as he surveyed the man before him and he took him into his study and closed the door.

He went to the decanter and poured Henry a stiff brandy. Henry hesitated.

'Go on, man,' said Herbert, 'you look like you need it.'

Henry downed it in one swig and thanked Herbert. The matter of his visit was plain, he said, and as it had taken him two days to summon up courage to knock on the door he'd better get it off his chest now whilst he had the courage.

'You see, Mr Everton, it's about my little girl, Emily,' he said.

Herbert said not unkindly, 'I heard about that, Carrot, and I'm sincerely sorry. My own little girl has grown to womanhood, thank God, and I can't imagine what it must mean to lose a little child like that. There seems no purpose to it.'

'Thank you, sir,' said Henry, 'Mrs Carrot an' me, we're goin' through a bad patch at the moment. There's been no decent work for weeks past an' it's been hard to get by. Then as you perhaps 'eard, I got in trouble with the law. They let me off, but it worries Mrs Carrot so that they might send me back to prison one day.

Now on top of it all, my little girl's dead an' there ain't the money to give 'er a proper burial.

In the name of all that's holy, Mr Everton, I can't 'ave 'er put in a pauper's grave, just tipped in there with dozens of others an' no marker to say who she was. Not my little girl. She was our baby, our youngest, and to see Mrs Carrot cryin' so breaks my 'eart.'

The big man wrung his cap in his hands and his shoulders shook with the grief of it all as he bowed his head.

Herbert waited until Henry was ready to talk again, refilling his glass and putting it on the table beside him.

Henry raised his head, his great eyes swollen with tears and his voice soft with emotion.

'Mr Everton, I'm a proud man, I've never 'umbled myself afore anyone in my life, but I'm at my wit's end. We've sold everythin' we 'ave that's worth a brass farthin' over the last few months an' still we 'aven't got anything, nothin' but a few shillings for rent and food. I'm askin' you, Mr Everton, nay, I'm beggin' you, give my Emily a proper funeral an' a proper place to rest in. I'll work off my debt to you, I swear; you know I'm a good worker, sir, an' I'll repay every last farthing, so help me God.

I was talkin' to the parson only this mornin', Mr Everton. "E says that every time we make a child smile, then St Peter up in 'eaven, 'e 'as a book, an' 'e puts a good mark against your name for when it's your turn to stand afront of 'im. If my Emily had a proper grave, then I know she'd be smilin' up in 'eaven, I just know it.

We're worlds apart, you an' me, sir, but our sons is friends, good friends, even tho' you don't approve of it. Even tho' we're livin' almost in different worlds, we're both fathers, you must know 'ow I feel, you must . . . you must . . . .' His voice quivered and then trailed away into silence. His words were now exhausted and he could think of nothing else to say.

Herbert looked at the man before him. In later life Will was to say that it was the only time his father ever put sentiment before money and he was never able to explain why he had done it.

236.

Herbert had seen strong men weep more than once and it was not normally a sight that moved him. As a member of the workhouse Board of Guardians he had learned that tears were not the prerogative of the female sex. Many a man will weep when he is at the end of his tether and can see no way out, particularly if his family is suffering more than he is.

'Stop blathering, Carrot, and get to your feet,' said Herbert. 'There's a pair of cottages at South Carlton that I've bought and they need doing up afore I can rent them out. We're starting next week and you be there on Monday morning at half past seven, sharp. Bring that lad of yours as well, there's plenty of humping and lifting for both of you for a couple of weeks at least.'

Then his voice dropped and he put one hand on Henry's shoulder.

'Your little girl shall be buried properly, I promise you. I'll make all the arrangements and we'll take the child from the hospital and lay her in church where she ought to be before this day is out. She shall be laid to rest in her own little plot and she'll have a stone to mark where she lies.'

Henry Carrot stood open-mouthed. He had come to Herbert only as a desperate last resort and had never believed that his prayers would be answered. His disbelief showed plainly in his face.

'I know, Carrot, I must be going soft in the head to be doing it, but I've said it shall be done, and so it shall. There is a friendship between our sons, despite all I've done to stop it, and that has to count for something. I'm not unaware that your home has always been open to Will, even when he's not been happy here, and for that I'm grateful to you and your wife. I can't recall that I've ever had a true friend in my life, Carrot, and I can't recall that I've ever wanted one either. Now go home and give Mrs Carrot a little bit of good news in these dark days.' He put his hand in his pocket and pulled out his purse, putting several coins in Henry's hand. 'Here, man, your wife'll want a new coat for the funeral and a new shirt and collar might tidy you up a bit.' He pushed another coin into his palm and said '. . . and buy those other kids of yours a few sweets or something and pray to God they haven't caught the cursed diptheria as well.'

Will made the tiny coffin himself and with each stroke of the plane he seemed to see the tiny girl who had sat on Henry's huge lap on that Christmas Day more than five years ago, long hair curling over her shoulders and deep blue eyes taking in everything going on around her. When it came to the lid, he added a touch of his own above the brass plate that carried the little girl's name and age, a tiny angel which he carved lovingly into the wood. The cherub's lips seemed to be blowing softly across the coffin top and feathered wings spread out behind him, each feather fine to the last detail.

'He's blowing the breath of Heaven across Emily to give her peace in her rest,' he explained to Mrs Carrot as they all stood, gazing down on the tiny child, swaddled in silk, her tiny hands clasping a single red rose on her breast.

Mrs Carrot took Will in her arms.

'God bless thee, Little Will,' she stammered amidst the tears, 'she'll like that. Wherever she is, she'll like that.'

'Aye, boy,' whispered Henry, 'I'll never forget what your father has done for us. Never.'

On a warm August day, Emily was laid to rest in Newport cemetery in a tiny plot of her own. Great white clouds chased each other in a blue sky and there was no sound other than the chirping of birds and the droning of the parson at the graveside. The Carrot home, always bursting at the seams, seemed strangely empty that night.

On the Monday morning Henry Carrot and Clink walked the road to South Carlton at the crack of dawn and were waiting by the cottages when Will and two other men arrived just before half past seven. Grandfather William had also walked out from Burton to supervise matters. He was getting old now, but his years of experience were invaluable and he was as tough and durable as a piece of weather beaten leather and could do a fair day's work with men young enough to be his grandsons.

The cottages were reputed to be at least two hundred years

238.

old and had been much neglected, having been empty for a long time before Herbert had purchased them cheaply. It took them a full day to clear out all the debris which had accumulated and then Grandfather William gave them a thorough examination. He immediately placed the upper floor out of bounds to everyone, explaining that there was rot in many of the floorboards. The plan of action was to complete the ground floor areas first and this took a full week. A further fortnight was spent in reflooring the upper rooms and in repairing the several leaks in the roof. When this was finished, there was a huge bonfire in the garden and all the rotted timbers were burned. At the end of this, Herbert set Will to replace the various inside fittings, helped by Henry and Clink.

The days were warm and sunny and the three of them working together seemed to strike up an even warmer friendship. Henry was mainly concerned with the labouring work, and he lifted and carried with a will, the hard work helping to take his mind off the death of his daughter. Thankfully, the other children had stayed free of infection, although Mrs Carrot had draped every doorway in the house with vinegar-soaked sheets for several days as a precaution, and for this they were thankful.

Will endeavoured to teach Clink some of the rudiments of woodwork, but Clink was a poor pupil, largely due to lack of interest. He did not really like being tied down to one spot all day long in a quiet village and he yearned for the busy city. Therefore he was not sorry when Herbert visited them one afternoon and said that the remaining jobs must be finished within the week as he had let the cottages to tenants from the following Monday.

'I can find a few days more work in Lincoln for your father, my lad,' said Herbert, 'but I shall have to let you go at the end of the week.'

It was later in the week when Will discovered the rotten window ledge at the back of the house. As he delved into it with his bradawl, it crumbled at his touch. The sash-cords were also almost worn through and further rot was discovered inside the sash runners. Will prodded about the lintel above the window and told Clink that he felt that the whole lot would have to be removed and replaced with a new frame. Henry was sent to get some stout timbers to give temporary support to the lintel whilst the rotten frame was removed. Whilst he and Clink were busy sawing them to length in the garden, Henry asked what they were to be used for. Will explained that the window frame was rotten and would have to be removed and burned and that was why they needed the timbers. He thought nothing of it when Henry nodded his head and disappeared inside the building.

Suddenly, there was a loud yell, followed by a resounding crash and the sound of falling bricks, whilst a great cloud of dust and dirt billowed through the cottage door.

Running inside, they found Henry sitting on the floor rubbing his head amidst a heap of rubble, the rotten timber frame around his shoulders and a gaping hole where the window had been. There was dust everywhere and as they dragged Henry to his feet he explained that he had tried to help by removing the window frame.

'You wanted it out, Will,' he said, 'so out it came! 'Course, I didn't know the whole damned house would fall on me!' And he coughed and spluttered as he cleared the dust from his throat. The lintel was still in place and Will directed the placing of the timbers to support the load, wedging them beneath so that they could not easily be knocked down; then he set Clink to clearing the brickwork where the window ledge had been. Clink brushed away the dust and broken stonework and bent down to look into a cavity in the wall.

"Ere, Will', he shouted, 'there's something down 'ere inside the wall.'

Clink reached down, straining to grasp the object and then pulled out a small, stone jar, some six inches in height. He shook it and it rattled. They put the jar on the floor and Will prodded the cork in the top of the jar. It crumbled into dust almost at once. Henry put a piece of board on the floor and Clink poured the contents out onto it.

A shaft of sunlight coming through the window space illuminated the board like a spotlight and they were all quiet for a min-

241.

ute, surveying the contents. Henry picked up one of the gold coins and turned it back and forth in his hands. 'Gold!' he said simply, 'Gold! It's a gold sovereign, tho' it's not like any sovereign I've ever seen before.'

Will took the flat disc of metal from him and examined it carefully. 'It's not a sovereign, it's a gold coin all right, but it's not a sovereign. Look, there's the king on a horse, and the words are all in Latin . . . see,' and he spelled out the words, turning the coin around as he did so, ' . . . C-A-R-O-L-U-S . . . R-E-X . . . Carolus . . . that means Charles . . . and Rex . . . that means King! It's King Charles! I bet it's King Charles the First, the one who was executed!'

'I've 'eard about 'im', said Henry: 'but what would 'e be doin' 'idin' his money in a little cottage like this?'

'No, no,' said Will, 'it doesn't mean that King Charles was in this house. If you stuffed the coins out of your pocket down the wall would it mean that Queen Victoria had lived here? I reckon what it does mean is that this house is older than people think. I bet it was about the time of the civil war between the Roundheads and the Cavaliers.

Just think of it, old Oliver Cromwell and his roundheads are coming down the road to set about Lincoln where all the King's troops are waiting for them. The owner of this house must have been scared stiff and so he hid his money under the window ledge. And there it's been all this time.'

'If I'd 'idden my money, then I'd come back for it,' said Clink. 'Why didn't this chap come back, then?'

'Who knows?' asked Will, 'Perhaps he was killed in the fighting and no one knew where he'd hidden it; perhaps he got knocked on the head and forgot. But here it is, just as he stowed it away about two hundred and fifty years ago.'

'Two hundred and fifty years ago?' said Clink, 'If these coins is that old, then they must be worth something. We can sell 'em in Lincoln and divide the money.'

'No,' said Will, 'these cottages belong to my father and we can do nothing without asking him. It wouldn't be honest to do anything else. Clink, you and your father hitch up the wagon and we'll go back to Motherby Lane and show him what we've found.'

Leaving the coins on the board, Will went out to the field where the old horse was grazing and brought her around for Henry to harness up. Then he went back into the cottage and put the coins back into the jar, counting them as he did so. There were eleven gold coins and seventeen silver ones.

'Here, Clink,' he shouted as he got onto the cart and took the reins, 'you take these until we get into Lincoln.'

When the coins were shown to Herbert, he was not sure of the legal position. As he owned the cottages, did that make him the owner of the coins? Or did they rightfully belong to the person from whom he had purchased the buildings? He went round to see Josiah Otter and was advised that it was up to the law to determine the owner of the coins. Although Herbert was now the rightful owner of the property the coins did not belong to him. The cottages had been purchased from the estate of a gentleman deceased who had died intestate and who, as far as was known, had no living relatives. As Josiah pointed out, if one followed that argument, then every person who had ever lived there during the last three hundred years or so could be held to have a claim to the treasure.

'No, Herbert,' he proclaimed, 'the find must be declared to the police and no doubt there will be an inquest to determine if the coins are treasure trove.'

Will's identification of the coins proved more or less correct. They were all of the reign of Charles I with the exception of two pieces of James I, Charles' predecessor, and one of Elizabeth. The coroner held that the coins were treasure trove as it had obviously been the intention of the original owner to conceal them and return to claim them for his own use at a later date.

'However', continued the coroner, 'the sum of these coins would represent a sum of money such as could not conceivably have belonged to a labourer living in a humble cottage. Perhaps it was some noble person fleeing from Cromwell's troops and fearing capture. Perhaps they were even taken from the corpse of some deceased Royalist and hidden away for fear of discovery by the finder. These facts we shall never know.

The museum authorities have declared a wish to purchase them for their collection and this they are prepared to do at the current market rate which, I gather, is £30 for the eight gold coins and £12 for the seventeen silver ones, a total of £42. It is my decision that the museum shall purchase them at this agreed figure, the proceeds to be divided equally between the owner of the property and the finders.'

Thus Herbert received twenty one pounds and the three lucky finders seven pounds each.

'Only one thing bothers me,' said Will as he and Clink sat on the Waterside discussing their good fortune, 'When I counted those coins I think that there were eleven gold ones, not eight. In fact, I'm sure of it. I counted them twice.' He turned to Clink as if seeking an explanation.

'Well, I ain't 'ad 'em, and that's a fact!' he said, 'All I can think of is that when you threw the jar to me on the cart, some dropped out. After all, the cork was gone and there was only a bit of rag to keep them in. I swear, Will, I 'aven't 'ad 'em! Let's go back to South Carlton. There's long grass in front of the cottages and if they're there, no one could 'ave found 'em.'

When they got to the cottages, the new tenants were tidying the small garden. They had already cut the long grass.

Will introduced himself and said that when they had been working there, he had lost something in the grass. Had they found anything when they cut it? No, said the tenant, he had found nothing at all except all the rubbish that Will and his friends had left behind for him to move. Certainly they had heard about the finding of the hoard, but although they had turned the house and garden inside out, they had found nothing else, much to their sorrow.

'Well, that's it, then,' declared Clink. 'Someone else must 'ave come along and found 'em, and that's the end of that.'

After his generosity to Henry Carrot, Will was surprised when his father took most of the two Carrots' share of the find as payment for the funeral.

'Will, being kind to Carrot was no more than a business transaction. Debts must be paid. Besides, Carrot will feel better now that he's repaid me. No honourable man likes to be in debt, it weighs heavily on his conscience; so, you see, I've really done Carrot a favour by taking the money from him. He'll walk straighter now that he doesn't owe me and his wife'll be pleased as well. Out of debt and he's got work! What more can a man want? Learn the lesson, Will, never owe anyone a penny and you can always walk with your head held high – but if you do owe anyone money, hold on to it to the last minute and make it earn every penny you can afore you part with it!' Thus delivered of this philosophy, Herbert went off down Burton Road to collect an overdue rent from a tenant in dire straits.

It was some three weeks later when Will arrived home from work in the early evening that he found Constable Peasgood sitting in the parlour with his father. The constable went carefully over the details of the find with Will, asking him carefully about every detail and making notes in a laborious hand every now and then.

'You're not going to take my money back, are you?' asked Will.

'No,' said the policeman, 'but I want you to think carefully now and tell me honestly. How many coins were there in that pot?'

Will thought carefully and then said, 'I felt sure I counted eleven gold ones and seventeen silver when we were at the cottage. In fact, I'm certain of it because I counted them twice. But when the museum saw them there were only eight gold coins, although all the silver ones were there.' And he went on to tell the constable how he and Clink had returned to South Carlton to search amongst the grass for the three missing items, but without success.

'Where's young Carrot now?' asked Peasgood.

'I don't know,' said Will, 'I've been at work all day and haven't seen him. He's at home, I suppose.'

'No, he isn't,' said the constable, 'he hasn't been home all day. If he comes here . . . '

'He never comes here,' said Herbert, 'I'm particular who I have in my house!'

'Well, then, if you see 'im tell 'im that I want a word with 'im and if 'e's got any sense 'e'll come round to see me straight away and make a clean breast of it.'

'Clean breast of what?' asked Will. 'What has he done? Is he in trouble?'

'I'm afraid 'e is,' said Peasgood, shaking his head sadly. 'I'm afraid that it's not just a piece of mischief this time, it's real trouble and if I 'ave to go out and find 'im, 'e'll make it ten times worse for 'imself.

Yesterday we had a visit from Mr Frederick Choice; Mr Choice is a pawnbroker and he tells us that early in the morning he was visited by one Edgar Carrot who offered for sale . . . er . . . '(and here he consulted his notebook) ' . . . er . . . one gold 'alf-unite of 'is Majesty King Charles the First . . . er . . . one gold ten-shillings, ditto, and . . . er . . . one gold angel, ditto. I 'asten to add that this 'ere angel ain't no cherub with wings and an 'arp; it is a gold coin of them times. This unite and them two dittos is valued at about fifteen pounds, one of 'em being a rare coin.'

He looked Will straight in the eye and said: 'Now, Will, you don't 'ave to be very brainy to guess where them coins came from, do you?

But it goes a lot deeper than that. Treasure trove is the property of the Queen until she decides what's to be done with it. That's why we tells the coroner; 'e makes the decision on be'alf of the Queen, like. There's no way I can sort this out with a clip across the ear like so many other matters 'e's 'ad 'is 'ands in.

'E's your mate, Will Everton, an' if you see 'im, you bring 'im straight around to me. Understand?'

Will nodded. He felt very miserable indeed for he had long suspected that the three coins had not been lost in the grass.

After tea he hurried round to Gordon Road to find Mrs Carrot in tears and Henry Carrot trying to console her. Of Clink there was no sign at all. He had not been seen since early morning.

Will knew that if Clink would be looking for him anywhere it would be on the Waterside where so many of their boyhood dreams had been discussed. There were parts of the Waterside which were not very pleasant, consisting largely of cheap lodging houses and being the haunt of tramps and vagrants. Some of these men Will knew by sight and he had occasionally given them a copper when he had one to spare. He had never come to any harm there, although he always made sure that he was away from the area before dark.

By the time he got there that evening it was dusk and he made his way gingerly towards Magpies' Bridge, prepared for flight at the first sign of trouble. He had gone as far as he dared and had reluctantly turned towards home when a voice hissed at him from the shadow of a doorway. It was Clink.

They talked for a long time and Clink, after at first denying that he had stolen the coins, eventually admitted it.

'I'd do the same again,' he said, 'I just knew that there'd be some way your father would get that money from us. 'E did nothing, but 'e got half anyway. Then my dad gave 'im nearly all our share as well, an' that's not fair . . . '

Will interrupted him and said: 'Your father didn't give mine anything. He repaid a loan and that's not giving.'

'Maybe not', responded Clink, 'but in the end we was left with bugger all as usual and your father 'ad almost everything. Why shouldn't I 'ave kept some of the coins? I found 'em, didn't I? No matter what you've got, there's always some toff schemin' to get it from you. They even do it to each other, swindlin' an' cheatin' all the time and no thought for working people except to work 'em 'arder and pay 'em less.

It was daft of me to offer them coins to Mr Choice. 'E knew me]cos we've been in his pawnshop many a time. I thought 'e'd just buy 'em and then sell 'em to make a profit like all 'is kind. I never dreamed 'e would go to the police and shop me.'

'Let's go home,' said Will. 'I'm sure that if you apologise it'll all come out right in the end. The best thing to do is to own up and take your punishment like a man, then make a clean start.'

'Aye, like my father,' said Clink. "'E did no more than try to stop his 'ome being sold to pay the rent, but they put 'im in prison all the same an' I watched my mother cry for "im, night after night. Then when 'e came out it 'adn't finished. No one would give 'im work, just 'cos 'e'd been in prison. Lucy knew that when she left us that money. She knew my Dad would never get work and so she gave 'im that money so as we could 'ave just a bit of time without 'avin' to worry 'ow to pay the rent.

There's no clean start for the likes of me, Will. We're meant for prison from the day we're born.'

'What will you do, then?' asked Will.

'I'm goin' to Doncaster,' he said. 'One of the Yorkshire regiments is recruiting there. They don't ask too many questions, I 'ear. They just gets you to take all your clothes off, counts that you've got two of everythin', gives you a shilling and then signs you on. They say that they're off to India soon and nobody's goin' to run after me to India, I'm sure. I'll 'ide out overnight and then get the workman's train early in the morning. That'll look less suspicious than me 'anging around the station 'alf the night.'

'But your mother', said Will, 'and your father. Aren't you going to see them before you go?'

'No,' said Clink, 'that's just what they'd expect me to do. After all that's happened this year, what with Emily dyin' an' everything, if they sent me down my mother would just about be finished. I don't reckon she could stand that. It's better that I leave now. They'll be watching Gordon Road, I'm sure, waitin' for me.

Just make me a promise, Will. Promise that you'll tell them at 'ome where I've gone and why I've done it. Tell my mother I'll write to 'er just as soon as I can. I ain't much at writin', but I reckon as I can find someone to 'elp me. Don't go to see my mother until I've left Lincoln; she'll only try to stop me.

You've been a good friend to me, Will, even though you're clever an' I'm not. I reckon you'll grow up to be a toff, but a proper toff, not like your father, an' I'll be proud to tell people that we're friends.'

248.

Will pressed on Clink the few coppers he had in his pocket and they shook hands. There was a great bond between these two young men and both struggled to hold back a tear.

By now it was getting quite dark and Clink promised to watch Will until he was safely off the Waterside. With a final embrace and promises to write to each other, Will turned his back on his only friend and walked slowly towards High Bridge. He did not look back until he reached the obelisk and then, as he leaned over the parapet, he caught a glimpse of Clink moving back into the shadows. Clink stopped for a moment, waved, and then was gone. Will looked at the pubs along the Waterside, light spilling out from the doors and the windows. From the Labourer's Arms there was the sound of a sing-song and a great deal of laughter and he felt glad that someone could be happy on this sad night.

After a sleepless night, Henry Carrot turned up for work early the next morning to find Herbert waiting for him. Herbert handed him an envelope.

'Here's your money, Carrot,' he said, 'you're fired. I won't have the father of a thief working for me. I treated you well and your son stole from me. You'll never work for me again. Take your thieving ways elsewhere.'

Henry's face went a deep red and he drew himself up to his full height. He towered over Herbert and for a brief second it seemed as if he would grab him and break him in half. Then he took the envelope very slowly and half turned away, then turned back.

'Mr Everton,' he said slowly and deliberately, 'me and Mrs Carrot, we'll never forget 'ow you 'elped us when little Emily died. But I've repaid the money side of that debt, the kindness I 'ave to repay with another kindness an' I'll do that right now.'

'What kindness can you do for me?' asked Herbert.

'The kindness not to break your back, mister, for callin' my lad a thief. But next time, I'll kill you with my own hands; as the good Lord's my witness, I swear it. Now my debt's repaid an' I'll be leavin' you.'

Henry walked away, leaving a pale and shaken Herbert sitting down to recover.

When Clink reached Doncaster he made straight for the recruiting office and presented himself to the officer in charge.

'Come to join the colours, have you?' asked the refined young officer seated behind the desk.

'That's right,' said Clink, 'just show me where I sign on and then I'll be off to the cookhouse for me breakfast; I 'aven't 'ad a bite to eat since last night an' I'm starvin' . . . an' me uniform, I could do with that 'cos I've got 'oles in me boots and the arse is damn nigh out of me breeches!'

The portly recruiting sergeant, face as red as the sash around his shoulders, came around from behind the desk, grabbed Clink by the collar and tapped him on the head with his swagger stick to emphasise every word spoken.

'When (crack!) you (crack!) speaks to the (crack!) hofficer (crack!) you calls 'im (crack!) SIR! You also (crack!) stands to hattention (crack!) hat hall times, me lad (crack!)'

Clink rubbed his head and wondered whether joining the army had been such a good idea after all. At the same time he had visions of the Greetwell Road prison and remembered some of the stories told by his father about the place and decided that anything was preferable to that.

The officer took up his pen, dipped it in the inkwell, and asked Clink, 'What's your name, lad?'

'Broke,' he said and then, seeing the sergeant's raised cane, 'Broke, SIR! Broke by name and broke by nature, sir, I ain't got a copper!'

'Christian name?' was the next question. 'John, sir.'

'Address?'

'Ain't got one, sir. That's why I want to join the army. To 'ave mates and somewhere to belong. I'm an orphan, sir, an' as long as I can remember I ain't 'ad nowhere to live.' Clink had taken a long time to invent his story and he had it off word perfect.

'How old are you?' asked the officer.

'Nineteen, sir,' answered Clink as the officer looked him up and down and had no hesitation in accepting that as his age.

250.

'In the event of anything happening to you, whom do you wish to be informed?' was the next question. It was one that Clink had not anticipated.

'Eh?' he said.

'Who do we write to if the henemy blows your bleedin' 'ead orf?' roared the sergeant.

The officer put on a pained expression and held his hand to his head, pen poised. 'As you are an orphan, I presume there is no one you wish to nominate as your next of kin in the event of your death?'

Clink had a brainwave.

'There's an aunt was once very kind to me when I was small,' he said, putting on a look of concentration intended to convey the impression that he was thinking very hard. 'Funny name, she 'ad, what was it now? Ah, yes, that's it! Carrot! Mrs Carrot, Gordon Road, Lincoln! If I snuffs it, you can tell 'er!' Clink was quite pleased with himself for thinking of this.

'Birth certificate?' asked the officer. 'Ain't got one, sir. Ain't never 'ad one.'

'Then how do you know how old you are, Broke?'

'They told me at the workhouse, sir. Me mother brought me there just after I was born. It was winter, sir, snowin' 'ard as 'ell and she was stiff as a board, frozen solid, but she 'ad me all wrapped up snug an' warm. As they took me from 'er, she dropped dead on the floor without saying a word. So you see, sir, I ain't got no birth certificate, just the date I went into the work 'ouse, 'an I can't remember that.'

'Any trouble with the police?' was the next question.

Despite himself, Clink gave a noticeable gulp and before he could answer the officer shot another question at him.

'Are you wanted by the police for anything serious, such as assault or violence of any kind?'

'No, sir,' answered Clink truthfully.

The two soldiers exchanged glances as Clink stood before them. The officer noticed that the boy's hands were trembling slightly and seemed about to say something, then changed his mind and pushed the form across the desk.

'If you can write, sign your name there. If you can't write, put a cross. Then the sergeant will ask you some more questions and take you to the medical officer who will examine you. Subject to a satisfactory examination, you will be accepted into the Regiment.'

A few days later Will received a letter from Doncaster. The message was very simple. 'I have joined the Army; your friend, Private John Broke.' He took the card around to Gordon Road and showed it to Mr and Mrs Carrot and only then did they know what had happened to their son.

'I'm sorry I didn't tell you earlier', he said, 'but you might have tried to get Clink back and he could never have lived in prison. I know that. Clink hates being cooped up anywhere and he wouldn't have survived. He'd have done something desperate.'

Will had two brief letters during the remainder of the year and then just before Christmas Clink wrote that his Christmas Day would be spent at sea as the Regiment would be sailing from Liverpool for India. Suddenly Will felt very lonely. At least with Clink in Yorkshire he had lived in hopes that perhaps, when the matter of the coins had faded into the past, Clink could come home on leave and that eventually he would leave the army and their friendship would be resumed. India was so far away that even a letter took weeks to arrive.

He visited the Carrots frequently. They were barely scraping by. In his own way Clink had always managed to contribute something to the household budget each week. Such work as came Henry's way was of a temporary nature and they barely scraped by from week to week. Even if food or coal went short, the rent was always paid. Henry never intended to be indebted to Herbert again in his life and after their last meeting he felt sure that Herbert would not hesitate to throw them into the street at the slightest excuse. With three children still to support there was little joy in the Carrot household that Christmas. One child dead and one on his way to the other end of the earth added a terrible burden that was hard to bear.

Always there was the thought of the workhouse and of the social stigma attached to entering its doors. When Henry passed the entrance drive at the bottom of Burton Road he would push back his shoulders and mutter to himself, 'Over my dead body!' and doggedly resume the search for work.

Will would occasionally give Mrs Carrot a florin or half crown. She would always refuse the money, which he was careful not to offer in front of her husband, but Will would press it upon her and she would eventually give in, saying: 'All right, then, Will, just this once. But it's a loan, mind you, and I'll give it back just as soon as 'Enry gets proper work.' A couple of times Will even said that he had received money for her from Clink and that this had been sent to him in case the police were still trying to track Clink down. Will wasn't really sure whether soldiers could send money from India, but Mrs Carrot never doubted his word.

With his only friend gone, more and more of his time would now be spent working on extra jobs put in his way by acquaintances. If you needed a door re-hanging or a couple of fine oak bookshelves, then Will would do a good job in the evening at a very keen price. He liked working with wood and did not find it tiresome after his day's work. In fact he rather liked the freedom to take his own time and to work without Simon Groom forever peering over his shoulder.

The money he earned from these jobs was carefully hoarded away in a secret compartment he had constructed for himself beneath the floorboards of his bedroom. He had had to work on the hiding place when the house was empty and it was beautifully made. The end of a floorboard was fitted with a concealed hinge beneath the skirting board. Pressure on the board caused the far end of it to rise on the hinge, revealing a tin box hidden between the joists. Will never went into his hiding place if anyone was in the house and was taking no chances of anyone finding it. When he took out money to buy the Carrot family presents that Christmas of 1892, he still had more than fifteen pounds left. This was a very considerable sum of money. The seven pounds awarded to him by the coroner had gone to his father and he had never seen it since.

In February of the following year there was a bitter winter spell with deep snow. Outdoor workers were laid off and many had to swallow their pride and present themselves at the workhouse gates. Things were desperate with the Carrot family and they had reached the stage where there was not even fire in the grate and Mrs Carrot was trying to keep the children warm by playing games, running round and round the tiny house to keep warm. Even then, when she stopped to gain breath, she would hear the plaintive cry, 'I'm cold and I'm hungry.'

Coming across this pathetic scene on his way home from work one evening, Will made straight home for his secret hiding place so that he might take some of his money to help them.

The tin box was empty. Not a single copper remained. He stood open-mouthed, the tin box in his hand. He turned to find Martha standing in the doorway. 'It's in the bank,' she snapped. 'It's in the bank. Not in your name, mind, it's in the firm's account.'

Will felt himself boiling with rage.

'I met Mrs Wainfleet in the market yesterday,' said Martha. 'She told me what a lovely job you'd made of the little bedside cabinet for her and how you'd mended the broken sashcords in her next door neighbour's parlour window. On my way home I checked the workshop job book. There was no mention of either Mrs Wainfleet or her neighbour, nor was there any record of the money they'd given you in the cashbook. I did a bit of checking around. Seems you've been doing quite a few little jobs on your own.'

'What I do in my own time is my own business,' fumed Will. 'How dare you take my money? I earned that with my own hands in my own time. Not a single penny belongs to the firm. Who told you where I kept the money?'

'I just looked,' said Martha. 'I figured if you were so clever with your hands, you'd have made somewhere to hide what you've stolen.'

'I didn't steal that money!' shouted Will. 'It was mine. It didn't belong to you and you had no right to take it.'

254.

'I'd every right to take it,' snapped Martha.' All the materials you used came from our workshop. Every bit of wood, every nail, and every screw was stolen from us, from your father and me. You're no better than that Carrot boy. You're a thief just like him.'

'I'm no thief,' yelled Will. 'Every nail I took from the workshop was paid for, aye, and every bit of timber. I paid Mr Groom for every single bit and you'll find it in the cash book under "Sundry Receipts". Now, give me back my money!'

'I've told you,' was the response, 'it's our money. You used the skills your father taught you to cheat him out of business. I don't care anything for your "Sundry Receipts" story and Simon Groom will say whatever I tell him to say. If I was your father, I'd kick you out of the house; but he's too soft by half.'

The conversation was halted by the sound of the front door slamming and Herbert came storming up the stairs.

'Ye Gods and little fishes,' he bellowed, 'what the hell is going on in this house? I could hear the pair of you bawling at each other half a mile away!'

Martha told him her story, which Will hotly denied, but his father silenced him immediately.

'The name of this firm is Herbert Everton,' he said. 'It's not Everton and Son, nor will it ever be. There's no working for yourself in this house. You work for me. I pay your wages and give you your board and lodgings. Do it again and I'll turf you out, neck and crop.'

He pulled out his purse and threw half a sovereign on the floor.

'There's pay for your labour in doing the work,' he said. 'The rest belongs to me. And you, woman, don't be presuming to put money in the bank without my say so. I've made sure you can't take it out, so I'm damned if I'll have you putting it in behind my back. You've gone too far this time and don't damn well interfere again.

Now, where's my dinner? It's bloody freezing outside, there's barely a glow in the grate inside and I'm bloody well clemmed. You, Will, go downstairs and build up the fire. Martha, get my meal ready.'

He bawled down the stairs, 'Annie! Get off your arse and stop tinkling on that flaming piano. I could fart a better tune! Go in the kitchen and help your mother and before you do that, pour me out a brandy.'

When Herbert was in this kind of rage no one was immune from a tongue-lashing.

Herbert stormed off down the stairs muttering to himself, 'Bloody women! They're only good for one thing! Bloody children, a pain up the arse from start to finish!'

Martha looked at Will, a grim smile of satisfaction on her thin lips.

'That'll teach you,' she said, 'I hope he does throw you out. Cheating your own mother and father like that. It's disgraceful.'

Will looked her straight in the face.

'I went to the service at Saxon Street Methodist Church last Sunday', he said, 'and the minister said he could see good in everyone; even murderers had some good in them if you looked for it. I don't reckon there's any good in you. You're mean and spiteful and wicked. As for being my mother, I'd hoped you would be when my father first said he was marrying you. But I remember you cracking me across the leg with that stick of yours when you came back from Mablethorpe. You couldn't be a mother to anyone; you'd rob a starving child in the gutter, let alone mother one.'

Martha turned white and took a step towards him, hand raised.

'And I'll tell you what I told my father,' continued Will, 'you ever strike me again and I'll knock you to the floor, woman or no.'

He picked up the half sovereign and left the house, muffling himself up against the biting wind which swirled the snow into drifts at the side of the road. He went into the shed at the side of the house and tied up a bundle of sticks, then put a few lumps of coal into a canvas bag. On the Bail, he was just in time to catch Brummitt's before closing. Having bought a chicken and some vegetables and fruit, he found a sweetshop and tobacconist still open and bought an ounce of tobacco for Henry and a tin of toffees for Mrs Carrot and the children and went back to Gordon Road, where he was greeted like the saviour he undoubtedly was.

After the meal, and with the children safely asleep, Henry sat in his armchair, puffing away at his pipe, whilst Mrs Carrot tried to mend the childrens' threadbare clothes yet again. The fire was glowing merrily, for whilst Will had lit it and Mrs Carrot was preparing the meal, Henry had gone down to the coalyard and carried a hundredweight sack on his back through the driving snow, a prodigious feat which would have defeated lesser men. For the moment the Carrot family was not hungry and for a day or two at least, they would not be cold.

'Will,' said Henry, when he had heard the story of the missing money, 'I'm mindful of your kindness to us and always will be. Me an' the missus is always glad to see you and we feel for you like one of our own, 'specially now that Clink's not at 'ome. You could stay 'ere with us, but I think that your father would 'ave the law drag you back again, so there's no point in it. I don't know what we could do to help, lad.'

'It's not long to my eighteenth birthday', said Will, 'and I've already worked out what I want to do then. Now I've no money, it's going to be a lot harder, but I'll still do it.'

'Well, whatever it is, and per'aps it's as well we don't know, good luck to you, Little Will,' said Mrs Carrot, 'Perhaps when you're eighteen, things 'll turn for the better. Oh, in all the excitement I forgot to tell you, Will, we've 'ad a letter from Clink – mind you, I don't think as he wrote it, 'cos it's too good for 'im to 'ave written – anyway, 'e's arrived in India safe and sound.

'Ere we are, freezing to death, an' out there the sun boils your brains all day and them 'eathens is runnin' round with no clothes on. It's a funny old world an' no mistake. Anyway, 'e says that it's safe to write now 'cos 'e reckons that the police won't want to drag 'im back all the way from India an' 'e says that Constable Peasgood is too fat to last out there. 'E says 'e'd melt in the sun!'

They all had a good laugh and by the time it came for Will to go home he felt a little brighter, although he was still seething over the loss of his money.

When he stepped out into the street the wind had died down and it had stopped snowing. There was a clear bright moon up above, the gleaming snow reflecting the light until it seemed almost as bright as day. His feet made a satisfying crunching sound and when he reached Bailgate, he hesitated and then turned right instead of left, walking down to the front of the Cathedral. As he stood there, the great bell chimed the hour and shimmers of snow powdered down from the tower, shaken loose by the vibration. Will looked at the stars, radiant in the clear sky, and for some inexplicable reason thought of Lucy Matchbox and turned his steps towards the Old Harlequin.

He stood outside the inn and looked up at the little window which had marked Lucy's old room. The cranberry coloured oil lamp had gone and the curtains were drawn, but he could still remember clearly the time that he and Clink had first met there. Now they were parted, perhaps for ever. An idea crossed his mind and suddenly he felt that he had the answer to his problems.

'Thank you, Lucy,' he said, touching his cap to the dark window and turned on his heels and hurried home.

Winter turned to spring and Will's eighteenth birthday was reached. He worked all day at Motherby Lane as usual, but when he left he found the workmen waiting for him at the end of the lane.

One of them stepped towards him and said: 'Master Will, we know it's your birthday and the lads and me, we'd like to ask you to come for a drink with us. You're old enough to go in the pub now and we hope you'll come wi' us and let us drink your health.'

Will didn't know quite what to say. He had always got on well with the workmen, although he had never been able to build up a relationship with anyone similar to that which he had had with old Walter. Although he worked the same as them and neither asked for nor received any privileges, he was still the master's son and as such the men had never really felt him to be one of them. He noticed that Simon Groom was not present and asked where he was.

'He chose not to come wi' us,' said the spokesman. 'Said as it

258.

would make your father mad to see his son drinking with the workpeople. We said we didn't mind that. If 'e finds out we'll know who's told 'im and 'e can't very well sack the lot of us. We told Mr Groom where 'e could stick 'is bowler 'at an' 'e went off in a huff. We're going to the Duke William on Newport, Will, on account of Sam 'ere is courtin' the servin' maid there an' the walk'll give us a thirst for the ale. Poor old Sam! 'E asn't seen 'er since last night and 'e's fair pinin' away!'

They all laughed and Sam took a swipe at those round him as they chided him all the way to the inn. His lady love turned out to be a buxom girl with long, dark hair and flashing brown eyes and it was very easy to see why Sam was pinin' away.'

She looked at Will's five feet three inches and shook her head in dismay. 'Sam Carter', she said, 'you'll get me thrown out if I serve 'im – 'e ain't eighteen years of age, not by a long chalk.' She stood firm on her decision until the landlord appeared on the scene. He knew Herbert by reputation although not as a customer and told the girl to serve Will, whom he recognised as Herbert's son.

Foaming tankards in hand the men stood in a circle around Will and Sam Carter proposed a toast.

'To Little Will — beggin' your pardon, master Will — a happy birthday an' may 'e grow up to be a better boss than his father!'

'That's not fair on the lad,' said one of them, 'It ain't for us to criticise the gaffer in front of his son, nor to turn the lad against 'is father. Let's just make it "Appy Birthday" and 'ave done. 'Appy Birthday, Will lad, an' many of 'em.'

Will thanked them all and took a draught from his tankard. Since his drinking bout with Clink he had been careful not to touch beer at all, but told himself that one drink on the way home from work could not do much harm. 'Mind you,' he said, 'I haven't got enough money to buy you all a drink in return today, but I will buy you one soon.'

Gradually the men drifted off home to their meal until only Will and Sam were left. Will had deliberately made his beer spin out so that he would not have to accept a second and Sam was hanging on because of the girl. Seeing that only the two of them were left, two men who had been sitting in the far corner came towards them.

'Ain't you the one that found them gold coins?' said one of them. 'I 'ear you got more than a hundred quid each for that lot. Wish it 'ad been me that found 'em. Seein' as you got all that money for nothin' and as 'ow your father is a rich man, you won't mind buyin' us workin' chaps a drink, will you?'

Sam Carter made to interfere but the second man stood between him and Will.

'I got seven pounds, not hundreds,' said Will, 'and in fact I've never even seen that; my father kept it. As for buying you a drink, Sam here will tell you that I've not got money to buy you anything, and even if I had, I wouldn't.'

Sensing what was developing, the barmaid ran into the back room for the landlord.

'Cocky young bugger, ain't you?' spat the ruffian. 'Too good for the likes of us, eh? You're no bigger than three 'aporth o' coppers, you little toff. You're no better than that mate o' yours whose Dad's always in jail. 'E's a thief, wanted by the law. Oh, yes, you can make friends with thieves, but not with honest working men. You're no better than a thief yourself!'

Will's right fist shot out straight into the man's left eye, knocking him backwards onto the floor. At the same time Sam Carter grabbed the second man, but not before he had caught Will a blow on the back of the head which sent him dizzy and knocked him into a bench, bruising his face. As the first man got to his feet, his eye already swelling, the landlord arrived with the cellarman. They made a formidable pair and soon had the two thrown outside on the pavement. Will was still sitting amongst the sawdust, shaking his head, Sam Carter regarding with alarm the bruise on Will's cheek.

'I think you'd best be off 'ome, young man,' said the landlord, 'Your father won't thank me for 'aving you 'ere after that little scrap. I'm glad I arrived in time to see that straight right. It was as good as a prizefight.'

260.

'I'll take you 'ome, master Will,' said Sam, 'tho' 'eaven knows what your father'll say about this.'

Will scrambled to his feet, a sorry sight, his clothes covered with sawdust, a bruised cheek and still shaking his head which rang like the cathedral bells.

'That's all right, Sam,' he said, 'I can find my own way home.'

An elderly man who had been sitting quietly in a corner with his drink and a newspaper came forward and brushed Will down with his hands.

'You could do with a wash and a brush on your clothes,' he said. 'Also, I think a spot of goose grease on that face might well relieve the swelling, whilst the lump on your head needs some attention.' He prodded both the bruise and the lump as he spoke and Will jumped away from him. 'I live just across the road on Tompitt Lane, possibly known to you, young sir, as East Bight,' continued the man, 'I'm sure that my wife would be pleased to dress your wounds, most honourably gained in protecting your reputation! If you have any doubts as to my character, mine host here will undoubtedly vouch for my good intentions.'

'I'd go with Mr Fletcher if I was you,' said the landlord. 'Like 'e says, 'e only lives over the road and you can't go 'ome in that state! Mind you, your 'ead will probably ache all the more tryin' to understand all those big words he uses all the time. You can tell 'e used to be a school master.'

'We have the most beautiful language in the world, landlord,' responded Mr Fletcher, putting his arm around Will's shoulders. 'Would that we would all use it, rather than abuse it, sir.'

Will accompanied Mr Fletcher over to East Bight and into the cottage where he lived, where Mrs Fletcher bathed his wounds and applied liberal dressings of goose grease. Then, sitting in a chair by a small fire to take the chill off the evening air, he enjoyed a mug of steaming tea and a slice of Mrs Fletcher's delicious fruit cake. In conversation it turned out that this was the same Mr Fletcher who had seen Spring Heeled Jack on top of Newport Arch the previous year and Will forgot his aches and pains as he described his own meeting with Jack in Newport cemetery.

'Bless my soul!' exclaimed Mrs Fletcher. 'That was a lucky escape you had and no mistake. I wonder whatever happened to Spring Heeled Jack. He's never been seen since that day, not hide nor hair of him. Probably we shall never know whether he was man or beast.'

Will kept a discreet silence and said that it was time he went home.

'You've both been very kind,' he said. 'I know you don't expect payment for your kindness, but I notice that you need a new sneck on the door and a couple of palings in the fence at the front of your garden. I'll be pleased to do those jobs for you.'

'There, mother,' said Mr Fletcher, 'What have I always said? Cast your bread upon the waters and it shall be repaid a thousandfold. Young man, I would appreciate that. Though there are those who would say that Joshua Fletcher has been well-endowed in the matter of brains, those who told the truth would equally say that his hands served little purpose except to convey food to his mouth! Will, I confess that if I were to try to nail two pieces of wood together, I should undoubtedly split them. Your offer is accepted with our thanks, although you must let me pay for the wood and any other materials.'

'I really would have to charge you for the wood, Mr Fletcher,' said Will, and added hastily: 'Not that I want to.' And he told the Fletchers the story of his savings and their confiscation. Despite having expressed his intention of going home, he found himself relating the story of his life and it soon became apparent to the Fletchers that he was not a happy young man, particularly since his only friend had left Lincoln to join the army. He told them in some detail of his endeavour to run away to sea and how his father had pursued him to Boston and brought him back home again.

'I'm still going to leave home,' he said. 'I don't intend to spend the rest of my life working for coppers for my father. I know that I'm a good craftsman. I just love working with wood and I can make things that people like to buy, nice things that they're proud to have in their homes. To tell the truth, I was saving that money to leave home and now it seems that I shall never have any money until I'm twenty-one and inherit my hundred pounds . . . . That means I have to work for my father another three years unless I do something now. Anyway, I've got an idea . . . '

Then he became silent and no one pried into his secret.

As he left the cottage Mrs Fletcher invited him to call for tea the following week as their niece, Polly, would be visiting them from Stafford. Mrs Fletcher explained that Polly's mother had died very suddenly, her father having passed away some years ago.

'Apart from a sister who is married, we are her only relatives,' said Mrs Fletcher. 'Mr Fletcher is her mother's brother, of course. She will probably be staying with us for some time and we are very anxious for her to have some young friends about her. Do say that you will come to meet her. She will be just as lonely as you seem to be.'

The following Saturday, Josiah Otter looked in his diary and saw that his clerk had penned a note to the effect that he had made an appointment for Mr Everton to consult with him at three o'clock that afternoon. Josiah was very surprised when he found that his client was Will rather than his father.

'Before I say a great deal', said Will, 'I understand that anything I say to you as my solicitor is in confidence and that you will not repeat it to anyone, even to my father; in fact, particularly to my father. I want you to promise me that, Mr Otter.'

Josiah conjured a silk handkerchief from up his sleeve, took a perfunctory pinch of snuff, and gazed out at the Cathedral towers before answering.

'It is true that dealings between a solicitor and his client are always held in confidence, unless there is a grave breach of the law, of course, but there are two things I would have to consider before I could give you advice.

Firstly, I have not yet agreed to be your solicitor; secondly, I have advised your father for some years now and I could not possibly act for you if by so doing I were to be acting against your father's best interests. That would not be proper at all. Perhaps it

263.

would be better if you were to tell me the nature of your problem and then I could say whether I would be able to assist you.'

'It's about my money,' said Will, 'the money that Lucy left me; the hundred pounds.'

Josiah held up his hand for silence and went to a cabinet from which he drew a bulky file and took out a small notebook. Returning to his desk he opened the book, secured his spectacles on the end of his nose and gave a loud 'Hrummmph!' as he studied the pages. Then he took his pen and made some quick calculations.

'In accordance with the wishes of my client, the late Miss Lucinda Letitia Hathergood-Smythe, I have invested the sum of one hundred pounds for you as instructed. According to my calculations that one hundred pounds, thanks to my strenuous efforts on your behalf, is now worth at this moment . . . er . . . er . . . approximately one hundred and twenty four pounds, four shillings and eightpence three farthings – less my fees of course. This is an appreciation of approximately three per cent, Will, a tidy building up of your fortune.

In matters appertaining to your inheritance, I can advise you, as in that respect I am acting on the instructions given to me by my late client, Miss Hathergood-Smythe, to protect your interests. Therefore I am technically not accepting instructions from you, if you follow me.'

'I don't see that it matters a jot whose instructions you are following Mr Otter, as long as they can pay your bill,' was the response.

Josiah Otter took off his spectacles and placed them on the desk in front of him. He wiped his pen nib carefully with a piece of blotting paper, wiped the edge of the inkwell, and then sat back in his chair, hands together on his chest and fingers drumming at each other. He looked up towards Heaven and gave a loud sigh.

'Ah,' said he, 'would that life were so simple, Will! There are professional ethics to be followed, I am afraid . . . *"Verbum sat sapienti"* . . . which translated means: "A word to the wise is enough."' And he winked one eye.

'I don't speak foreign languages, Mr Otter,' said Will, 'but I'm sure you're right. Now about my hundred and twenty five pounds . . .'

Josiah held up his hand again. 'One hundred and twenty four pounds, four shillings and eightpence three farthings . . . er . . . less my fees, of course.'

'Of course,' said Will. 'About my money. Can I have it now?'

The spectacles were replaced on the end of his nose and Josiah peered incredulously over the top of them at Will. 'Have it now? Have it now!' he repeated: 'Absolutely not, sir! Miss Hathergoode-Smythe's instructions in that respect were quite clear. You are to receive the money when you reach twenty one years of age, not before.' He put the file back in the cabinet, closing the door with a bang as if to terminate the matter.

'Mr Otter,' persisted Will, 'if Lucy said that you were to act in my best interests and it was in my best interests to have the money now, rather than in three years, wouldn't that be reason enough to give it to me?'

'It might,' said Josiah, 'but only under the most extreme circumstances. What YOU judge to be in your best interests might differ very greatly from my own opinion; and my opinion is final. My client's will made that very clear, no doubt realising that young men are very headstrong. However, *errare est humanum*, as they say. Explain to me why you want the money now.'

When Will had explained, Josiah thought for a few moments, dabbed his nose with the silk handkerchief and then shook his head.

'No, sir,' he said, 'I could not release the money to you on that basis. What you propose to engage upon is a speculative venture, by no means liable to succeed. Secondly, it might be held that such a course of action would be very definitely against your father's best interests and against whom I could not possibly act. Thirdly, and this I believe to be the nub of the matter, you are still a minor in the eyes of the law and will be held to be so until you reach your majority.'

Josiah was not unmindful of what Will was trying to achieve

and secretly had every sympathy with his endeavours. He looked across the desk and saw the disappointment on the young face before him. The deep brown eyes flared with anger as well as discontent, and there was already a ruddy flush to his face. 'Like father, like son,' thought Josiah.

Out loud he said: 'However, I believe that there is a middle course in all things and there can be no doubt that your inheritance represents a tangible asset against which a suitable person might be inclined to advance a loan. In all probability they would demand a first charge against your capital and most certainly would demand a rate of interest which would rapidly eat away the gains which I have so carefully and diligently acquired for you.

Whether it would be proper for any establishment to advance a loan to a minor under such circumstances is open to doubt and about that I cannot comment for the reasons which I have explained.'

He put a sheet of paper before him, dipped his pen into the inkwell and, resting his hand across a sheet of blotting paper, wrote a short letter. This he placed in an envelope which he sealed and then wrote a name and address on the front. He handed it to Will.

'Take this to that gentleman and explain your proposition. I give you no assurance that you will succeed, however, but do not hesitate to remind him that you made a fine corner cabinet for his wife last year.' A flicker of a smile crossed the solicitor's face. The story of Will's endeavours to do work on his own account and the eventual fate of his money had been recounted by Herbert in the White Hart on more than one occasion.

Josiah wiped the pen and the inkwell as Will stood to his feet. He shook the young man's hand and wished him well. Will was almost through the door when he suddenly turned and said with a grin: 'Don't forget, Mr Otter, less your fee, less your fee . . . '

The solicitor sighed and flipped back the lid of the inkwell yet again. He opened his day book and wrote in his slow and deliberate copperplate hand, 'Master William Everton: to consultation and advice, the sum of two shillings and threepence. To be debited against his account with this house.' On reflection he thought that perhaps Will's idea had a little more merit than he had given it credit for and crossed out 'two shillings and threepence' with a neat, straight line and replaced it with 'three shillings'. Then he wiped his pen and inkwell all over again.

By the time that Will had experienced his second interview it was quite late in the afternoon. He had to get to Burton to see Grandfather William that evening and was lucky to get a lift on a farm cart travelling that way. He sat up front with the driver and, lulled by the pleasant evening sunshine, allowed his mind to wander on what might be. Before he realised it, they were in the village main street and he was bidding the driver farewell.

Grandfather William had always promised him that, when he retired, Will should have his tools. Will had now come to ask him whether he might have just one or two pieces almost immediately. He had some of his own tools, oddments he had purchased at the pawnbrokers shops or been given by friends, but in the main he had to rely upon the firm's tools from the workshop and this did not satisfy his future needs.

The old man was tidying his garden when Will arrived and he got a warm welcome, for his grandfather had a genuine affection for him.

'I didn't expect to see you today, Will,' he exclaimed, 'We're all coming to tea tomorrow to celebrate your birthday. You're getting quite a man now, aren't you?'

Will felt embarrassed to ask his grandfather for the tools, but now that he had made up his mind there was no turning back. They were sitting on the garden seat in front of the cottage window, the old man enjoying the warmth of the evening. He did not give Will an immediate answer but seemed deep in thought as he filled his pipe and lit it, watching the fragrant blue smoke disappear towards the sky.

Eventually he spoke.

'Will, a man's life is just like a summer day. You get up at the crack of dawn and watch that great, red sun rise over the fields and you wonder what lies ahead for you. Then, as the day goes on, you get wrapped up in your work and nothing seems to matter except the thing you're doing at that moment. All sorts of things happen during that day, some good, some bad, but eventually it comes to an end and the sun goes down again, just like it's done every day since the good Lord made the earth and everything on it.

What I'm really saying, Will, is that I'm an old man now, well past sixty and every day when I watch the sun go down I know that there won't be a great many more sunsets for me. What days I have left, I want to spend in peace and quiet with your grand-mother. I've saved a little bit and this cottage is paid for. All my children are off my hands except Fanny and I doubt she'll ever marry, so when we're both gone she'll get this cottage and every-thing in it.'

His lips broke into a sly smile.

'That'll upset your father! But if he never earned another penny I reckon he's got enough to last for a few years. I always intended you to have my tools, Will, so take what you need and the rest you can have just as soon as I've tidied up the odd couple of jobs I have on hand. You might as well have the benefit of them now as when I'm dead. When I fancy a bit of work to keep my hand in, I'll come to you and borrow them back again!'

They went into the house and Grandfather William opened his tool cabinet. To Will there was no more beautiful sight than the row upon row of tools which now lay before his eyes. Some of the tools were more than a hundred years old and had been handed down from father to son with loving care. The wooden handles had been stained with a century of sweat and hard work and no-where could the most minute inspection have found a speck of rust.

Grandfather picked up a chisel and turned it this way and that so that it caught the light coming through the window. He tested the edge with his thumb and nodded with satisfaction.

'This was my own grandfather's,' he said. 'It must have been almost an inch longer when it was new, when he was an appren-tice. I can't remember how many times it's been sharpened in my lifetime, but it could tell some tales if it could speak.'

He picked up another and examined it carefully, putting it tenderly back in its place and suddenly Will realised the magnitude of the gift which he was to receive from the old man. They were not just his tools, they were also his memories. Will was about to say something, but the old man was lost in his dreams. He picked up a tenon saw and turned to his wife.

'Do you remember this, mother?' he asked.

Ann smiled her shy smile and nodded.

'I bought that with my first week's wages when I'd done my apprenticeship; and this, just look at this.' He picked up a claw hammer. 'Do you remember, I was working with this when you came out of the house and told me you were expecting our Herbert. I was so shaken I hit my blasted thumb with it. My God, it was painful, turned black and blue it did.' They both laughed.

Will took the old man by the arm.

'I'm sorry, grandfather,' he said, 'it was very selfish of me. I couldn't possibly take your tools. They mean too much to you.'

The rheumy old eyes looked straight into his and old William smiled.

'Rubbish, lad. You shall have them and when you're married and got a home of your own, I shall come and visit you and mother and me will look into your tool cabinet and remember our memories and you can tell us yours. Besides, I've a feeling that something's afoot with you. I've never known you to ask me for anything since the day you were born.'

'I'll tell you tomorrow, I promise,' said Will.

The birthday party was not a very jolly occasion. Martha brooded over everything in her long, black dress and seemed to frown on everyone. She had been against the birthday celebration when Herbert had first decreed that it would take place. According to her, it was positively wicked to enjoy yourself on the Sabbath. However, Herbert had been determined. He had sensed that Will's character had changed tremendously over the last few months and had suddenly realised what an asset to the business he really was. The confiscation of the money by Martha he realised to have been a gross error but, having got his hands on it, it was totally against his nature to give it back.

At her father's insistence, Annie had baked a birthday cake. It had failed to rise on one side and presented a peculiarly lop-sided appearance. The almond paste was gritty and the icing was bone hard and splintered at the first touch of the knife. The whole confection shouted aloud the lack of interest which had gone into its making and the largest proportion remained uneaten upon the plates.

Will thanked everyone for their presents, noting that neither his father nor Martha had apparently given him anything.

'Thought I'd forgotten you, didn't you?' said his father. Will said nothing.

Herbert drew from his pocket a small brown envelope which he gave to Will.

'Will, you're such a good worker that I've decided that you shall not wait until you are twenty one to get full money. As from tomorrow you're on a man's full wages. Twenty five shillings a week! Now then, lad, how's that for a birthday present, a full week's wages in advance? Now you're really a member of the firm!'

Will hesitated and then put the envelope in his pocket. He seemed to be thinking very carefully what he should say. At last he spoke.

'Thank you, father,' he said, 'I'll keep the wage packet because it will go a little way to make up for the money that was stolen from me. As for being a member of the firm, I have to tell you that I'm going into business on my own account.

Will you want me to work a week's notice, father?'

270.

CHAPTER EIGHT

THE END OF ONE FRIENDSHIP . . .
AND THE BEGINNING OF ANOTHER

THE SMALL RECONNAISSANCE PATROL had turned for base an hour ago and was now wending its way down a rocky valley with steep boulder-strewn slopes on each side. They had been away from camp for more than a day following an intelligence report of armed insurgent tribesmen who had been seen in the area, but they had found nothing. During the worst heat of the day Lieutenant Greenwood normally ordered a rest, but for a reason which he could not explain he felt very tense and nervous and, amid much grumbling under their breath from the men, he had allowed them to stop only for a brief meal at midday. Earlier that morning he had thought that he had caught the glimpse of the sun reflecting on something high up the hill, but a careful examination through his field glasses had failed to reveal the source and this did nothing to quell his unease.

For Private John Broke this was his first patrol. He had been told all about soldiering in India whilst he was in training at Richmond, but never in all his wildest dreams had he imagined that the heat would be like this. When they had stopped to eat, he had touched the metal of his pack and almost burned his fingers on the buckle. He was dry and parched and his water bottle was almost empty whilst his feet seemed so swollen that he was sure he would never be able to take off his boots. He looked at the officer mounted on his horse.

'Bloody toffs again!' he muttered to himself. "'E rides an 'orse an' we sweat our bollocks off walking.'

It seemed almost as if Mr Greenwood had read his thoughts for he signalled a halt and turned to his men.

'Another fifteen minutes or so and we shall be out of this valley and by the stream. Then we can fill our water bottles and you can dip your feet for ten minutes.'

There was a muffled cheer at this announcement and the refreshing thought of the cool water ahead. They had passed the spot on their way out the previous day. The stream tumbling down from the hillside widened out into a deep pool and the water was icy cold from the mountain snows above. Clink pulled back his shoulders and marched a little faster.

There was a puff of smoke from the left, a sharp crack and the officer's horse dropped dead, catapulting Mr Greenwood over its neck onto the ground and dazing him. Then firing broke out from both sides and the men scattered for cover, but they were caught in a withering cross fire where there was little cover and the well concealed tribesmen gave little target to shoot at.

Lieutenant Greenwood staggered to his feet and drew his revolver. He looked about him and quickly assessed that if they stayed where they were it was only a matter of time before they were annihilated. He glanced desperately from side to side and spotted a narrow defile leading off the valley. It appeared to rise steeply at the far end and terminate in a cave under the cliff face.

He pointed to it and shouted above the confusion to make for the cave.

'Bring your water bottles,' he yelled at the top of his voice. 'Don't leave them behind.' And he charged for the defile waving his men on. He never got to the cave. He was hit in the back and gave a muffled cry, falling forward to drape himself over a large rock. He made a visible effort to get back to his feet and then fell back over the boulder.

They lost a further six men in the dash to the cave, two of them wounded and shouting for their comrades not to leave them. Clink turned to go back, but the corporal pushed him forward again. 'You can do nothing for them except get yourself killed,' he screamed. 'Get to the bloody cave.'

The survivors scrambled over the rocks at the entrance to the cave, chests heaving at the effort of the climb, and looked around them. The cave did not go more than a few yards back, but the boulders scattered at the entrance made a natural parapet. It was shady and the temperature was considerably lower than it had been outside.

Clink looked around at his colleagues. Only four of them had made it.

In civilian life Private Matthew Braithwaite had worked in a Sheffield iron foundry. On his twenty first birthday he had decided that he had no intention of spending the rest of his days roasted by the furnaces and turned into an old man before he was forty. He had enlisted at Doncaster the day after Clink and they had become friends. Right now Matthew was licking his parched and swollen lips and wishing that he had a pint of Yorkshire bitter in front of him.

'I used to come out of that bloody foundry so parched that I'd down three pints afore me throat got oiled,' he had often said. At the present moment he would have given everything he possessed for a cup of water. He up-ended his water bottle in a vain gesture and when nothing emerged he shrugged his shoulders and threw it on the ground.

Private Joseph Broadbent had nothing to say. He was by nature a surly man who did not have many friends. He had accepted the army as an alternative to the workhouse but he hated the discipline and longed for the day when he could return to his home in the Yorkshire Dales. 'You should see it in spring;' he would say, 'it's so beautiful, you feel you want to put it in your pocket an' keep it forever.'

'I wish I were back 'ome' now,' he said, spat on the floor and gingerly raised his head above the rim. The angry 'pow' of a bullet ricocheting from the rocks above his head made him duck down quickly.

Corporal Job Palmer was a Cockney of twelve years service who had somehow found himself in a Yorkshire Regiment. As he had tumbled into the cave he had been shot in the abdomen, but the bullet had passed through without hitting anything vital only to lodge against the base of his spine. 'I can't feel anything,' he told Clink, 'but I can't move my legs either; everythin' down there is just numb.' Clink put a field dressing over the stomach wound and then they propped him behind the most secure part of the parapet, his rifle in front of him.

'Cor, look at that!' he exclaimed in wonderment as he examined the wet stain spreading over the front of his trousers, 'Pee'd meself an' didn't even know it. There ain't no water goin' in, but there's plenty comin' out.' He laughed drily and coughed. 'Me mother always told me as my name meant: "'E who is to be persecuted". Now that's a bleedin' larf an' no mistake, ain't it? I reckon I've been persecuted in this 'ole ever since I arrived. It ain't dignified, peein' yourself without knowin' it.'

'Right,' said the corporal,' let's see 'ow we are. 'Ow much water 'ave we got?'

They had only two water bottles between them, the other two having been lost in the dash for shelter. Altogether they had just over two hundred rounds of ammunition. The position was not good; in fact Corporal Palmer said it was 'bleedin' desperate!'

'Private Broke' ordered the corporal, 'stick your 'ead carefully over the top an' tell me if you can see them two poor bleeders moanin' down there . . . an' don't get your ruddy 'ead shot off doin' it! An' tell me if they've still got their rifles with 'em.'

Clink peered gingerly through a gap in the rocks. He could see one poor fellow with his back against a rock and his hands clutching at his stomach. The blood oozed slowly between his fingers as he rocked back and forth moaning to himself. The second man had been hit in both legs and was trying to drag himself along the ground towards the cave. Each move made him cry out in pain and eventually he gave it up and lay face down in the dust, his shoulders heaving. Of their weapons there was no sign.

'Ave you got a clear shot at 'em?' asked the corporal. Clink looked astonished, but nodded.

'You're a good shot, Private Broke,' said Palmer. 'Shoot 'em both now, afore them 'eathens gets 'old of 'em. I'd do it myself, but I can't get sight from 'ere an' my eyes is gettin' blurred.'

Clink looked horrified. 'Shoot our own men?' he queried, 'I can't do that. Them two is Potter and Southam. I trained with them. I can't shoot 'em. When it gets dark we can drag 'em in,

274.

Corporal.'

The corporal dragged his senseless legs to one side so that he could point his rifle straight at Clink's chest.

'Me eyes may be goin' funny', he said quietly, 'but I can 'ardly miss you from 'ere, Broke. I'm givin' you a direct order to shoot them two afore the enemy takes 'em. If you disobey me, I can shoot you 'ere an' now. You're on active service, lad, and disobeyin' my order is mutiny. As for draggin' 'em in tonight, we may never see tonight, an' even if we do you won't get five yards down that gulley afore they slit your throat.'

His gaze softened.

'Listen 'ere, lad,' he said, 'I've been on this frontier for four years an' I know what they does to prisoners. If I were down there I'd be prayin' real 'ard that me mates would kill me, quick and clean. Now you do it, private, do it for your mates while you still can.'

The two stared at each other for a full thirty seconds and the problem was only resolved when Broadbent yelled: 'Here they come.'

The tribesmen charged up the defile, but Lieutenant Greenwood had picked his spot well. The way was so narrow that no more than two could get up abreast. From their sheltered position the soldiers poured a hail of fire into the enemy who broke and ran, leaving several dead behind them. When the smoke cleared the two wounded men had gone. Their screams echoed round the valley for more than an hour before their severed heads were thrown on the ground at the foot of the gulley. In the cave, no one spoke.

During the rest of the afternoon the enemy tried to make his way up to the cave by dodging from rock to rock. Although trying to conserve ammunition the little party had no option but to fire and drive the enemy back, but as the sun began to dip low in the sky they were down to their last few rounds and the position was made worse by the fact that neither water bottle had contained more than a mouthful or two and they were now empty.

As the sun was setting Joseph Broadbent looked warily over

the rocky parapet towards the body of Lieutenant Greenwood. It was about ten yards down the slope and draped over a boulder just as it had fallen when he had been shot in the back as he ran for cover. His staring eyes seemed to gaze towards their retreat although they had long since ceased to see anything, and a lank forelock of brown hair hung over his brow, occasionally stirring as a gentle evening breeze blew down the valley. Of much more interest was the fact that he held a water bottle firmly in a death grip in his left hand and a revolver in his right. Every now and then the water bottle tapped gently against the rock.

'I reckon that by tomorrow the search patrol will get 'ere,' said Broadbent, 'but if they're late, then we'll all be even more bloody thirsty than we are now. Now, if what they told us is true, this 'ere 'alf light is the worst to shoot by. Them shadows an' everythin' causes you to sight all wrong an' it takes you ages to get used to it. So, mates, I'm goin' to get that water bottle. I'd as soon be shot as die o' thirst.'

Before anyone could stop him he vaulted over the parapet and dashed the few yards to the body. The agonal grip of death held the bottle firmly and as he struggled to release it the first shots rang out. Two bullets whined away off the boulder no more than six inches from him and a splinter cut him across the cheek. As he finally prised the bottle and pistol from the iron grip a further shot clipped the lobe from his left ear, but with a yell of triumph he dashed back up the slope and on to the top of the parapet. The next bullet hit him in the back of the head, continued on its downward trajectory, and passed out of the base of his throat, the flattened soft lead scything through the water bottle and splitting it almost in half. 'Christ!' gurgled Broadbent, 'Ain't it 'ot.'

Then he crashed over the parapet like a felled tree and was dead before he hit the ground. They carried him to the back of the cave and covered his head with a handkerchief.

They had barely laid him down when another charge took place.

About a dozen of them charged up towards the redoubt, wav-

276.

ing their tulwars and screaming in frenzy. Five of them were dropped in quick succession and most of the remainder turned and ran. However, two of them reached the redoubt and leaped over the parapet. The first, a huge, bearded fellow with a red turban, slashed down with his sword at Braithwaite who skewered him through the belly on his bayonet and then turned to help Clink who was locked in a desperate struggle with the second. Braithwaite smashed the man on the back of the head with his rifle butt and Clink finished him off with a thrust through the chest. Meanwhile Corporal Palmer had dragged himself across the ground and stabbed the first native through the heart with his bayonet as he lay clutching his belly.

A cautious peep over the top confirmed that there was no further attack pending and they propped the Corporal back into his sitting position, but when they handed him his rifle he shook his head.

'I ain't got a single round left,' he said. "Ow about you two?'

Clink shook his head.

'If I'd 'ad another round that great 'eathen there would never 'ave reached us,' he said, pointing to the body of the fellow in the red turban.

Braithwaite said nothing. He was peering over the top and aiming at a mark on the far hillside. His rifle cracked out and there was a muffled scream. He lifted his head to look and said 'I've been after that bastard all day!' As he turned towards them, there was a single shot and he fell dead with a bullet through the temple, his rifle arcing through the air and clattering onto the ground. Clink picked it up and examined it.

'That was his last round as well,' he said.

'What about the officer's revolver?' asked the Corporal.

Clink broke it open and showed the cylinder to Job. There were just two rounds left.

'I'm not making this an order, my lad', said the Corporal, 'but as me bleedin' legs ain't workin' I ain't got nowhere to go. Don't let 'em take me alive, boy, whatever you do, don't let 'em take me alive.'

'No, corporal, I won't,' said Clink. He snapped the breech closed and, putting the revolver to the side of the NCO's head, he blew his brains out.

He took out his silver pocket watch and looked at the time. It was almost six o'clock.

'If it's the same time in Lincoln,' he thought, 'my mother will be puttin' out Dad's meal an' she'll be hearin' Big Tom strike the hour; an' I can almost see Little Will trampin' 'ome up Union Road.'

He sniffed the air, almost sure he could smell steak and kidney pudding.

* • * • * • *

When Will announced his decision to go into business on his own account there was an absolute silence which lasted for several seconds as they all stared at him. He looked at his father's face. It was turning bright red and he was clenching his fists as he spluttered for words.

'Goin' to work on your own account?' he eventually exploded. 'What the hell are you talking about, Will? You work for me and you always will. My God, boy, you try my patience with your damned nonsense.'

'What a wicked thing to say to your father,' snapped Martha, her long nose prodding forward like an angry crow. 'After all the trouble we've gone to for your birthday and the lovely surprise your father's just given you.'

'Aye,' murmured Grandfather William, 'but not half as big a surprise as Will's given his father.'

'Herbert,' continued Martha, 'I absolutely forbid you to give him full wages after that. He doesn't deserve them. He's thoroughly wicked and ungrateful.'

'I don't want them,' said Will, the enormity of what he had just said dawning upon him in all its majesty. 'I don't want them,' he repeated. 'After this week I shall be making my own money. In fact, if you don't want me to work notice I shall start earning for

278.

myself tomorrow. I've got a shed in Butchery Street that I'm renting. I've paid a month's rent in advance. It's got a bench, a gaslight and a good, strong lock on the door. Anything else it needs, I can make it or buy it from a second-hand shop.'

'Buy!' screamed Herbert. 'Buy? Where the hell have you got money from to buy? Renting sheds! Going into business! All that takes money, money you haven't got. Your mother saw to that when she found your ill gotten savings. Where would you get the money to pay a month's rent and fit up a workshop?'

'From the money Lucy left me,' said Will, 'I can't have it yet, Mr Otter won't give it to me until I'm twenty-one. He was very firm about that.'

'Thank God for that,' boomed Herbert.

'But he did give me an introduction to another gentleman who loaned me thirty pounds. I had to sign a paper to say that he had first call on the money from Lucy in case I can't pay it back, but pay it back I shall, every last penny piece just as quickly as I can,' continued Will.

'That bloody Josiah Otter,' interrupted Herbert, 'I'll take his damned legal jargon and ram it up his arse! What's he doing, sending you to borrow money? You're a minor, you can't borrow money. And another thing — where are you going to live? You'll not live here, that's for certain. You go into business against me and I'll stop you soon enough, but you'll not live under this roof while you're doing it.'

'I thought that you might say that, father', said Will, 'so I've rented a room. In case you should need me, the address is thirty-three Waldeck Street. She's a very respectable widow lady and there's just me and a lady schoolteacher living there. I have my own room with a lock on the door.'

Herbert fumed and raged and his language was so dreadful that the birthday party guests made their excuses and left. Grandfather William was straight-faced, whilst his wife was openly crying. Annie had joined her father in the tirade against Will until her father had clipped her across the ear and told her to mind her own business. She stared at him, mouth wide open. She could never recall that he had struck her before and with a scream she burst into tears and ran upstairs to her room.

Will walked slowly upstairs after her. If ever he had had any doubts, it was now that they began to niggle at his mind. Would he succeed? If not, where would he go and what would he do? He thrust such thoughts from his mind and packed his meagre belongings into a battered suitcase.

He passed his father standing in the hallway, Martha hovering behind like an evil shadow.

'Bear in mind, Will Everton,' said his father, 'once you go through that door, you never come back again. Never, do you hear, never. I'll see you on the streets first, damn you.'

Will looked his father straight in the face.

'I know that, father,' he said quietly, 'I know that.'

Then he turned his back and walked out of the door and through the garden into Burton Road. He turned and took a last look at the house where he had been born and where his mother had died. He knew that he would never return there as long as he lived and suddenly he felt as if a great burden had been taken from his shoulders. He could not remember a single happy moment in that place since the day he had been born.

Will's next few days were very busy. He fitted out the shed, buying various things he needed such as a vice and a set of pure bristle paint brushes. He scoured the second-hand shops and procured a battered stool and a small desk in which to keep his papers. Grandfather William brought him the tools he had promised, and Will constructed neat racks along the walls to hold them. He bought pen and ink and writing paper which he put in the desk and then he made a sign to put on the door. It said: 'WILLIAM EVERTON, JOINER AND CABINET MAKER'. When he had put the sign on the shed door he stood back for a minute to admire it, hands on hips. At that moment he felt considerably taller than his five feet three.

He was brought back to earth by the voice of an old man who lived opposite and had been standing on his doorstep watching.

'All you want now, young master, is a few customers!' he said.

'That I do,' said Will. 'But I'll get them. If I have to drag them in from the streets, I'll get them.' And he locked up the shed and went into town to place a small advertisement in the paper. By the time he had done this, all he had left was a month's rent for the shed, a month's rent for his lodgings and ten pounds to purchase the wood and materials for whatever work he might obtain. This latter money he sealed in an envelope and resolved that no matter how impecunious he became it would not be touched except for its intended purpose. He looked at the few shillings remaining in his pocket and said a silent prayer.

The clerk at the newspaper office was very helpful and eventually they had the small insertion to their liking.

'I want to emphasise repairs,' Will told him. 'I haven't got a lot of money to last me and I can't afford to be making pieces of furniture that might take me a fortnight before I get my money. Repairs are generally smaller jobs and they'll bring me in a bit of cash until I'm properly on my feet. Once I've got established, then I can go for the bigger jobs.'

'Quite so,' said the clerk. 'Why not use something like . . . er . . . I know. Why not say: 'No repair too small for my personal attention'?

Will paid over his one and threepence and the clerk promised him that if he called on the Friday, he would give him a free copy of the newspaper, and this Will did, being waiting at the newspaper office when the door was opened. He took the newspaper back to his shed and eventually found his advertisement. Carefully he cut it out and then pinned it to the wall above his desk and stared at it. He felt quite proud.

'Newly established', he read, 'William Everton, joiner and cabinet maker, is now open for business. No job too large, no repair too small for my personal attention. Call to see me without delay at my Butchery Street offices.' Having read it over several dozen times he awaited the stream of customers he felt sure would arrive.

It was two o'clock before an old lady, bent almost double, knocked at the door of the shed and came inside, dragging a three-legged kitchen chair behind her.

'Good afternoon, madam,' said Will, drawing forward a chair for her to sit. 'You've no doubt read my advertisement in the paper?'

'No,' she said, 'that old chap opposite said you'd just started up and you were bound to be cheaper than anyone else, so I've brought this chair for you to repair. It's a favourite of mine and it just fits me back when I'm at the table. Anyway, yesterday our Walter stood on it to reach something and the leg snapped off. Then, to make matters worse, the daft lad used the broken leg to light the fire this morning. 'E's a bit soft, is our Walter, 'armless, but soft.'

Will nodded understandingly and examined the chair. The dowel of the broken leg was still jammed in the seat and would have to be chiselled out. Then a new leg would have to be made, stained and varnished, glued in the seat and clamped. It was a simple, square-legged construction which would not give Will any difficulty. He explained what would have to be done and quoted ninepence for doing the job, having observed to his delight that his own battered office chair was of the same construction.

'Ninepence?' queried the customer. 'Do you think I'm made of money? It shouldn't cost more than sixpence at the most, it's only a bit of wood.'

'Tell you what,' said Will, 'pay me ninepence and that chair'll be ready for you this time tomorrow, stained and varnished — mind you, you'll find the varnish tacky for a day or two. As you're my first customer, that's a special job I'm doing for you. I wouldn't do that for everyone.'

'Make it eightpence and I'll pay you now, 'said the old lady and they agreed on this.

The customer was barely out of the shed before Will put his gluepot on the gas ring and had the office chair dismantled and the required leg in his hand. He glued in into the socket, rubbed it down with a bit of sandpaper and applied stain to almost the same shade. Then he clamped it up and hung it on the wall to set. Later he would apply a thin veneer of varnish. He could make a leg for his own chair in his own time. At the moment, the eightpence was very important. He had no customers for the rest of the day and on his way back to Waldeck Street that evening he hoped that this would not be a bad omen for him.

The old lady came back for her chair the next morning.

'You're a bit early,' said Will. "Two o'clock it was supposed to be, wasn't it? Anyway, it's ready for you, and he handed her the chair.

She turned it this way and that, carefully examining it.

'By golly!' she exclaimed. 'That new leg's exactly the same as the old one. 'Owever did you do that? Mind you, the colour's a bit different to the rest of it.'

'Give it a month or two to absorb the stain and varnish properly and you won't see the difference,' responded the craftsman, touching the leg gently with his finger. 'See, it's even dried quicker than I thought it would do. You can take it straight home and sit on it.'

The old lady delved into her purse and gave Will a penny.

'That's a very good job, Mr Everton, and I'm well pleased wi' it. 'Ere's the other penny I bargained you out of. I'll tell other folk about you for sure. I 'ope you do very well in your new business.' And with this she went off down the street, dragging the chair behind her.

Will examined the penny and on an impulse, took a hammer and nail and pinned it to the wall. He couldn't recall that anyone had ever called him 'Mr Everton' before and he wanted a permanent reminder of the occasion.

Before lunch he had a response to his advertisement from a widow lady who had a broken sashcord. As it was only in the next street, he went straight away, leaving a notice on the shed door, 'Back Soon'. It was quite straightforward except that he had no sashcord and had to go into the city to buy some. He took a chance and bought a spare length in case anyone else should want the same job doing. When he had finished the work, he returned to the shed to find a gentleman waiting for him, newspaper in hand.

'Is Mr Everton about?' he asked.

'I'm William Everton,' said Will proudly pointing to his sign. 'What can I do for you?'

The man eyed his diminutive stature up and down and raised his eyebrows. He pointed to the newspaper and asked: 'Is it you that's advertising, then?'

'It's me,' said Will, 'and I'm working on my own now. I can do any job that my father's firm would do.'

'Good!' exclaimed the gentleman. 'No offence, lad, but I hate your father's guts and wouldn't give him a penn'orth of business. If you can do a good job, I think I can find a few things for you to do. My name's Jacob Down from the Saracen's Head. I'm pleased to meet you, Mr Everton,' and he held out his hand.

Will took the hand and said: 'The pleasure is mine, sir.' To be called 'Mr Everton' twice in one day filled his cup to overflowing. 'How may I help you, Mr Down?'

It appeared that Mr Down had a number of small jobs which needed attention, such as items of furniture for repair, doors to be rehung and the construction of a secure cash drawer beneath one of the bars. It was arranged that Will should go along on the Monday morning to assess the work and tell Mr Down his price. 'It should keep you busy for a week,' was his customer's final remark and they shook hands and parted.

Will mentally patted himself on the back. Things looked considerably brighter than they had when he had walked home the previous evening. Thus he concluded his first week's business. He had not actually put much into his cashbox, but the thought of a week's work at the Saracen's Head was very comforting. He sat in his room that evening and pondered what he would do with all the money he was going to earn, then put that thought out of his mind and concentrated on what he would do the following day, which was Sunday.

As long as he could remember, he had always gone to the Saxon Street Methodist Church on Sunday morning, together with the rest of the family. He remembered what his father had always told him when he had complained about having to go.

'It's not good enough to be a Christian, Will. If you're in business in this city you also have to be SEEN to be a Christian, even if you do have to sit with a lot of hypocrites to do it.'

He knew that if he went to Saxon Street he would be bound to meet his father and that, he felt, might well be a very unpleasant confrontation. On the other hand, Sunday would not seem right if he did not go to church, business or not. He had hardly missed a Sunday in his life and saw no reason to start now. The fact that there had been no word from his father worried him. Will might have won the battle, but he did not deceive himself that he had won the war. He knew his father far too well to think that he would allow himself to be bested by anyone. For one fleeting moment when he had left the house he had seen a look in his father's eyes which almost pleaded with him to stay, but it had vanished as quickly as it had appeared.

Eventually he decided to attend the new Wesleyan church on Bailgate. It was always known as the 'New Church', even though it had now been in operation for some fourteen years. It was a splendid building, its frontage centred around a huge stained glass window and the gable roof surmounted by four towers. It soared above Newport Arch and the surrounding terraced houses and shops until it seemed almost like a small cathedral, whilst the tiny cottages in East Bight were positively dwarfed.

Before the morning service began Will said a small prayer on behalf of himself, that his business might succeed, for in truth he had no idea what he would do if it failed. Certainly he would never be able to humble himself by returning home; that tie had been severed forever and whatever else might happen, he would never return to Burton Road. He felt rather guilty to be asking God for favours, but with the departure of Clink he had no friends of his own age with whom he might share his worries. Remembering Clink, now absent in a foreign land, he prayed that his friend would be kept safe from harm.

On leaving church he stepped out into bright sunshine. Will looked across the road at the Duke William where he had had his battle and decided that he would go straight back to his room in

Waldeck Street and make himself a lunch, then go into his work-shop and potter about for the rest of the day. In truth, he was very lonely. His reverie was interrupted by a hand on his shoulder and he turned to see Mr and Mrs Fletcher.

'I saw your notice in the newspaper on Friday. Off to the White Hart for lunch, Will?' asked Mr Fletcher. 'Now that you're a businessman no doubt you'll be wanting to mix with the gentry.'

Before Will could answer, Mr Fletcher turned to his wife and said: 'Such a shame, my dear, that Will can't join us. Roast beef, sprouts, and cabbage, carrots from the garden, roast potatoes . . . oh, those delicious roast potatoes. Then there's the apple and blackberry pie with custard. Hurry, my dear, I'm feeling hungry at the thought of it.' He grabbed his wife by the arm and took a couple of steps towards home, then turned round to Will and said: 'Of course, young sir, if mixing with the gentry is not what you had in mind, I think we could make a place for you at the table.'

'I'm a long way from taking lunch at the White Hart, sir,' said Will. 'It's a bit of bread and cheese for my Sunday meal, I'm afraid. That is unless Mrs Fletcher really doesn't mind me coming home with you?'

'Mind?' queried the good lady. 'There's so little of you that you can do with a good feed. It's my Christian duty to fatten you up a bit, young man, then you might grow!' Seeing that he was sensitive about his height she quickly added: 'My mother always said that good things come in small parcels, Will Everton, so you're very welcome.'

When Will entered the Fletchers' house his immediate impression was that he had never seen so many books in his life. They were on shelves, piled on small tables, heaped on the chairs and even in piles on the floor. Before Mrs Fletcher could set the table she had to move several books and as soon as she had disappeared into the kitchen Mr Fletcher absent mindedly put them all back again. Noticing his glances towards them, Mr Fletcher wagged a finger at him and said: 'Never underestimate the power of the written word, Will. In these books there is the knowledge that it has taken many a man a lifetime to collect. Books, Will,

286.

books are both meat and bread to a man with a soul. A man can deny what he has said, for the spoken word fades with the passage of time, but he can never deny what he has written, nor should he want to do so.'

It was indeed an excellent lunch and afterwards as Mrs Fletcher washed the dishes Will and Joshua Fletcher sat in easy chairs and discussed Will's venture into the world of commerce. Will said that he was quite disappointed that he had spent his money on the advertisement but that it had not brought him any business except for the sashcord job and that didn't even cover the cost of advertising. The enquiry from the Saracen's Head had not yet put any money into his pocket and there was no certainty that he would be given the work. Thus, argued Will, he would have to quote the bare minimum in order to ensure that he got it.

Mr Fletcher puffed at his pipe, stuck his fingers in the edges of his waistcoat, and expounded one or two of the principles of successful business.

'Never sell yourself cheap,' he said. 'Work out a price to show yourself a fair profit and stick to it. If you start off doing cheap work, then that's all you'll ever have to do. People will come to you purely because you do cheap work. Mind you, I said cheap, not low priced. There is a very big difference. In the mind of a successful business man, the word cheap is synonymous with shoddy. Did you ever know your father to quote a price that didn't have a fat profit? Of course not. He started as he meant to go on. People don't go to your father because he's cheap. They go because he does a good job.

In fairness to your father, he always has, and that's something you can learn from him. Never under-sell yourself and never be a party to a poor job at a low price.

You see, Will, you have been talking about your advertisement and saying that it's been a waste of money because you haven't put any cash in your pocket yet. The finest advertising you can get is what people say about you, and that costs nothing except honesty and hard work. Get that job at the Saracen's Head, price it fair and do it well and it will reach the ears of other people. Folks will seek out a good craftsman, no matter where he hides himself.'

'I hadn't thought of it like that,' said Will, 'but even if I get the work, I'll have to put in a bill and wait to be paid and that's what's worrying me. I have only a few pounds left to buy materials and I must do some work to put money in my purse, otherwise how will I pay my rent and buy my food, let alone clothes and boots?'

'Get your materials, but don't pay for them,' said Mr Fletcher.

As Will looked astonished, Joshua Fletcher rubbed his brow in frustration.

'When you went to fetch wood, or nails, or anything else for your father's business, did you ever take any money with you?' he asked.

'No,' said Will, 'I used to sign for things and then they sent the bill to my father and I suppose he paid it, or perhaps Martha did because she looked after most of the book work.'

'There you are, then!' exclaimed Joshua triumphantly. 'It is possible to get your supplies without paying. Business runs on credit, not cash, my lad. Tomorrow morning, don't be sitting in your office waiting for the world to bring work to you. Go out and organise your finances! Get you to the printer first thing and have him print you some business cards with your name and occupation on — don't forget your address, mind.

Then go to the merchants and the timber yard and present your card and introduce yourself, even if they already know you. Present your card and speak to no one but the proprietor. You are above the underlings now, my lad, you negotiate only with the principal. Open credit accounts wherever you can, but do not buy more than you need, ever. That's money lying idle and earning nothing.

If you run into difficulties with one firm, go somewhere else until you succeed. Then, once you have no worries about your finances, then is the time to push for work. Be honest with the fellow at the Saracen's Head; he knows that you've only just gone into business for yourself, so tell him that if he will put a small

288.

deposit down on the work, you will give him a small discount on the price, say two and a half percent.'

'But isn't that reducing my prices?' asked Will, 'Just what you've told me I shouldn't do?'

'Will Everton,' said his mentor, 'you are without doubt a fine craftsman, but you are without comprehension of the world of business. You are offering an exchange, not reducing your prices. If he will help you by a small advance, you will help him by giving a discount. The one pays for the other!'

He sighed heavily and concluded: 'I am told that just across the border in Yorkshire they have a saying, "Ne'er do owt for nowt, but if tha' does, then do it for thee sen!" You will find that to be very true. There is little, if anything, that is free in this life. One thing buys another.'

During this long dissertation Mr Fletcher's pipe had gone out and he lit it with some show of irritability that Will had not realised these things for himself.

Mrs Fletcher had heard all this as she worked in the kitchen and she came in wiping her hands on the tea towel, put her arm around Will's shoulder and said: 'Mr Fletcher was always a good teacher, Will.'

Mr Fletcher nodded his head in agreement, but his wife added a few more words: 'but he was never very patient with anyone who wasn't as brainy as he is!'

'I'm sure I've learned a great deal today, Mrs Fletcher,' said Will, 'and I'm very grateful to your husband for the instruction. Everything he has told me is very sensible, I'm sure, and I shall do my best to be guided by him. Once again, I'm in your debt, both of you, and I don't know how I shall repay you.'

Monday morning saw Will at the timber yard, where he asked to see the proprietor.

'The proprietor?' laughed the workman. 'Look lads, Little Will wants to see the gaffer! We ain't good enough for 'im now, 'e wants the boss.'

Will let the laughter die down and then seized the man by the lapels and thrust his nose within an inch of the man's face.

'I want to see your master,' he hissed, 'I have business to discuss with him and if you value your job you'll tell him I'm here without any further delay. I'm my own master now, and I don't take insolence from workmen like you. Now be off with you and find him!' And he thrust the man from him.

For a moment it seemed that the workman would strike him, but Will stood firm and eventually the man, ashen faced with anger, went off to find his boss. Will had made his first enemy in business and, like his father, he was to make many more.

'Why should I give you credit?' was the immediate response from Ellis Wentworth, the proprietor. 'Why don't you go to your father's yard and buy your timber there?'

Will explained that he had left home and had set up his own business. It was his intention to be beholden to no one, least of all his father. Already, said Will with a perfectly straight face, he had a contract to do work at the Saracen's Head and a number of other jobs were pending until he had sorted out the matter of his finances. His father would have described this statement with one of his favourite business maxims — 'Never tell a lie, but always present a half-truth in the light most favourable to yourself.'

'You're a minor,' responded Mr Wentworth. 'Your father won't let you go that easily. Until you're twenty-one he can grab you back into that workshop of his and there'll be nothing you can do about it. Then where would my money be? Your father wouldn't give it back to me, that's for certain!'

This was a snag that Will had not anticipated and he paused a moment before answering.

'My father has already told me that I'm never to set foot in his house again. Does that sound as if he wants me back? Added to this I have received advice from my solicitor' (Ellis' eyebrows shot up) 'and I am advised that under the circumstances it is not likely that he would be able to force me to return.'

Will half rose from his seat.

'Mr Wentworth,' he said, 'my father wants me to fail. In fact, he's sure I'll fail, but I'm damned if I will. I'll work night and day, seven days a week if I have to, but I'll not fail. I'll not!'

He banged the desk in his determination and sat down red faced.

'By golly, I do believe that you mean it,' said Mr Wentworth. 'Tell you what I'll do. You can have credit up to ten pounds a month and see how we go from there! Mind you, not a penny more and see you pay me promptly. The seventh day of the month is settling day here, so keep that in mind.'

He held out his hand. 'Congratulations, Mr Everton, may you prosper in your venture.'

After a quick visit to the printers to order some business cards, Will made straight for Jacob Down at the Saracen's Head and was shown around the various small jobs to be done. He made careful notes as he progressed around the building and they then adjourned to the kitchens where a pot of tea was served to them.

'Well?' said Jacob Down. 'How much?'

Will scribbled busily and scratched his head. He estimated that the materials required would cost four pounds and that the work would take him the best part of a week. He knew that the average wage for a joiner was no more than thirty shillings a week, but reckoned that as he was working for himself he should draw at least twice that amount. If he had to knock off two and a half percent discount, he was business wise enough to add it on in the first place. He couldn't calculate what two and a half percent was very quickly and as Jacob Down was now tapping his fingers on the table he decided to play safe.

'Seven pounds seven and sixpence,' he said.

Mr Down looked him straight in the eye and said: 'Seven pounds.'

Here Will was not out of his depth for he had seen his father bartering many a time and he stared straight back at him and replied, 'Seven pounds five shillings — and if you advance me three pounds I'll knock two and a half percent off that.'

'Done!' said his adversary and held out his hand.

Thus was Will's first important job put in hand. He worked like a Trojan and had the whole job finished in four days, Mr

Down declaring himself well pleased with the work, and adding that there would undoubtedly be further work for him in future. On the last day he was fitting the secure drawer to the bar till, watched by a number of interested customers. One man seemed particularly fascinated by the way he worked and bombarded him with questions which Will was only too pleased to answer, for he never tired of talking about his work nor of showing his skills to interested onlookers.

'Very interesting, young man,' said his interrogator. 'You obviously know your trade. Here's my card. I've just bought a house on Bailgate and my missus is moaning about the kitchen. Needs new shelves and cupboards, she says, and I don't doubt she'll find lots more to spend money on. Pop round and see her when you have a minute. Mind you, don't start any work until we've agreed a price. Jacob Down says you're a hard bargainer.'

It was as Joshua Fletcher had said. His satisfied customers brought him a steady flow of enquiries and after a few weeks he found that he was beginning to pay his way. The Sunday service at the Wesleyan Chapel became a regular habit, as did the visits to the Fletcher household for Sunday lunch. For their part, the Fletchers were pleased to see him, for they had no children of their own and took a keen interest in his progress. Joshua kept a wary eye on his finances and helped him with a simple cash book, showing him how to keep track of his income and expenditure.

In the Smoke Room of the White Hart, Herbert began to receive a measure of not so gentle chiding.

'How's that lad of yours, Bert? I hear he's getting on quite nicely since he left home. Surprised you haven't dragged him back yet. He's only eighteen and I thought you'd have had him back in Motherby Lane as quick as the blink of an eye.'

'Mind your own damned business!' snapped Herbert. 'I'll get him back in my own time and in my own way without any advice from you, thank you.' He rammed his cigar out in the ornate brass ashtray and called for another bottle of claret to be brought to the table. Martha never stopped nagging him about Will when he was at home and he was in no mood to have the subject raised when he was at leisure. 'I'll get him back', he repeated, 'in my own time and in my own way.'

'God help poor Little Will,' murmured more than one under his breath.

One Sunday morning Will missed the Fletchers at church. As he gazed anxiously around him at the departing throng, he heard a voice behind him.

'You'll be Will Everton, I do believe.'

He turned around and found himself gazing into a pair of blue eyes. The owner was a young lady whom he judged to be about his own age. She was at least three or four inches taller than he was, slender and with a ready smile. Her auburn hair peeped out from beneath the rim of her bonnet and the richness of her velveteen coat seemed to make the perfect foil for those wonderful blue eyes. Will wouldn't have called her beautiful. That would have been too lowly a term for her.

He turned rather red and continued to stare at her. 'Well', she said, 'are you Will Everton or are you not?'

Her voice seemed to hold all the laughter of her pleasant smile and Will remembered a sentence from a book he had once read. 'She had a voice like the tinkling of temple bells at twilight,' he said under his breath. Then he remembered the word for which he had been searching.

'Handsome,' he said out loud, 'handsome is the word.'

'Pardon?' said the young lady. 'Did you say something?'

Will took off his cap. For some reason his face felt very flushed and he stammered: 'No. That is, no I didn't say anything, but yes I am Will Everton.'

'I'm Polly Johnson,' said the young lady. 'Mr and Mrs Fletcher are my uncle and aunt. Mr Fletcher isn't very well today and so they've stayed at home, but you are to come to lunch. They told me you'd be waiting outside the church for them.'

Will held out his hand and mumbled: 'Pleased to meet you Miss Johnson, I'm sure,' and they walked the few yards back to East Bight together and in silence.

Mr Fletcher suffered from angina and his attacks tended to

make him irritable and impatient. This, he said, was the curse bestowed upon him by teaching generations of schoolchildren who did not appreciate the blessings of knowledge which he had bestowed upon them and preferred to waste their time on fruitless pastimes such as kites, marbles and hopscotch. Mrs Fletcher shrugged her shoulders behind her husband's back and indicated to Will that he should listen silently. Sure enough, Mr Fletcher soon tired himself out and fell asleep in his chair, commenting that he had never seen Will so silent in all their brief acquaintance.

Lunch was served a little late to allow Mr Fletcher to enjoy his snooze. His sleep had refreshed him and he questioned Will about his business as they ate. Polly remained largely silent but every now and then Will caught her eye across the table and turned red. She gave a hint of a smile and looked down at her plate, but the glances were not lost on Mrs Fletcher although Mr Fletcher kept asking Will if he was feeling well, pointing out that he kept going red in the face as if he were running a temperature.

The meal over, Polly rose to help Mrs Fletcher with the pots, but the offer was refused.

'It's a pleasant afternoon,' she said, 'why don't you take Polly and show her around the town, Will? She's never been here before and I'm sure she'd love to see all the sights. A walk will do you more good than sitting here with my husband. He needs his rest, anyway!' And before Mr Fletcher could stop her she had put on his slippers, taken away his book, rested his feet on a small stool and instructed him to sleep.

Will was not used to walking around the town with young ladies. He was very conscious that his clothes looked rather shabby beside hers and as they walked he self-consciously kept pulling at his jacket and straightening his tie.

'I've just ordered a new suit,' he lied. 'Made to measure, it is.'

'The one you are wearing looks perfectly adequate to me, Mr Everton,' she said. 'Don't you think that's a waste of money when you've just started in business on your own?'

'Oh, no,' he blustered, 'I'm hoping to do business with some of the best places in town and when I go to see the proprietors I can hardly go in my overalls. When I have men working for me, I'll have to look like the master, not like a workman, so I might as well get the suit now and be prepared, Miss Johnson.' He looked up and caught a glimpse of that elusive smile again.

'You can laugh', he said, 'but I'll do it. I will have men working for me one day, and a big house and carriage and pair.'

'I wasn't laughing,' said Polly gently. 'Well, not at that anyway. I was laughing that at last I've discovered how to make you say something. If you won't talk about anything else, at least you'll talk about your work. You hardly said a word at lunch time, and we've walked past all these interesting places and you haven't told me a word about them. Yet as soon as work is mentioned you find your tongue! I don't understand you, Will — I may call you Will? And you must call me Polly.'

'There was an old sea captain used to live on Burton Road,' said Will without thinking, 'he had a parrot called Polly.'

'So, you think I chatter like a parrot, do you?' asked Polly.

Will went positively scarlet and wished that the ground would open up and swallow him. He stammered 'I didn't mean that. You see well, what I meant was . . . this sea captain . . . ' He felt positively wretched.

'I know you didn't mean that,' laughed Polly, 'I was only joking. I know what you meant.'

By now they were at the Cathedral and they walked inside. Will was on surer ground now and was able to tell Polly much about the history of the beautiful building. He also told her how he had sat at the organ and thrilled as the giant gave voice to his commands on the keys, the notes soaring off into the great roof as if to Heaven itself.

'It was like talking to God,' he said, his eyes sparkling with the memory. 'I would have loved to study music, but my father wouldn't let me. He said it was a waste of time and he couldn't afford it.'

'I'm not sure you should talk about God like that,' said Polly, 'especially in here. I'm not at all sure that's right and proper.'

'I don't think God would mind us talking to him,' said Will. 'When Jesus was on earth he talked to everyone. I believe that God could understand what was in my heart when I was playing that organ just as clearly as if I had been speaking to Him face to face, just as I'm sure He can understand what I'm thinking when I'm making a fine piece of furniture and sing a hymn as I work.'

Will looked Polly straight in the eye.

'After all, if we can't talk to God and if He doesn't understand our thoughts, then everything we are taught at church is wrong,' he concluded. Much to his embarassment, Polly grabbed him by the arm and hustled him out of the Cathedral and back up the Bail to East Bight, not speaking a word as they walked. Will left her at the door and, making hurried excuses to the Fletchers, went quickly away, his face showing his bewilderment. Polly had had a strict religious upbringing and what Will had said had deeply shocked her, particularly as he had expressed his thoughts in the Cathedral.

Will found it difficult to sleep that night, his slumbers strangely disturbed by the thoughts of those deep blue eyes and long, auburn hair. He was genuinely sorry that he had upset Polly and grappled with thoughts as to how he might make amends to her.

Early next morning, his mind still thinking of Polly, he was visited at his workshop by an ashen-faced Henry Carrot. Henry said nothing but held out a letter to Will to read and then sat down, his head in his hands.

Will read silently.

'As Commanding Officer it is my sad duty to inform you of the death in action of your nephew, Private John Broke. He was a member of a patrol ambushed in the hills by rebel tribesmen and from which there were no survivors. We believe that Private Broke was the last to be killed and there is evidence that he died gallantly defending his wounded corporal.

He has been buried in the Regimental Cemetery, together with his comrades, with full military honours. I am sure you will be proud . . . '

The words blurred on the page as Will's eyes filled with tears. He felt terribly numb and he collapsed onto an upturned box beside Henry, his legs shaking and the letter trembling in his hand. Large tears ran down his cheeks as he strove to stifle the sobs.

Henry Carrot raised his head, his eyes red-rimmed and swollen.

'Clink's dead, Will,' he said. 'He ain't comin' 'ome, e's dead. My missus is grievin' fit to break your 'eart an' I feel like I got nothin' left in me. First the little 'un and then Clink, God knows it's a cruel world an' that's for sure. Even amidst all the tears, my missus sent me down 'ere to tell you. 'Go tell Little Will,' she said. 'They was friends, good friends. Go an' tell 'im right away!'

Any passer-by looking into the shed must have wondered at the sight of them, their arms around each others shoulders, the tears flowing as they gave vent to their grief. Eventually Will locked up the shed. With a shaking hand he scrawled a note on a piece of cardboard, 'Closed for the day', and pinned it to the door.

When he had gone a few yards up the street, he turned round, came back, and altered the notice to read: 'Closed — due to the death of my friend'.

In later life Will was to remember little of the weeks that followed. He could not really believe that Clink would never return to Lincoln and frequently he was to be found on the Waterside, hoping against futile hope that some miracle would return his friend to him and that they would once again sit in their favourite spot and discuss their future together. His work became his life and he threw himself into it as if nothing else existed, working frequently by candlelight and oil lamp.

Before the end of the year he had paid off the loan, largely due to the guidance of Joshua Fletcher who remained his firm friend and guided him through the troubled period after Clink's death. For some weeks after the tiff with Polly, Will had not gone to church on Sundays, but one day as he was working in his shed on Butchery Street a shadow had fallen across the door and he had looked up to see Mr Fletcher smiling down at him.

'We were sorry to hear about your friend, Will,' he said. 'We know how you must feel and we want you to know that we're truly sorry. The death of a friend is always a great blow, particularly when you're young. You'll make other friends, Will.'

'Not like Clink,' said Will, furiously planing a piece of wood. 'There'll never be another friend like Clink. He was my friend when I had no one and his parents always made me welcome. Now he's dead and somewhere on the other side of the world. There isn't even a grave to visit.'

He lifted up the piece of wood and examined it with a critical eye.

'Damn!' he said and threw it out into the street. 'It isn't true!'

Joshua Fletcher went slowly into the street and retrieved it, handing it back to Will.

'No, Will', he said gently, 'it isn't true, but with your skill you can make it true, and if you can't make it true then you can save it and use it for something else. You see, Will, you can't take out your anger against the world on a piece of wood. Your friend's gone, God rest him, but his family is still there. They've been good friends to you over the years from what I hear. How do you think they feel? They need your friendship now more than ever they did.

At the moment every memory of that boy hurts them, but as time passes and the wound heals, then it will be those very same memories that become more precious than gold. Oh, yes, each memory will hurt but they'll hurt a little less with the passing of each year, and when they're old it will be one of the few pleasures left in life to them.'

He put his arm around Will's shoulder.

'You see, Will, that's all they've got now, memories; and you're part of them, Will. When you're young, death seems the most terrible thing in the world. It's so final, so awful. One minute a bright, young life with everything stretching out ahead. The next, finished and gone. Nothing, just nothing.'

Mr Fletcher took out his handkerchief and blew his nose.

'I'll tell you a secret, Will, a secret you must mention to no one. We had a child once. Oh, it's many a long year past now. A little boy. Like you, he was called William, but he died before he reached his first birthday. Mrs Fletcher keeps a little box in the bottom of a cupboard with some of his clothes in it. Every now and then, she goes to that box and takes out a little woollen coat and washes it. She dries it in front of the fire and then she irons it, all neat and tidy, and puts it back in the box.

I watch her Will, I watch her and I say nothing, but my heart's fit to burst with sadness. That little coat, there's hardly a bit of shape left in it now, but to her it's not a coat, it's a memory. She smiles to herself and I know she's thinking of what might have been. I've often thought that one day I might take that box of clothes and destroy it. But it wouldn't be just clothes that went up in smoke, it would be all my lady's memories and even though it hurts me, I don't have the right to take away her memories.'

He blew his nose and wiped the corner of his eye.

'Polly's been asking after you,' he muttered in a hoarse voice: 'I think she understands what you meant now, even if she doesn't agree with you. We'd be very pleased to see you after church on Sunday, Will. Shall I tell Mrs Fletcher that you'll come?'

Will nodded and, as Mr Fletcher made to leave, grasped him by the arm and said, 'I owe you a lot, sir; thank you for coming to see me.'

Mr Fletcher's face lit up with a smile as he patted Will on the shoulder.

As the year moved to a close, Will began to pull himself around. There hardly seemed a place in the city which did not bring back a memory of Clink and he realised that there was a great deal of truth in the advice given to him by his friend, Joshua Fletcher. He took to having the occasional drink after work had finished, for it was at this time that the memories seemed to be the strongest, tugging at him like some positive force determined never to let him go. He found that the company in the ale house seemed to send him home in a better and more cheerful frame of mind.

His Sunday visits to the Fletchers renewed, his friendship with Polly grew, and he looked forward tremendously to the walk which inevitably followed the Sunday lunch. There was no romance between them, although Will felt that if he had shown affection, it might have been returned. Sometimes, when their hands touched, or when Polly took his arm to cross the road, he felt a strange tingling in his limbs and on one occasion actually shuddered. This disturbed him greatly.

He introduced her to the Carrots where she immediately won their hearts and was always made welcome and on one occasion they went to the music hall together. In the darkness he gently took her hand and felt very relieved when she grasped his in return. Afterwards he reflected that Polly might have gained the wrong idea from this and resolved not to do it again.

One Sunday afternoon, wandering a little further afield than they had intended, they found themselves on Wragby Road. Will was telling her about an order he had received to make a dining table and chairs when he heard Polly give a gasp of horror. Her eyes were riveted on the sign above a public house, the Adam and Eve. As might have been expected, the sign depicted Adam and Eve in the Garden of Eden. A fig leaf covered Adam's manhood and a strategically placed vine twined around Eve's loins and one breast, the tip of the other peeping through in a provocative manner.

Polly's face was scarlet.

'Will Everton,' she exclaimed in a shaky voice, 'I do believe that you've brought me here just to embarass me. It's disgusting! They've got no clothes on! Someone should tell them about it.'

'In actual fact, if I recall correctly, there has been a bit of a fuss about it. Someone told me that the clergy have already made representations to Mr Thomas Harrison, the landlord, to have it removed and . . . '

Polly didn't give Will time to finish.

'There you are,' she snapped triumphantly, 'not only did you know this sign was here, you even know the landlord by name.'

She flounced back up the road, long skirts swishing round her ankles, head held high and the ribbons from her broad-brimmed hat streaming behind her. Will ran after her.

300.

'Polly!' he cried, 'Polly! Wait for me, please. I didn't realise we were coming this way. I was busy talking and didn't notice or I'd have gone a different way. Please, Polly, don't be angry. I'm always so proud to be seen out with you. I love you, Polly, really I do!'

Polly stopped dead in her tracks and turned around as Will caught up with her.

'At least I think I do,' said Will lamely, wringing his cap in his hands, 'You make me go all funny sometimes and it's either that or I've got some sort of a fever . . . perhaps I'm wrong. But don't be angry again, please.'

Polly looked into his eyes and saw the tenderness striving to express itself. On an impulse she leaned down and kissed him gently on the cheek.

'Disgusting!' roared a peppery gentleman passing by with his wife. 'Damned disgusting. Fornication in the streets, no less! The whole damned city'll be running about with no clothes on next. Some public spirited person ought to burn that damned ale house to the ground. The country's going to the dogs, my dear, going to the dogs I say!'

Will wasn't really sure whether the man was referring to the sign or Polly's peck on the cheek. Either way it didn't seem to matter to him as Polly took his arm and they walked back home together. For a young lady to take your arm publicly indicated that you were 'walking out' together and for Will this was a totally new experience. He felt three feet taller and kept glancing around him to make sure that everyone was observing the handsome young lady on his arm.

He felt so happy that when he got back to his room in Waldeck Street he hardly absorbed the information given to him by Mrs Gresford, his landlady. Mrs Gresford was getting on in years and had decided to sell her house and move to Gainsborough to live with her widowed sister. She assured Will that the new landlord had no intention of depriving the lodgers of their rooms. He was, she said, quite well off and had no intention of living in the house. Of this the solicitor dealing with the sale had assured her,

301.

although she had no idea who the landlord might be. Will wished her every happiness in her new home and thought no more of the matter, his mind full of Polly.

Of course, he reasoned, Polly had not said that she loved him, but she had taken his arm in the street for everyone to see and when they had turned into East Bight neither Mr nor Mrs Fletcher who were standing talking to a neighbour had passed any comment. Thus, he concluded, her guardians obviously had no objection to the friendship blossoming into something stronger.

As that Christmas of 1893 approached, Will felt happier than he had done for some time. His friendship with Polly had filled a huge gap in his life and he found himself spending more and more of his spare time with her. Occasionally, when she was shopping in town with Mrs Fletcher, Polly would pay a brief visit to his workshop and the three of them would sit on whatever was handy and enjoy a mug of tea.

'Don't you worry, Polly', he would say, 'I won't always be working in a shed like this. One day I'll have a proper joiner's workshop and men working for me. When I'm twenty-one I get my hundred pounds and that, together with what I've saved, that will set me up in a proper place. Until then, I'll work hard and save whatever I can. Mark my words, Polly, I'll do it.'

Polly would take his hand and say: 'I know you will, I believe you, Will.'

When Will arrived to spend Christmas Day with the Fletchers he was greeted with a huge surprise. There, crammed into the tiny cottage, was the huge bulk of Henry Carrot, his wife and children. Even to move round the rooms was difficult and the children with their new toys got under everyones feet. It was a merry Christmas indeed and when it came time for the Carrot family to depart, complete with presents and food enough to see them over the rest of the week, Mrs Carrot took the Fletchers both by the hand.

'Neither me nor 'enry is much good with words,' she said, 'an' you a school teacher, as well, Mr Fletcher. But we all thanks you for this wonderful Christmas Day and we know as 'ow you've thought of us, an' our poor lad what ain't 'ere an' . . . an' . . . '

The impromptu speech stammered into silence as the lump in her throat seemed fit to choke her.

Henry endeavoured to complete the thanks, 'What we means is . . . ', he commenced.

Mrs Fletcher stretched up to put both her arms around the huge man and kiss him gently on the cheek.

'We know what you mean, Mr Carrot,' she said. 'We know exactly what you mean and we thank you for your kind thoughts, all of us. May the New Year prove a little kinder to you than the old one. God bless you, Henry Carrot and Mrs Carrot and your lovely children. God bless you all.'

Early in the New Year Will and Polly volunteered to help at the first of the Robin dinners to be held in Lincoln. The local lodge of the Royal Antediluvian Order of Buffaloes ('Poor man's bloody Freemasons!' scoffed Henry Carrot) had obtained the use of the Masonic Hall for a Christmas dinner for poor children and had started the subscriptions for the event with a magnificent donation of eight pounds ten shillings. By the time that the subscriptions had all been collected a sum of no less than seventy pounds was to hand, sufficient to provide a right royal dinner for some fifteen hundred children. However, as the Hall could hold no more than five hundred with comfort, no fewer than three events had to be arranged.

When Will and Polly arrived at the Hall there was already a huge queue of eager children at the doors, stamping on the pavements to keep out the bitter January weather and banging their arms on their sides. Some wore shabby top coats and there were others with pullovers and jumpers ragged with holes. Mufflers were wrapped around mouths, luminous nose-ends peeking forth from the wrappings and eager eyes scanning every new arrival admitted by the doorkeeper.

As Polly made to enter, she felt a hand tugging at her coat. 'Please, lady', said a piping voice, 'is it true that we can all eat as much as we want and no one will take it away?'

She looked down to see a little girl at the head of the queue.

She was perhaps five years of age, her tiny pinched face white with the cold, but her eyes shining brightly at the thought of the treat in store. Long golden ringlets hung down from under a boy's cap perched on her head and she had a piece of blanket hanging around her shoulders to keep out the cold. Her shoes had seen much better days and a tiny toe stuck uncovered from the hole in the front of the left one. She was shivering with the cold and when Polly took her hand it was like seizing a block of ice.

'Oh, Will!,' she cried, looking down at the poor mite. 'Oh, Will, however can this sort of thing happen?' She picked the little girl up in her arms and took off her own scarf and wrapped it around the child's shoulders.

'It's very easy,' said Will. 'Their fathers have no work or perhaps they're in prison and the mother just can't manage. Maybe the father is ill and can't work and has had to go on the parish. One day I'll take you to see the workhouse and then you'll really cry.'

Polly looked the little girl straight in the eye and said, 'I promise you that today you shall eat roast beef and plum pudding until you feel fit to burst and that you shall have a pair of stout shoes to keep your feet warm. Now come with me.' And despite the protestations of the doorkeeper she carried the waif into the hall and sat her beside the open fire which roared at one end of the room. The attendant who came forward to put the child out again took one look at the anger blazing in Polly's eyes and beat a quick retreat.

The next hour was spent finishing the decoration of the hall with holly and paper chains and the laying of the tables.

Mr Hatton of the Arcade Coffee Palace dashed about as if demented, organising the strategic placing of the huge sides of roast beef and steaming vegetables in huge hot plates, kept warm by the hot coals underneath and, as the hour for opening drew nearer, placing his staff and the volunteers at their appointed stations. Polly had slipped out to the nearest shoe shop and the little girl, now as warm as toast, sat in front of the great fire gazing in wonderment at the pair of bright red leather boots which covered her feet and clung snugly at her ankles.

When Polly had put on the new shoes, Amy, as she was now known to be, had given a quick curtsy to Polly and made as if to leave the hall. When Polly had asked her where she was going, Amy had said that she was going home. She had never had a new pair of shoes before and although she would sooner have had the dinner, she thanked her for the shoes and made for the door. Polly explained that she could keep the shoes and have the dinner as well, but it was obvious that the child did not believe her and she sat by the fire, half in rapture and half believing that the dream would soon end and she would be out in the cold again.

The Malleable Iron Works Prize Band took its place on the rostrum and to the strains of *O, Come, All Ye Faithful* the doors were opened and the children streamed into the hall. They needed no bidding to sit at the tables and there was excited chatter as they sat, knives and forks in hand, to await the arrival of the dinner, the aroma of which was positively mouth watering.

The music stopped and Canon Fowler said grace, then, with a fanfare from the band, Mr Hatton marched around the hall holding a platter of steaming hot roast beef on high and, to a great cheer, set it at the head of the first table. Further dishes followed and the excited chatter settled down to a gentle hum as the serious business of eating began. True to her word, Polly sat the little girl at the head of a table and kept her plate replenished as fast as she emptied it, whilst Will found a new joy in seeing the happiness of children who, for the first time in months, found themselves warm and well-fed. He had brought with him a small cart he had made, meaning to give it to some needy child, but with so many around him he felt that it would have been a sin to pick out just one for his gift.

The dilemma was solved when Polly took his arm and guided him to a corner of the room where a small table had been set up on its own. Here sat a small group of children who were handicapped and crippled.

'This is Benjamin, and this is his brother, Arthur,' said Polly.

Benjamin's crooked frame was wrapped awkwardly around

the chair; one spindly leg was at least six inches shorter than the other and the strain of walking like this for his seven years had given him a permanent lean to one side. As if this was not enough, his right hand was clenched like a talon, fingers bravely striving to handle a fork, whilst his head had a permanent palsy which made it continually shake. Arthur was plainly very backward. He seemed unable to speak and his constant drooling was gently mopped by the elderly lady at his side.

'Wouldn't think 'e was ten, would you, master?' she said, 'but 'e was a lovely baby, lovely, 'e really was. Then when he was three, 'e was out with his father and strayed away from 'im in the street. Straight under a cart, 'e was goin' but 'is father ran and pushed 'im out of the way. The cart went straight over 'is father's 'ead, crushed it like a walnut an 'e saw it. 'E's never spoken an' they say 'e never will. Some kind of shock, it is, master, some kind of shock.'

Will put the little cart on the table in front of Benjamin. The claw dropped the fork and the hand grasped the cart and held it to his chest, stroking it lovingly.

'Thank you, master,' said the little boy,' me an' Arthur, we can play with this together. Thank you, sir.'

'Perhaps there'll be another Robin dinner next year', said Will, 'and then I can make another one, so that you can have one each.'

The children being full to bursting, the places were cleared and they prepared themselves for the promised entertainment. However, before this took place, Canon Fowler called for three hearty cheers for those who had arranged the dinner and those who had presented it. The rafters rang as the children, now warm and no longer hungry, gave vent to their feelings. Then the Canon went on to tell them how fortunate they were and how much better life was for them than it had been for their forefathers. He concluded by telling them to avoid strong drink, ('Which has brought many a strong man and his family to grief'), to be kind to their brothers and sisters, obedient to their parents and, above all, to be grateful to their Heavenly Father for all his mercies.

'Mercies!' muttered Will under his breath. 'Dear God, look at the state of some of these poor mites. Mercies, indeed!'

By now, the balcony of the hall had been filled by the general public and a fine minstrel entertainment began.

The children joined in the choruses of some of the popular songs of the day and howled with laughter at the comic sketches, particularly Mr J J Hobbs' 'Painless Dentistry', although Mr Doughty's 'Come Where My Love Lies Dreaming' was hardly to the taste of small boys and girls.

The entertainment concluded with another series of hearty cheers for their benefactors and the rendering of *God Save The Queen* could be heard miles away, whilst the bag of sweets and an orange given to every child leaving the hall was but a distant memory by the time they got home.

Polly and Will helped to clear the hall afterwards and both of them had clearly been moved by the plight of many of the children. Even Will, hardened as he was by his visits to the workhouse, had been surprised at the condition of some of the children and was strangely silent as he wielded his brush, sweeping up the wrappings and general debris. His silent reverie was interrupted by a voice he knew well.

'Hello, Will,' said his father.

Will looked up. He had not seen his father for some time, but Herbert was unchanged. His topcoat had a wool collar and he wore a tall hat, shining with careful application of a stiff brush. His spotless white collar pushed foward a grey silk cravat and the usual diamond stickpin glistened in the gaslight which had been lit to ward off the shadows of impending evening. His black shoes shone like glass and the silver-topped cane tapped impatiently upon the floor.

'Hello, Father,' said Will and as an afterthought added, 'and a Happy New Year to you.'

His father reached inside his coat and handed Will a long envelope.

'Here's your Christmas present, Will,' he said. 'I'm sorry it's late, but these things take time to arrange.'

Will was not quite sure what to say. A present from his father

308.

was the last thing he had expected, particularly as he had had neither sight nor sound of him for several weeks. It made him feel mean that he had not even sent a Christmas greeting to his old home, much less thought of giving anyone a present.

The matter was resolved when his father turned his back and without another word walked out of the hall.

Polly came over and said: 'That was your father, wasn't it? I'd have recognised him anywhere from your description of him. What did he want? I thought that you were not speaking to each other.'

Will explained that his father had brought him a Christmas present and showed Polly the envelope. Warily he tore open the flap and read the contents, his face turning ashen as he absorbed the words. Finally he screwed the paper into a ball and threw it into the heap of rubbish he had been sweeping up.

'My father was the person who bought the house in Waldeck Street', he said grimly, 'and that letter was to give me notice to quit in seven days. He has also bought the bit of land in Butchery Street where my shed is, and that's being pulled down in a fortnight.'

His face turned purple and he stamped angrily on the floor.

'Damn him!' he shouted. 'Damn my father and all he stands for!'

Polly took him outside, away from the inquisitive glances of the other helpers, and they walked silently through the streets, Will's mind racing as he strove to cope with the enormity of his father's actions. Every now and then he clenched his fist and muttered to himself, 'Damn him!' When the expresssion got to 'Damn him to hell and back!' Polly stopped and told him that if he used that expression again, she would leave him and go home.

By this time it was quite dark and the January cold was biting deeply at both of them. There was the distinct sparkle of frost twinkling on the cobblestones in the gaslight and Polly shuddered as they stood silently together. The joy that had been Will's for so many days past now seemed to have evaporated and he felt that his father's shadow would dog him all his life. Once again, a feeling of deep loneliness overwhelmed him and he instinctively moved to Polly's side.

They were standing a few yards down Steep Hill, he suddenly realised, and he looked down towards the Old Harlequin. It seemed centuries ago that he had first met Clink there and, thinking of Lucy Matchbox, he took out the silver pocket watch which she had bequeathed to him and flipped open the cover, turning towards the light to read the time. It was six o'clock.

As Big Tom boomed out the hour, someone lit a cranberry coloured lamp in the upstairs window of the inn and Will felt the tears start hot to his eyes as he saw someone outlined against the window before the curtains were drawn. 'Marry me, Polly,' he cried, 'for God's sake, marry me!'

Polly turned towards him and looked him straight in the eyes.

'One day, perhaps I will marry you', she said, 'but it will be because I want to marry you, not because I feel sorry for you. It will be because you stop letting your father overshadow your life. You've made a good start in your own business, Will, but you've got to have the strength to carry on being your own man. I won't marry you just because you're lonely.'

And with that, she turned on her heel and walked back up the hill, leaving Will sobbing quietly.

THE END